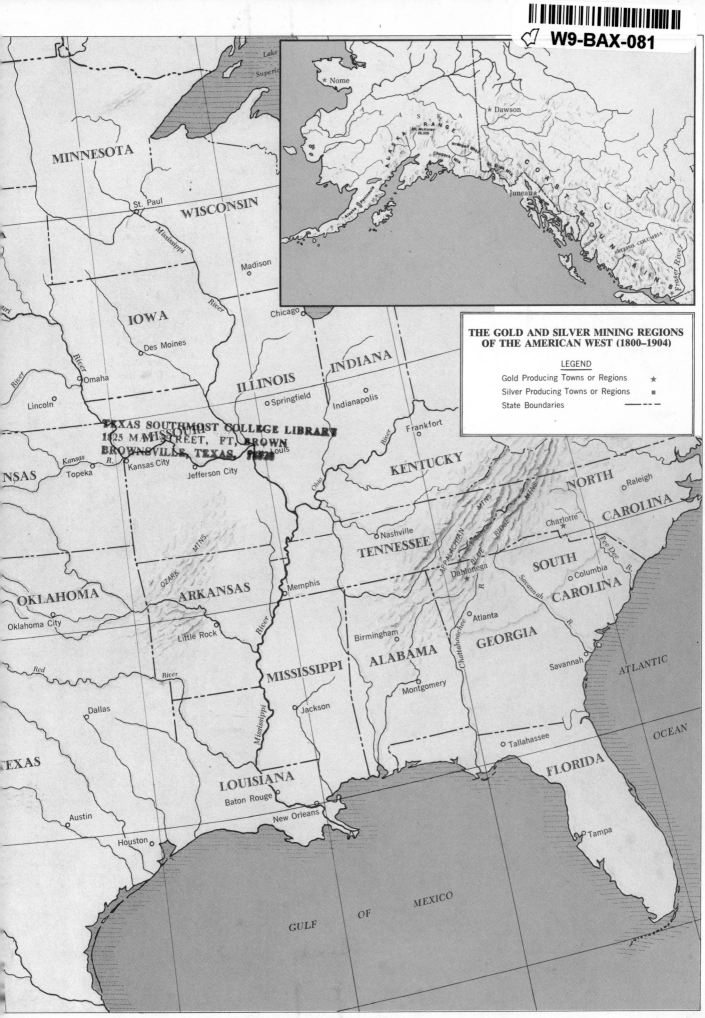

THE GOLD AND SILVER MINING REGIONS
OF THE AMERICAN WEST (1800–1904)

LEGEND

Gold Producing Towns or Regions ★

Silver Producing Towns or Regions ■

State Boundaries — · — · —

MINNESOTA

WISCONSIN

St. Paul

Madison

IOWA

Des Moines

Chicago

ILLINOIS

INDIANA

Springfield

Indianapolis

Omaha

Lincoln

NSAS

Topeka

Kansas City

Jefferson City

Frankfort

KENTUCKY

NORTH
CAROLINA

Raleigh

Charlotte

SOUTH
CAROLINA

Columbia

Nashville

TENNESSEE

Dahlonega

OKLAHOMA

Oklahoma City

ARKANSAS

Little Rock

Memphis

Birmingham

Atlanta

GEORGIA

Savannah

ATLANTIC

MISSISSIPPI

ALABAMA

Montgomery

Dallas

Jackson

Tallahassee

OCEAN

EXAS

Austin

LOUISIANA

Baton Rouge

New Orleans

FLORIDA

Tampa

Houston

GULF   OF   MEXICO

Nome

Dawson

ALASKA

Mt. McKinley
20,320

Wrangell Mts.

Chugach Mts.

Alaska Peninsula

St. Elias Mts.

Juneau

BRITISH COLUMBIA

Fraser River

GOLD AND SILVER IN THE WEST

...AN AMERICAN DREAM

"*Ours is a story mad with
the impossible, it is by chaos
out of dream, it began as
dream and it has continued
as dream down to the last
headlines you read in a
newspaper. And of our dreams
there are two things above
all others to be said, that
only madmen could have dreamed
them or would have dared to—
and that we have shown
a considerable faculty for
making them come true....*"

—BERNARD DeVOTO

*This page: Placer mining on Foster's Bar,
Yuba River, California.*

*Following two pages: Surface workings of
the Homestake Mine, Lead, South Dakota.*

GOLD AND SILVER IN THE WEST

The Illustrated History of an American Dream

By T. H. Watkins

AMERICAN WEST
PUBLISHING COMPANY

PALO ALTO, CALIFORNIA

This book is dedicated to my mother and father.

Library of Congress Card Number 70-158953
ISBN 0-910118-21-3

CONTENTS

INTRODUCTION *by David Lavender*

Another of the casualties of our consumer society is the ancient hope of simply leaning over and plucking material happiness from the earth itself. No more. Today, charge-o-plates and credit cards provide the instant money that brings, so we are assured, instant fulfillment.

It is too easy. Bored, we have lost all sense of the challenge that a century ago must have flickered now and then across the consciousness of every hard-pressed American—or for that matter, of every Occidental and many Orientals: he might, if he dared, transform his life by traveling to one of the mining camps of the American or Canadian West and there producing his own instant success. For in those wondrous spots, as a San Francisco newspaper triumphantly proclaimed in 1850, the stern law that man must earn his living by the sweat of his brow had at last been repealed.

I would hate to guess how many thousands of books have been churned out about various aspects of that dream and about the gold and silver rushes it initiated—their excitements, excesses, and inevitable failures. Yet none of these innumerable accounts, so far as I know, combines text and lavish pictorial documentation in quite the way this one by T. H. Watkins does.

It is a matter of both scope and depth. Writers trying to resurrect the past have always dredged up reports by contemporary observers in order to buttress their own summaries, and many have tossed in a clutch of pictures to boot. Watkins, a practised historian and associate editor of *The American West,* goes farther, weaving carefully chosen lithographs, paintings, and photographs into his narrative, not as embellishments, in the manner of the coffee-table non-book, but as integral parts of his presentation. The result is almost a tactile as well as a visual experience—the sort of response a tapestry might stir under your fingers, as compared to the feelings aroused by the flat, enameled surfaces characteristic of all too many books about the trans-Mississippi West.

This is not to imply that the author has fallen into the ways of some documentarians, simply heaping up materials bound loosely together by means of a running commentary. Faced by an overwhelming store of material, Watkins has been forced into rigid selection and tight patterning. Both operations entail personal judgment. How far one goes in striving to mingle objectivity with such decisions depends in part, I suppose, on the genes of the composer. Watkins has not bridled himself unduly. Whenever it suits his purpose to do so, he pushes matter-of-factness aside and resorts to sharp irony, broad humor, even, at times, to bits of overt editorializing. For he is fascinated—and occasionally repelled—by what went on during the mineral rushes, and his candor in giving expression to his own ambivalences furnishes another element in the texture of this work.

His pattern is to present, in the first half of the book, a chronological account to the major stampedes of the New World. To be sure, the ancients are mentioned, but the story of the dream (dream is his unifying thread) really begins with the Spanish *conquistadores*. He touches on the Americans in the southeastern United States during the early 1800s, and then jumps quickly ahead to the explosive years of the last half of the century, when prospectors, developers, swindlers, and assorted camp followers washed across the land from San Francisco to South Dakota, and from southern Arizona to the frozen tundra of the Seward Peninsula in Alaska.

Some readers will miss favorite spots. As a transplanted but unreconstructed Coloradoan, I felt deprived of Aspen and of Tom Walsh's fabulous Camp Bird mine above Ouray. More surprising than the omissions, however, is the amount of coverage that Watkins does achieve in a relatively limited space. If the writing seems a bit excited at times, so were the events that the writing describes. If the rushes occasionally sound repetitious, that was the hope of the participants. Above all, they wanted another California.

They didn't get a repetition. This story begins almost at its climaxes—California for placer diggings, the Comstock Lode for deep bonanzas. Even if a full duplication of those strikes had appeared somewhere else at a later date, it would not have sufficed. The threnody that runs throughout the book is the lament that always the rushes were paralyzed in the end by too many people questing for too little gold. Death from excessive demands has been the common fate of many a dream.

The temptation to settle for narrative alone must have been great, especially since graphic details without number, both in words and pictures, could easily have been added to the tale. Watkins resists. He uses the second half of the book to put the rushes into their geologic, technologic, economic, and social places. To me this is the more satisfying section, for it involves looking long and hard and not always coolly at the interplay of forces that brought about both the era's enormous technical success and its equally resounding human failures.

The author sees very clearly, underneath the rationalizations of that exuberant frontier industrialism, the five relentless horsemen of every mining apocalypse: greed, waste, hardship, social breakdown, and environmental butchery. He states quite candidly that the most vaunted of our mining areas never produced a fraction of the wealth that agriculture has. Poignantly, he traces the human agonies that accompanied the shrinking of what began as a search for personal fulfillment down into a corporate routine replete with all the impersonal cruelties of nineteenth-century urbanism. This pervading sense of a lost faith is another haunting part of the book's texture.

Fifty frenetic years—from '48 in California to '98 in Alaska—wrapped it all up, leaving behind innumerable legends, a few sagging ghost towns, and a handful of gold "factories" like the giant Homestake Mine in South Dakota. Then, almost like an afterthought, came the uranium rush of the 1950s. Beginning as a brand-new lottery for everyday people and ending as usual in a corporate take-over, the amazing episode lets Watkins remind us, in an ironic reprise, that although times have changed, the unreasonable stuff of our longings has not, plastic credit cards notwithstanding. We would still dream and act and lose in the same old ways—if just we could.

A far less painful reminder, and one certain to stir responses from anyone who has ever slowed his car to marvel at a gray tailing dump on a hillside or a weathered headframe leaning over the desert sage, is this book with its stunning evocation of the exaltations and wrenches that the mining rushes of the West brought to the very human hearts of those who participated in them. For in those hearts, if not in the events, we see ourselves.

PART ONE

THE DREAM-SEEKERS

"Bell, book, and candle shall not drive me back,
When gold and silver becks me to come on."
—William Shakespeare

In the long course of human history—or at least that portion of it which we have chosen to call civilized—the quest for treasure runs like a glittering thread through the literature and traditions of nearly all cultures. It has been the stuff of magic, strung with the gossamer of legend and woven into one epic tapestry after another, typified by Jason's odyssey in search of the golden fleece and the golden apples of the sun.

As civilizations expanded, reaching out for conquest and enlarging the outlines of the known world, myth and reality forever mingled, until men operated on the working assumption that beyond the next river or over the next mountain range lay a land of richness beyond measure. Just often enough to keep the dream living in the human mind, it came true, or nearly true. Alexander the Great, coursing his bloody way east from Macedonia to the valley of the Indus River in the third century before Christ, conquered Susa, the capital of the Persian Empire, and found there gold and silver ingots beyond all expectation; he found more in Persepolis, and again and again piles of treasure fell into his hands before the mountains of Kashmir turned his army back to its homeland.

Once implanted in history, the vision of Asia as a storehouse of riches was never abandoned. Seventeen hundred years later, the emerging nations of fifteenth-century Europe vibrated with legends of wealth outside the power of comprehension, and rulers of countries large and small leaned forward eagerly to hear them, as historian Allan Nevins has written: "By letters, word of mouth, and the first printed books, they learned with delight from Ser Marco Polo, Friar Oderic, and other travelers that cities existed with 'walles of silver and roofes of gold'; that Kublai Khan heaped in great storerooms his ingots, his masses of pearls, and his hillocks of diamonds; that Cambaluc, later called Peking, and Cipangu, now known as Japan, were seats of opulence and power that made Europe seem squalid." He who could tap these barbaric treasures would win the world, or so it was believed. In 1488, Portugal sent Vasco da Gama around the Cape of Good Hope to Calicut, India; and in 1492, Spain sent Christopher Columbus "to the countries of India, so that I might see what they were like, the lands and the people, and might seek out and know the nature of everything that is there...."

Vasco da Gama traveled east and returned with a cargo of treasure; Columbus traveled west and returned with an empire, for in his traveling he had "discovered" the New World whose existence would change the history of Western man. What is more, he had found a

land whose mineral wealth seemingly justified the long, mystic dream that had haunted civilization; here, finally, was Golconda, the land of gold and silver. For nearly four centuries thereafter, the dream ebbed and flowed with the tides of history, fading to myth here and bursting into explosive reality there, until its bright strokes had colored the whole fabric of the American narrative. It reached its climax in the last fifty years of the nineteenth century, when the North American West produced more gold and silver than any region before in the history of mankind.

The chapters which follow document the incredible sweep of history between that moment when Cortés surveyed the wealth of Montezuma and the time when twentieth-century men erected jerry-built cities on the deserts of Nevada. It is an enormously complex story, one tangled in the economics, morals, and politics of at least three distinct civilizations; but one factor remains constant throughout its four hundred years: the power of the dream and its ability to shape the lives of those who followed it. Whether a helmeted *conquistador* with a mind like an axe and an affection for spilling blood, or a grubby prospector sifting through the debris of other men's workings, all who married the dream were helpless, entrapped in visions. "It seemed that

every rock had a yellow tinge," a California miner wrote in 1852, "and even our camp kettle, that I had thought in the morning the most filthy one I had ever seen, now appeared to be gilded. . . . During the night, yellow was the prevailing color in my dreams. . . ." For many, the dream lasted a lifetime. Norman Wheeler, a Denver prospector who had spent fifty fruitless years seeking the hidebound treasures of the mountains, suffered a stroke in 1918; one night he demanded that he be placed in a chair in front of a window where he could see the mountains. Gene Fowler, his grandson, related the story in *A Solo in Tom-Toms:*

> The old man was obdurate. Aunt Etta's son Delford lifted Grandpa from the bed and carried him to an easy chair, and turned the chair around to face the window. Grandpa motioned with the unparalyzed hand for my aunt to raise the window-shade. She obeyed him and tiptoed away. When sunlight came, my aunt looked in upon Grandpa. She thought him asleep. He was asleep forever, his eyes fixed upon the distant snowcaps of the hills he had roved so many times.

Such men were the dream-seekers. And this is the story of how they helped to shape the history of a continent.

CHAPTER ONE

FROM TENOCHTITLÁN TO APPALACHIA

Myths, conquistadores, and Georgia Crackers

"I tell thee, gold is more plentiful there than copper is with us; and for as much red copper as I can bring, I'll have thrice the weight in gold. Why, man, all their dripping pans and their chamber pots are pure gold; and all the chains with which they chain up their streets are massy gold; all the prisoners they take are fettered in gold. . . ."

At the beginning of the sixteenth century, the Aztec empire held control of over ten thousand square miles of central Mexico by a *fiat* of death. This complex, but not altogether admirable, civilization was in fact a tyranny whose iron-handed rule over the native population was bitterly resented; like all despotisms, that of the Aztecs stood on a foundation of fear. Too often the Spanish conquest of Mexico is seen as nothing less than the brutal extinction of a race whose innocence would have justified all of Rousseau's lambent vision of the Noble Savage; one social historian has even gone so far as to lament "four centuries and more of cringing abjection in a land where once civilized men walked free, fearless, and masters of their destiny." In *Many Mexicos*, Lesley Byrd Simpson gently demurred: "Ancient Mexico may have been such a paradise, but the evidence is not conclusive. On the contrary, it is pretty clear that Cortés was able to carry out his awe-inspiring feat only because most of the Mexican people welcomed him as

their deliverer from the unbearable exactions of the Aztecs."

Which is not to say that the Aztec civilization was not impressive; it was indeed. The temples, palaces, causeways, lakes, and floating gardens of Mexico-Tenochtitlán, the seat of Aztec power, comprised one of the wonders of the world, and the gold and silver carved out of mines scattered from the eastern seacoast to the western mountains made it one of the most abundantly rich civilizations on the North American continent; their arts were highly developed, and a kind of literature existed in the form of picture-records whose sophisticated intricacy was a match for those of the Egyptians in ancient times. Nor should the Spanish legions of conquest be viewed as an army of liberation. The Spanish had their reasons, few of them having to do with anyone's freedom but their own.

One of their prime motivations was that very treasure on which the Aztecs had built an empire. Rumors of its existence came to Hernán Cortés not long after he landed on the east coast of Mexico in 1519. The town council of Villa Rica de la Vera Cruz, which Cortés had founded that year (making it the oldest European settlement on the North American continent), sent word of these rumors to Queen Dona Juana and Emperor Charles V of Spain; Cortés, they said, had "found a land very rich in gold. The captain said that all the natives wore it, some in their noses, some in their ears, and some in other parts.... In our judgment, it is en-

Cortés shackles Montezuma, the Aztec despot of central Mexico.
(From William Prescott's Conquest of Mexico, 1844*)*

tirely possible that this country has everything which existed in that land from which Solomon is said to have brought the gold for the Temple."

Strong words, those, and to seek out their truth, Cortés led his soldiers and his Indian allies into Mexico-Tenochtitlán for what at first appeared to be a peaceful confrontation with Montezuma, ruler of the Aztecs. Montezuma, fearful of Spanish power (and very likely sobered by the presence of the conquistadores' redskinned companions), attempted to appease Cortés with gifts indicating his subservience to Spanish rule.

Montezuma and his lords, Cortés reported to the Queen and Emperor, "all gave very willingly in bars and sheets of gold, jewels of gold, silver, and featherwork, and precious stones, and many other things of value...which amounted to one hundred thousand ducats and more. Besides their value, these things are so marvellous that for novelty and strangeness they have no price, nor is it likely that any prince in the world possesses such treasures." Montezuma also allowed Cortés to send out men to the Aztec mines in Cuzula, Tamazulapa, Malinaltepic, Teniz, and Tuchitepeque, and the reports they brought back fired the imagination. This was indeed a country to rival Solomon's treasure trove.

Unfortunately, Cortés made the gross error of attempting to enforce Spanish rule by placing Montezuma under arrest. The Aztec population of the city rebelled, and in the long march of retreat called the *Noche Triste,* the Spanish lost 450 soldiers and several thousand Indians. It took Cortés a year to reassemble a fighting force, but when he returned in August, 1521, the fall of Mexico was brutal, bloody, and brief. The kingdom of the Aztecs now became New Spain, and to discover what other treasures the land might hold, Cortés sent his lieutenants to explore the far corners of Mexico from the Gulf of California (named the Red Sea of Cortés) to Guatemala, and from northern Vera Cruz to Honduras.

What they found was not enough; it would never be enough. It was not even enough when Pizarro looted the kingdom of the Incas in 1533—the Incas, the most advanced civilization in the New World, whose king had attempted to ransom himself by filling a room seventeen by twenty-two feet full of gold. According to William Prescott, writing in the nineteenth century there were: "... ewers, salvers, vases ... curious imita-

tions of different plants and animals . . . Indian corn in which the golden ear was sheathed in broad leaves of silver from which hung a rich tassel of threads of the same precious metal . . . a fountain which sent up a sparkling jet of gold." The Hapsburgs, Spain's monarchs and rulers also of the crumbling Holy Roman Empire, had committed themselves to a ruinous series of wars, contesting with France, England, and the Turkish Empire on a score of fronts; the bullion of the New World was supposed to finance them, but it could not. The "King's Fifth" of American treasure was too little—in fact, historian Bernard DeVoto has maintained that "the crown's share and its levies on private loot barely covered the expense of the Spanish New World, the Department of the Indies." Moreover, the rich placer mines found by the Aztecs were quickly exhausted by the intense efforts of the Spanish; there had to be more—there *must be* more. The imperative of *must be* became the theme of Spanish exploration of the New World. It became the prime duty of each of Mexico's Spanish viceroys to follow this imperative, and the fifty years after the conquest were characterized by some of the most remarkable episodes of mythchasing in human history.

The legends, some of them ancient, were manifold and appealing. There was the rumor of mystic islands somewhere in the South Sea; Cortés believed it, and sent men to find the ocean (they found instead the Sea of Cortés), "for everybody who has any knowledge and experience of navigation in the Indies is certain that the discovery of the South Sea would lead to the discovery of many islands rich in gold, pearls, precious stones, spices, and other unknown and wonderful things." Among these wondrous islands was one supposed to be inhabited by man-hating Amazons. They cut off their right breasts for more effective use of a bow, and allowed men to visit the island on occasion for purposes of conception, but killed all male children born after such interludes.

Another rumor concerned El Dorado, the gilded man of Cundinamarca, a king who ruled the people of the Columbian plateaus and who coated himself in gold dust once a year to give tribute to the goddess of Lake Guatavita. For two centuries, men believed in El Dorado with incredible stubbornness. Not only the

Spanish, but the phlegmatic Germans and even the redoubtable Sir Walter Raleigh followed the myth into the jungles of Central America. And as late as 1844, an American published a book, *El Dorado,* which argued for his existence.

Another told of Gran Quivira, a land somewhere to the north whose people ate from plates of gold and silver, and whose king was lulled to sleep beneath a tree hung with tiny golden bells, which tinkled richly in the wind. Coronado chased this one all the way to the Kansas plains of North America in 1542.

Yet another was encountered by Hernán De Soto in his explorations of Florida and the American southeast in 1539 and 1540. In western Florida one of De Soto's lieutenants encountered a band of thirty Indians. According to the expedition's chronicler, "He asked them if they knew or had any information of any rich land where there was gold or silver. They said yes, that there was a province toward the west called Cale, and that the people of the land were hostile to others living in other lands where it was summer most of the year. That land had gold in abundance, and when those people came to make war on the people of Cale, they wore hats of gold resembling helmets. . . ."

De Soto marched toward Cale, and there learned of a land called Apalache, seven days further west. He went on to Apalache, where a captured Indian boy reported "that he was not of that land, but that he was from another very distant one lying in the direction of the sunrise . . . and that his land was called Yupaha and a woman ruled it; that the town where she lived was of wonderful size, and that the Chieftainess collected tribute from many of neighboring chiefs, some of whom gave her clothing and others gold in abundance. He told how it was taken from the mines, melted, and refined, just as if he had seen it done . . . so that all who knew anything of this said it was impossible to give so good an account of it unless one had seen it. . . ." The land of Yupaha was doubtless the gold region of what would later be North Carolina, Georgia, and Alabama, but before he could find it, De Soto was lost on the banks of the Great River, the Mississippi, and shortly afterwards he died.

But of all the shimmering myths that echoed in the Spanish New World in this fifty-year period, none was more compelling than that of the Seven Cities of Cíbola, a legend with its origins deep in the Spanish

consciousness. When the Mohammedan Moors of North Africa crossed the Strait of Gilbraltar in the eighth century and conquered Spain, legend had it, a Christian archbishop and six bishops led their faithful out into the western sea to a great island, where each established a city; the island was called Antillia, and for centuries its ghostly presence floated about the edges of maps depicting the unknown lands to the west. "Whoever should reach Antillia," Bernard DeVoto has written, "would find the Seven Cities there. Since they were cities beyond the horizon and of miracle, the sands they stood on would be gold."

The dream of Antillia was part of the mental baggage carried over to the New World by the Spanish. It did not take long for it to be revived. In the early 1530s, Beltrán Nuño de Guzmán, a particularly vicious *conquistador* who had practically depopulated the western region of Mexico, encountered news of seven rich cities lying somewhere in the north. In 1536, the rumors were corroborated by four emaciated Spaniards, the only survivors of the ill-fated Narvaéz expedition to conquer Florida eight years before, who stumbled out of the north with news of a land called Cíbola, where there were seven rich cities shining with gold.

Don Antonio de Mendoza, who became viceroy of New Spain in 1535 and knew where his duty lay, responded to this latest tale of wondrous possibility by sending a scouting expedition to investigate, headed up by Fray Marcos de Niza, a Franciscan monk, and one Estevánico, a black slave who had been one of the four survivors of the Narvaéz expedition. Meanwhile, he appointed Francisco Valasquez de Coronado to organize a major force to conquer the Seven Cities, should Marcos and Estevánico discover them. Coronado had no trouble finding volunteers; everyone in New Spain, seemingly, wanted a chance to lay hands on Cíbola's treasure, and those who could not go themselves sent servants in their name. In February, 1540, the expedition was ready to go; it was the most impressive such enterprise in the history of New Spain, comprising 336 soldiers and civilian volunteers, together with nearly a thousand Indians and fifteen hundred head of livestock.

By then, Fray Marcos had returned. Estevánico, he reported, had disappeared, presumably done in by

The land of the myth-chasers, as rendered by cartographer Henricus Hondius in 1642, before the legends (among them the island of California) had a chance to fade.

Indians, but the good priest had other news; he, himself, had seen one of the golden cities of Cíbola, glittering under the desert sun like a midday dream. In an air of electric excitement, the expedition set out from Culiacán on the west coast for the nearly three-hundred-mile journey north to the deserts of Sonora. In April, Coronado set out ahead of the slow-moving main force with a column of about one hundred. In July, they came to the first of the Seven Cities; stolid and earth-colored, it could not have looked less like a city of dreams. It was in fact the Indian pueblo of Hawíkuh,

one of six scattered across the desert of southern Arizona, primitive villages which legend and wish had transformed into the golden capitals of a rich nation.

The Indians put up a resistance that was as brief as it was useless. The conquerors found maize and food for their animals—but no treasure, no rooms filled with gold to match that of Pizarro. Pedro de Castañeda, the expedition's chronicler, recorded their disappointment: "When they saw the first village . . . such were the curses that some hurled at Friar Marcos that I pray God may protect him from them. . . ."And Coronado himself bitterly reported to Mendoza that "Fray Marcos has not told the truth in a single thing he said." It was the same story at each of the six pueblos which Coronado encountered—nothing. There was still Gran Quivira, somewhere to the northeast; and with an almost manic determination to find *something* to justify the expedition's efforts, Coronado led his men clear up to the Kansas plains, where they found nothing but great herds of "hunch-backed cows." There were no more myths to follow, and the glorious expedition straggled back to Mexico in 1542, carrying the wreckage of its dreams with it.

Coronado's ruinous adventure made it clear even to the credible Spanish of the New World that scurrying after legends was generally unprofitable. With his failure, myth-chasing on a national scale waned, replaced by a period of steady growth in the areas of agriculture and husbandry, by intense missionary activity that spread the Spanish version of civilization throughout Mexico, and by the slow building of a working government. Gold and silver took their place as integral parts of a producing country—they were no longer the prime reason for its existence.

Still, there were excitements to come. In 1543 and 1544, gold and silver mines were discovered in the mountains of New Galicia to the north of Mexico City; and while their production was less than spectacular, they did help to replenish the supply that had dwindled after Montezuma's placers had been worked out. Of far more significance was the discovery of silver ore at Zacatecas, near the center of New Galicia, by a group of soldiers in 1546. Hampered by a communications link with Mexico City that traveled through the country of the perennially hostile Chichimeca Indians, news of the ore's incredible richness did not become general knowledge for more than two years; but by 1549 (almost precisely three centuries, curiously enough, before the California Gold Rush), the first genuine "rush" in the history of the North American continent was well under way.

Thousands streamed north to the mines; new strikes were discovered all over the mountains; Zacatecas became a noisy boomtown, with all the paraphernalia that would become typical of such towns in the future —lawlessness, speculation, vice, and a generalized air of barely-restrained greed. By 1550 it was reported that there were thirty-four individual companies operating mines, *arrastras,* smelters, and foundries in the Zacatecas area, with labor supplied by Negro slaves and free Indians. Competition between the companies was so fierce that a wage ceiling for free workers finally had to be imposed by the government—surely the first example of inflation control exercised in the New World.

The discoveries at Zacatecas ushered in New Spain's Age of Silver; from Taxco to Guanajuato, new strikes fed silver into Mexico City, creating a "silver aristocracy" of immense wealth, as described by Lesley Byrd Simpson in *Many Mexicos:* "A silver nobility appeared in New Spain, complete with purchased titles and shaky coats of arms. Antonio Obregon spent a few thousand of the two hundred million pesos he had taken from La Valencia Mine of Guanajuato and became Condé de Matehuala. Jesus Salado went him one better and became Condé de Matehuala and Marqués de Guadiana. The Marqués de Mal Paso, the Condé de Regla, the Marqués de Apartado, the Marqués de Vivanco, the Marqués de Jaral, and the Condé de Santiago were among the glittering dignities bought by the miners from the bankrupt Crown, together with the privilege of painting a crest on their carriages and having their ears titillated by a murmured 'Señor Marqués' or 'Señor Condé'." The Church, replete with gifts for assurance of Heaven, grew fat with wealth; Mexico City became a vast metropolis unmatched in the New World; a class of paupers—*leperos*—developed, the sure sign of national prosperity.

From 1550 to 1820, when Spain lost control of her New World empire, silver ruled New Spain. In that time, her mints coined more than two billion dollars, and another two billion was exported in the form of ingots. Two-thirds of the silver supply of the world was shipped from the port of Vera Cruz, and Zacatecas alone accounted for a fifth of the world's silver.

Pizarro notwithstanding, the rooms of New Spain had not been filled with gold—they had been filled with silver.

The light cast by the gold and silver of New Spain illuminated the world—and inflamed its imagination, particularly that of England, Spain's arch-rival in the arenas of world power. Elizabeth I, determined to lift her country to a position of leadership, was intrigued by Spain's success and concluded, with superficial logic,

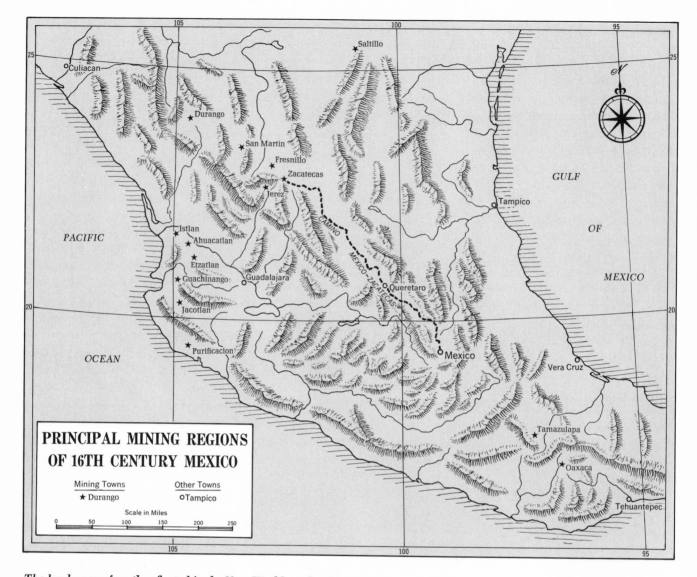

PRINCIPAL MINING REGIONS
OF 16TH CENTURY MEXICO

Mining Towns   Other Towns
★ Durango   ○ Tampico

Scale in Miles
0   50   100   150   200   250

*The landscape of myth reflected in the New World, as the shimmering legends
of the conquistadores were translated into solid reality.*

that if there was such treasure to be found in New Spain, then it might also exist in the northern latitudes. In 1576, she sent Martin Frobisher on a voyage of exploration to the northeast coast of America. He returned with a load of what he maintained was rich gold ore, and on the strength of that conviction, he was sent out on another voyage—in which Elizabeth herself invested one thousand pounds. Again he returned with a cargo of gold ore, and it seemed that England was destined to challenge Spain's dominance in the exploitation of the New World. In 1578, Frobisher

was sent out again.

By the time he returned, Elibabeth's lambent hopes had been stricken dead by exhaustive analysis of Frobisher's ore: it was worthless. Spain's King Philip, as Elizabethan historian A. L. Rowse put it, "could well afford to laugh—except that he was never known to laugh openly."

Elizabeth died in 1603, but the dream survived her. The vision of New England as a country rich in all that had fed the coffers of Spain was irresistible, as suggested by Ben Jonson and John Marston's contemporary play, *Eastward Ho!* in which one of the characters extolls the mineral virtues of the country: "I tell thee, gold is more plentiful there than copper is with us; and for as much red copper as I can bring, I'll have thrice the weight in gold. Why, man, all their dripping pans and their chamber pots are pure gold; and all the chains with which they chain up their streets are massy gold. . . ." The canny James I, Elizabeth's successor and never one to discount possibilities, specified in the royal charters he granted to various American colonization companies that one-fifth of all the gold and silver discovered by them in America would accrue to the crown.

The settlers of Jamestown in 1607 had hardly landed before they were around and about, digging after gold. One member of the colony complained in 1608 that there was "no talk, no hope, no work but to dig gold, wash gold, refine gold, load gold." That same year, Captain John Smith discovered what he thought was rich ore during an expedition up the Chickahominy River. He sent a load back to London, but his ore, like that of Frobisher, was worthless. The Jamestown colonists went on to the more immediate problem of surviving in the American wilderness, a task that left little time for chasing after someone else's hopes.

Those who followed them had no better luck, and gradually the dream of gold faded from the New England consciousness, until by the time of the American Revolution it was considered an incontestable fact of life that there were no precious metals on the American continent, as Benjamin Franklin testified in 1790: "Gold and silver are not the produce of North America, which has no mines."

Nine years later, the first gold mine in America was discovered on the Rocky River of central North Carolina. A small boy shot an arrow into the air, and where it fell he discovered a two-and-one-half-pound lump of gold, which he took to his father, a farmer by the name of Reed. Reed used the lump as a door-stop for a couple of years before a neighbor pointed out to him the fact that it might be useful for something else —like money. Inspired, Reed went down to the river and started mining, and in ten years he had pulled out something like 115 pounds of gold. By then, other strikes had been made in the area, and a minuscule

rush was under way.

Over the next fifteen years, the mining region spread to include about one thousand square miles, centering at the junction of the Uwharre and Pee Dee rivers. The area got another push in 1827, when the price of cotton took one of its several dives, and hard-pressed plantation owners loaded up their slaves and put them to work in the North Carolina mines. By 1829, the mines in Mecklenberg County alone were producing two thousand dollars a week in good quality ore, most of it from placer locations. Gold became a common medium of commerce, as the *Niles Register* for May 16, 1829, reported: "It is common for the merchants of the town of Charlotte, when they go to make their purchases, to carry from ten to forty pounds of the precious metal. It can readily be imagined what life and activity is infused in every department of business, where the only bank which is required to relieve the people's want is a bank of earth."

"The digging for precious metal," the magazine added in a later issue, "seems to be running into a mania in North Carolina. . . . A Major Harris is said to realize $100 per day by the labor of four Negroes— fifty mines are worked in one county and perhaps twenty counties are named in North Carolina where gold is found—some also in South Carolina and Virginia."

The biggest was yet to come. In the latter part of 1829, a new strike was made in Georgia on Ward's Creek, within the boundaries of the Cherokee Nation —which had been granted to the Cherokees by the United States in 1785 with all the usual assurances of permanence ("as long as the grass shall grow and the rivers shall run," etc.). As usual, these assurances meant nothing. By 1830, an observer reported, "It is said that 4,000 persons are engaged in gathering gold at the Yahoola mines, in the Cherokee country, and that their daily products are worth $10,000." Georgia promptly rescinded the guarantees of the federal government, and President Andrew Jackson, a hardheaded old warrior who had spent a good deal of his early career fighting Indians, capitulated to the state's action. In 1838, the Cherokees were summarily removed to the region of Oklahoma along the miserable route that has since entered the folklore as the "Trail of Tears."

While truly successful placer mining in the Appalachian goldfields died out in the middle of the 1860s, stubborn hopefuls continued to dig around in the creeks of Georgia well into the 1870s, as seen above near Dahlonega.

The miners couldn't wait that long. In 1831, a survey divided the entire Cherokee portion of northern Georgia into ten new counties, which in turn were subdivided into "gold" lots of 40 acres and "land" lots of 150 acres. The 35,000 gold lots were then given away via a public lottery beginning in 1832 and ending in 1833. This enormous giveaway extended the mining region all along the Appalachian Piedmont from the Rappahannock River to the Coosa, skirting the base of the Blue Ridge Mountains and including parts of Alabama. The richest locality was Lumpkin County, Georgia, where Auraria and Dahlonega emerged as first-class boom towns surrounded by a minor galaxy of camps with names like Gold Hill, Brindletown, Arbacoochee, and Goldville—each of them carrying on the dubious traditions established by the mines of Zacatecas nearly three centuries before. "I can hardly conceive of a more unmoral community than exists around these mines," a *Niles Register* reporter said in 1831. "Drunkenness, gambling, fighting, lewdness, and every other vice exist here to an awful extent. Many of the men, by working three days in the week, make several dollars, and then devote the remaining four to every species of vice."

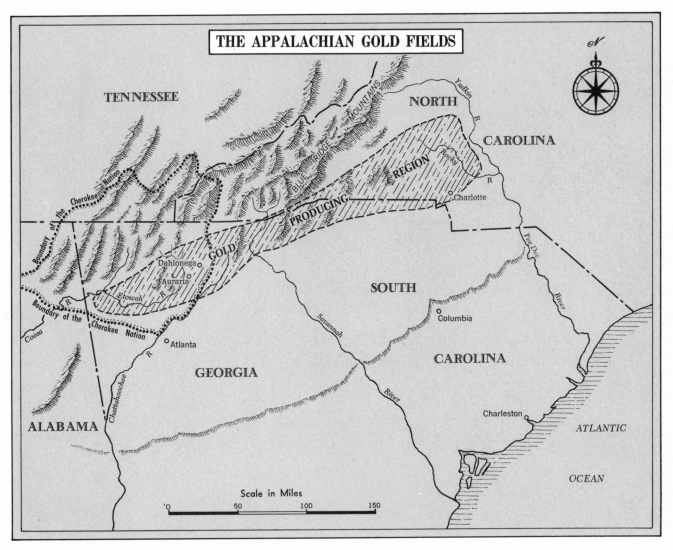

THE APPALACHIAN GOLD FIELDS

The Appalachian goldfields, the first expression of genuine gold mining in the continental United States.

Affection for vice in its sundry forms, however, was one of the few similarities between the Appalachian gold region and the Zacatecan silver region. For all its local excitement, the Appalachian mines simply did not produce that much gold. Between 1802 and 1845, according to *Freeman Hunt's Merchants Magazine* of August, 1846, the region accounted for only $7,100,663 of the gold deposited at United States mints. By 1847, most of the placer mines had been worked out completely, and only a few quartz deposits kept the region producing any gold at all—and by 1866 most of these, too, had been exhausted. In the more than sixty years since their discovery, the Appalachian mines produced exactly $19,375,890 in gold bullion—or an average of less than three hundred thousand dollars a year, a figure that would not have galvanized even the gold-hungry soldiers of Hernán De Soto, who had heard of this "land of Yupaha" more than three centuries before.

And in 1849, the first gold mines in America were rendered more insignificant by a phenomenon that put even the silver mines of Zacatecas in the pale: the California Gold Rush, the most stupendous mining strike in human history.

CHAPTER TWO

THE GRAND CATHARSIS

The California Gold Rush and a dream reborn

"The farmers have thrown aside their plows, the lawyers their briefs, the doctors their pills, the priests, their prayerbooks, and all are now digging gold."

It was a time for large excitements. The American 1840s was a decade as filled with tumult, change, and contrast as any in the nation's history. Ferment of one kind or another touched every area of life. Politically, the Whig Party—born as the last gasp of Federalism—was steadily crumbling, shaking down its components into what would become the Republican Party in the mid-1850s and, with startling regularity, alternating power with the Democratic Party, itself struggling in a welter of factionalism. The slavery issue began to take on the overtones of the emotional battleground it would become, as politicians of every ilk set up a cacophony over the question of the annexation of Texas and its effect on the balance of power between North and South. And in the great cities mechanics of political corruption, of votes bought and sold, of payoffs and graft at all levels were a harbinger of days to come.

It was a decade that saw America's first large push across the great unknown of the trans-Mississippi West to hopeful Edens in Oregon and California. By 1845 the American population in Oregon alone had reached six thousand, with another two thousand in California.

Pioneers in the true sense, entire families had yanked up their eastern roots and replanted them in a new land with an eye toward building the country—and, not incidentally, increasing their lot in this world. The emigration combined with a time of national muscle, the nation's first thrust toward continentalism. With a combination of belligerence and negotiation, the territory of Oregon was carved out of British land in 1846; and in May of that same year, war with Mexico was commenced, ostensibly because American lives had been taken at Matamoros, near the Texas-Mexican border, but in fact as a deliberate extension of the expansionist policies of James K. Polk and his supporters; they called it "Manifest Destiny."

Two years, one hundred million dollars, and eleven thousand American lives later (and no one knows how many dead Mexicans), the United States owned most of what would come to be known as the American West, including California. It did not come without cost to America's self-satisfied image as a nonaggressive nation; Ulysses S. Grant, who had fought on the plains of Mexico, echoed a wide base of opinion when he said, "I do not think there was ever a more wicked war than that waged by the United States on Mexico." But it was done, dissent notwithstanding, and no one was about to give the West back.

Economically, the country was in a miasma of confusion. Banking and currency had never quite recovered from the assaults of the administration of Andrew

The definitive goldseeker pauses in a San Francisco daguerreotype studio to immortalize himself for the folks back home, ca. 1851.

Jackson in the 1830s, when he set out to cripple the Bank of the United States on antimonopolistic grounds. Moreover, a rising industrialism was beginning to challenge the dominance of agriculture in American life, a conflict reflected in the question of the tariff, which was picked up and booted about by politicians. Speculation in land, stocks, and bonds flourished almost without restriction, lending an air of generalized hysteria to the economic scene; bubbles burst all around, and bankruptcies of entire states were the order of the day.

Adding to the confusion was the country's first significant experience in mass immigration, as refugees from Old World agonies, most of them Irish and German, poured into the cities of the Atlantic seaboard. Annual immigration into the country during the 1840s frequently exceeded 100,000, and in 1848, the year of the Irish potato famine, more than 296,000 arrived—this in a country with a population of only a little over twenty million. The Irish in particular had little to offer their new homeland but muscle, and labor was a glut on the market. Those who could not make their way to the Old Northwest, where employment waited, clustered in enclaves of poverty in New York, Boston, Philadelphia, and Washington, exchanging one misery for another; ghetto was not yet an American word, but it was a reality.

Amid this tangle of political and economic conditions, social ferment sputtered like the witches' cauldron in *Macbeth*. Virulent heresies assaulted the tenets of respectable Protestantism; Wesleyism proliferated and Millerites stood on a hill in baskets, waiting for God to pluck them up to heaven like so many bushels of grapes. Mesmerism, phrenology, and any odd number of supernatural manifestations excited the public imagination, and reformers promulgated the restructuring of civilization, chief among them the Fourierites, who advocated the redivision of society into phalanxes of not less than three hundred persons and not more than eighteen hundred.

More significant agitation, however, was brought to bear on such questions as prison reform, welfare, medicine, elimination of the death penalty, abolition of slavery, and women's rights, with varying degrees of success. Perhaps the most dramatic of all the social phenomena exhibited in these years was the anti-Catholic Native American movement, a reaction to

Irish immigration that produced a dismal series of riots throughout the urbanized East, culminating in the Philadelphia riots of 1844, in which thirteen people died.

Accelerating more rapidly than could be chronicled, alternatively arrogant and insecure, confused and purposeful, the American civilization was experiencing a kind of adolescence in the 1840s, making a painful transition from the agrarian age to the industrial age. It would be a mistake to assume—as some historians have done—that the unsettled nature of life in this period somehow "caused" the California Gold Rush, that it would not have been a catharsis on so grand a scale had it occurred at a more stable period. Given the amount of gold that the new territory provided, and given man's long history of dreaming out the golden fleece, the Gold Rush would have been a phenomenon to alter history no matter when it occurred. It is fitting, however, that its excitement rounded out one of the most profoundly complex decades in American history.

It was the climax of an era—and the beginning of another.

It was a January morning in 1848, one of those bitter, crackling-cold mornings typical of winter in the Sacramento Valley. James Marshall, an itinerant carpenter who was constructing a sawmill on the South Fork of the American River for Johann Augustus Sutter, was taking his usual walk along the new millrace when he spotted "something shining in the bottom of the ditch," as he later recalled it. "I reached my hand down and picked it up; it made my heart thump, for I was certain it was gold. The piece was about half the size and the shape of a pea. Then I saw another piece in the water. After taking it out, I sat down and began to think right hard." After thinking, he took the gold and showed it to his workmen. "Boys," he said, "I believe I have found a gold mine!"

A few days later he rode down to New Helvetia, Sutter's walled outpost of empire near the confluence of the Sacramento and American rivers. Sutter, a Swiss emigré who had persuaded the Mexican authorities to grant him a stupendous amount of land in the valley, was nearly as excited as Marshall, but fearful that news of the discovery would inundate his land with eager hopefuls. He attempted to enforce some kind of

A pencil sketch of James Marshall, whose wandering eye discovered an empire in a mill-race.

it. One day near the end of the month, legend has it, Brannan came galloping into San Francisco, waving a bottle full of nuggets over his head and shouting, "Gold! Gold on the American River!" The story has the ring of apocrypha, but *something* had certainly occurred. San Francisco and Monterey witnessed an exodus of hysterical proportions as able-bodied gold-seekers laid hands on whatever was available for getting at the stuff and headed for the American River. Walter Colton, the *alcalde* at Monterey, remarked in disgust that "the farmers have thrown aside their plows, the lawyers their briefs, the doctors their pills, the priests their prayerbooks, and all are now digging gold."

Sutter's nervous fears were justified by the middle of July, as more than three thousand miners trampled what he liked to think of as his land. Colonel Richard B. Mason, interim military governor of California, investigated the situation in that month, and described one of the diggings in a dispatch to the Secretary of War in Washington: "The hill sides were thickly strewn with canvass tents and bush arbours; a store was erected, and several boarding shanties in operation. The day was intensely hot, yet about two hundred men were at work in the full glare of the sun, washing for gold." As word spread down the coast, thousands more streamed into California from Mexico and South America, until by the end of the year there were at least thirteen thousand scrambling over the foothills like so many beetles on a corpse.

They were chasing no gossamer fable. The gold was there in quantities never before heard of on the American continent. Men were hauling out of the ground as much as eight hundred dollars a day in such locations as Woods' Dry Diggings, near the present town of Auburn northeast of Sacramento, and it has been estimated that by the end of 1848 no less—and possibly more—than six million dollars had been grubbed out by the fortunate early arrivals. This was the stuff of empire, and the military authorities in California made haste to send word east to Washington.

In July, Commodore Thomas ap Catesby Jones sent Naval Lieutenant Edward F. Beale across Mexico with letters and a sample of California gold. In August, Colonel Mason sent Army Lieutenant Lucien Loeser from San Francisco with similar letters—and a tea caddy packed with 230 ounces of gold. Beale made it to the states first, arriving in Mobile, Alabama, in early

secrecy on the whole business, but could not resist prattling about it himself to his servants. By March, the news was out—and was greeted by a thundering skepticism. On May 20 the *California Star*, one of San Francisco's two minuscule newspapers, said, with regrettable grammar and spelling, that it was all a "sham, a supurb takein as was ever got up to guzzle the gullible."

After all, this was not California's first gold discovery. In 1842, one Francisco Lopez, who had studied mining in Mexico City, had discovered gold in San Feliciano Canyon in the San Fernando Valley, causing a minor rush from Sonora, Mexico. But the deposits in the San Fernando hills had been so shallow that they were worked out in three years. Surely, Marshall's discovery would prove just another flash-in-the-pan.

But it didn't, and by the end of May attitudes had changed considerably. One of the reasons may well have been Sam Brannan, an entrepreneur and Mormon backslider who had started a small general store near New Helvetia and who knew a good thing when he saw

September, after a wild and frequently dangerous journey. Somewhat more casually, Loeser sailed around the Horn and arrived in New Orleans in late November. Beale went on to Washington in plenty of time to pass along his report before President James K. Polk's annual message to Congress on December 5, and Polk was able to give official sanction to rumors already spreading like a cholera epidemic: "The accounts of the abundance of gold in that territory are of such an extraordinary character as would scarcely command belief, were they not corroborated by the authentic reports of officers in the public service. . . ." A few days later, Loeser arrived with his 230 ounces of gold, worth at least $3,500 on the open market. The combination was irresistible; the dream was revived.

The California Gold Rush was a national experience rarely matched in American history—and in the nineteenth century only the Civil War surpassed its impact. It was a kind of madness, a thirst for treasure, which such critics of the movement as Henry David Thoreau characterized as nothing more or less than simple-minded greed. Throughout the winter and spring of 1849, newspaper columns throughout the country fairly screamed news of California and its gold, together with comment on the effect it was having. "The coming of the Messiah, or the dawn of the Millenium," one editor exclaimed in awe, "would not have excited anything like the interest." And James Gordon Bennett's New York *Herald*, the most influential paper in the country, proclaimed as early as January that "men are rushing head over heels towards the El Dorado on the Pacific—that wonderful California, which sets the public mind almost on the highway to insanity. . . . Every day, men of property and means are advertising their possessions for sale, in order to furnish them with means to reach that golden land."

They were, indeed. In December and January, thousands of easterners streamed into seaport towns, booking passage on anything that would float—and not a few on tubs whose seaworthiness was questionable at best. Between December 14, 1848, and January 18, 1849, 61 ships with an average of 50 passengers each sailed for California from New York City, Boston, Salem, Philadelphia, Baltimore, and Norfolk. Ships in ports all over the world, encountering news of the rush,

This was no way to get to California (then or now), but the forty-niners might have tried.

canceled their commitments and sailed for the east coast of the United States, eager to grab off their share of the passenger explosion. In February, 60 ships sailed from New York alone, and 70 from Philadelphia. In that same month, a Pacific Mail Company steamship entered the Golden Gate with 365 passengers, the first argonauts; not long afterwards, one day saw no less than 45 shiploads of passengers anchor off Yerba Buena Cove, and by the end of the year more than 700 ships had arrived, bearing a total of at least 45,000 gold-seekers.*

Those who went by sea had two basic choices. The first was to board a ship at one or another eastern port, sail to Chagres or Aspinwall on the east coast of the Isthmus of Panama, cross the Isthmus by foot, mule-back, and *bungoes* poled by natives through the boggy, mosquito-ridden interior, arrive at the venerable white city of Panama, gleaming like a mirage above the ocean, and finally catch a San Francisco-bound steamer for the last leg of the journey. Thousands chose this

*The demand for transportation during these months provided a good living for New York cartoonists, who lampooned the obsession by coming up with any number of outlandish devices for travel, including enormous rubber bands and miniature rocket ships, but at least one inventor, Rufus Porter, quite seriously proposed the construction of what he called an "Aerial Transport," a dirigible-like airship which, he maintained, would "have a capacity to carry from 50 to 100 passengers, at a speed of 60 to 100 miles per hour. . . . The Transport is expected to make a trip to the gold region and back in seven days." For one reason or another, including the utter impossibility of the whole thing, Porter's airship was never built.

route, on the conviction that it was the quickest way to the California mines—and everyone was in a crashing hurry, as Bayard Taylor, one of the travelers in late 1849, reported in *El Dorado; or, Adventures in the Path of Empire.* At Chagres, he wrote, a returning Californian had just arrived "with a box containing $22,000 in gold-dust, and a four-pound lump in one hand. The impatience and excitement of the passengers, already at a high pitch, was greatly increased by his appearance. Life and death were small matters compared with immediate departures from Chagres. Men ran up and down the beach, shouting, gesticulating and getting feverishly impatient at the deliberate habits of the natives, as if their arrival in California would thereby be at all hastened."

Hurry, at this point, was wasted effort, as most of them learned on arrival in Panama City. Hundreds of anxious, waiting goldseekers clustered in and about the city, living in scraps of tents and watching their precious pokes being eaten away to nothing as the weeks passed. The experience of one of them, Howard C. Gardiner, was typical. He left New York on March 15, 1849, with eight hundred other passengers and $475; he arrived in San Francisco on July 26 with exactly six dollars left—most of the rest having disappeared during his six-week delay in Panama City. Delay was more than frustrating, however—it was dangerous. Panama City was a death-trap. The creeping horror of cholera, which would haunt all the land and sea routes of the Gold Rush, took its toll of both

Fighting for dinner in the hold of a steamer bound for San Francisco from Panama in 1849; many people survived. (From Century *Magazine, 1891)*

Overleaf: City made of gold—this panorama of San Francisco's waterfront and the "forest" of Yerba Buena Cove was made in late 1850 or early 1851 and is very likely the first photograph of the city ever taken.

GOLD AND SILVER IN THE WEST

Panamanians and travelers throughout the late spring and summer of 1849, adding its grisly impetus to the generalized anxiety, as Bayard Taylor noted: "There were about seven hundred emigrants waiting for passage when I reached Panama. All the tickets the steamer could possibly receive had been issued and so great was the anxiety to get on, that double price, $600, was frequently paid for a ticket to San Francisco. . . . I was well satisfied to leave Panama at that time; the cholera, which had already carried off one-fourth of the native population, was making havoc among the Americans, and several . . . lay at the point of death."

The second route was entirely by sea, south to Cape Horn at the tip of South America and north to San Francisco—through some of the meanest and most unpredictable waters then known to navigation. It was an 18,000-mile voyage and took anywhere from six to eight months (it would be several years before the great clipper ships cut it down to a little over three months). Many of the vessels were in foul condition, a matter blithely ignored by shipowners hungry for the passenger trade, as historian John Bach McMaster reported: "Every ship, brig, schooner, sloop that was half fit to go to sea was scraped, painted, fitted with bunks or cabins, and advertised as an A-1 fast-sailing, copper-bottomed, copper-nailed vessel, bound for San Francisco. . . ." They were inadequately rigged for long journeys, displayed a tendency to roll badly in heavy seas (and called "butter tubs" for that reason), possessed a collection of leaks that kept pumps busy for months, and were manned by crews patched together with hopelessly inexperienced hands whose only visible qualification was a desire to get their hands on gold the minute anchor was dropped in San Francisco Bay (a few thousand did precisely that, or attempted to; by the end of 1849, the bay was jammed with some six hundred ships whose crews had lit out for the foothills, sometimes with their captains a step or two ahead of them).

Conditions on board these floating incompetents were dismal in the extreme. Passengers were crammed into every available crevice; hundreds were booked passage on ships designed for scores. Food was as primitive as expedience could make it, and there was rarely enough, even for those willing and able to pay extra. Water supplies invariably reached the point of rationing long before sight of the Golden Gate. Over-crowding, hunger, thirst, scurvy, dysentery, seasickness, and the dark presence of cholera combined with boredom and frustration to give most ships the characteristics of a purgatory; for most, only the hope of gold enabled them to tolerate a situation that otherwise would have disintegrated their nerves.

For overland travelers, conditions were no better, although a man was somewhat less at the mercy of the elements and usually subject to no one's incompetence but his own. At least half, and probably more, of those who came to California in 1849 journeyed by one or another of several land routes. One took them through the Southwest, over the Santa Fe Trail to Santa Fe, then west across the deserts to the Gila River, down that to its juncture with the Colorado, across another desert to San Diego, and finally north to the mines. Probably fewer than ten thousand made this journey.

One of the three routes across Mexico attracted others: in the north, from Brownsville, Texas, across the states of Tamaulipas, Nuevo Leon, Coahuila, Chihuahua, and Sonora to the Colorado River; in the center, from Vera Cruz or Tampico to Mexico City, then up the Central Plateau; or in the south, across the continent to the western seaports of Acapulco, San Blas, or Mazatlán, where sea passage to California might (and, too often, might not) be obtained. Until recent years, it has been assumed that very few took any of the Mexican routes, but in *The El Dorado Trail*, historian Ferol Egan estimates that at least fifteen thousand trekked across the broken desert stretches of Mexico.

Most land travelers, however, followed the old Emigrant Trail that had taken land-seeking pioneers to Oregon and California during the previous fifteen years. From various jumping-off points on the Missouri River, this followed the valley of the Platte River to the North Fork, crossed to Chimney Rock and Fort Laramie, then past Independence Rock, through the Devil's Gate and South Pass to Fort Bridger.

Here, the emigrant had two choices for getting to the Humboldt River in northern Nevada: he could take the Hastings Cut-off along the south shore of the Great Salt Lake, across the desert, around the Humboldt Mountains, and down the south branch to the main river; or he could go from Fort Hall, down the Snake or Lewis River to the headwaters of the Humboldt, then down that to its sink (some left the river

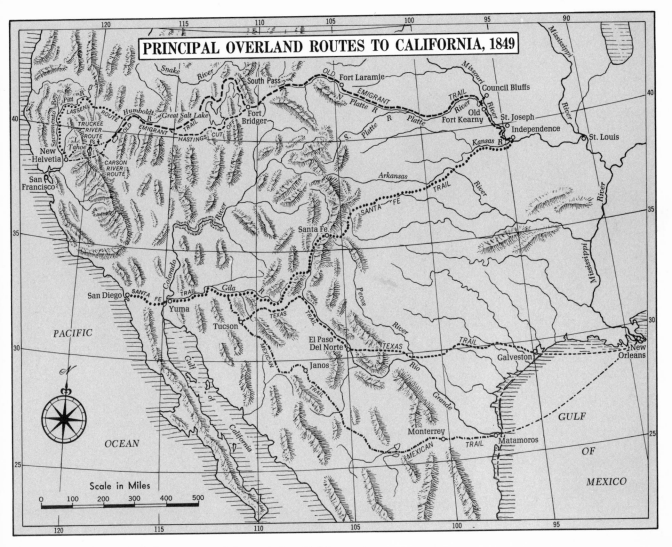

PRINCIPAL OVERLAND ROUTES TO CALIFORNIA, 1849

The trails to El Dorado led over some of the most formidable country in the West, a geography outside the pioneer experience.

at the great bend and headed north through Lassen's Pass to the Pitt River and the Sacramento Valley). Like those who used the Hastings Cut-off, they then headed west across the forty-mile stretch of desert to the Truckee River, and finally across the Sierra Nevada into the land of yellow promise.

In the spring, thousands poured into outfitting points on the Missouri River—Independence, Westport, St. Joseph, St. Louis—clamoring in the narrow streets and gladdening the mercantile hearts of tradesmen in wagons, horses, mules, oxen, guns, powder, broadcloth, salt pork, bacon, flour, sugar, tobacco, picks, pans, shovels, and miserably complicated and utterly useless contraptions peddled as sure-fire gold extractors. Some came as individual adventurers, but most as members of traveling companies formed in their hometowns (in some cases practically depopulating towns of their eligible bachelors), representing a geographical spectrum from New England, through the Old Northwest, the Mississippi Valley, and the South.

The names they gave these companies matched the grandiloquence of their dreams. Typical were the Congress and California Mutual Protective Association and the Sagamore and California Mining and Trading

The remarkable feature of this unfinished and unidentified drawing, probably done in 1850 or 1851, is not the dead and dying oxen—it is the presence of women and children, a rarity on the trek to California.

Company, both of which were armed and uniformed and operating under strict military rules (which, also typically, tended to disintegrate under the pressures of the trail, leaving most wagon companies riven by strife and bickering of feline dimensions).

Estimates on the number of wagons that crossed over the Missouri throughout the month of May and the first two weeks of June vary considerably; the Missouri *Republican* announced the total as nearly 5,800—but another contemporary observer estimated it at 12,000 for the month of May alone. Since each wagon generally had a complement of four men (and in very rare cases, women and children), these figures would put the total of emigrants somewhere between 23,000 and 48,000.

Whatever the total was, it was enough to make this the greatest transcontinental migration in American history. It was three to five months of brutal travel by wagon, over deserts, rivers, and mountains of a magnitude unknown to the pioneer experience. Thirst,

hunger, and simple exhaustion all took their toll, and while the Indians proved to be less of a problem than many had anticipated, they did have the unnerving habit of picking off stragglers. More emigrants, however, died as victims of their own inexperience; the number of drownings and accidental shootings reached appalling heights. The greatest killer of them all, of course, was cholera, carried west from the disease-ridden valley of the Mississippi. At least two thousand, and perhaps as many as five thousand, died of this agony before they ever reached the Continental Divide at South Pass in Wyoming.

The trail to California was a great highway, crowded with a sea of wagons. The prairies two hundred miles west of St. Joseph, one observer reported, were "glittering with wagons, carriages, tents, and animals." And they left behind far more than ruts to mark their passing. Among the other stupidities put forward as cold fact by dozens of so-called "guide" books thrown together by publishing sharks and purchased by the fistful, were lists of necessary equipment for the overland traveler. Some of these smacked of something straight out of *Alice in Wonderland,* noted Ray Allen Billington (in the August 1967 issue of *The American West*); many of these mendacious pamphlets, he says, "encouraged the natural proclivity of the emigrants to overload their wagons with nonessentials; travelers were advised not only to burden themselves with excessive quantities of flour and bacon, but to take an alcohol stove for use when buffalo chips were wet, a sheet iron stove, two India-rubber boats large enough to float a wagon across swollen streams, wading boots, mosquito bars, an air mattress, a rubber cloth to protect the wagon during rains, a fly trap, and even (in one English guide book) an Etna stove large enough to boil water for two cups of tea, 'the most refreshing thing possible after a long and fatiguing day's journey.'"

The result of all this was highway littering on a scale that passes belief, even in this age of discarded beer cans and abandoned automobiles. The farther they went, the more they threw away; for three thousand miles, the trail was cluttered with boxes, barrels, trunks, wagon wheels, cooking utensils, stoves, gridirons, carpenter's tools, anvils, crowbars, picks, shovels, gold-washing machines and bake-ovens, together with abandoned and burned wagons, rotting food, including great piles of rancid bacon slabs, and the carcasses of hundreds and hundreds of dead animals—enough, in fact, that a blind man might have been able to make it to California with nothing but the stench to show him the way. "If I had the property which has been sacrificed within 50 miles of here by those who followed the directions of the 'Guides,'" one traveler commented, "I would never go on to California."

By the time most of them did arrive, they had gone through the closest thing to hell on earth that any would ever experience, as suggested by the letter of one J. L. Stephens, an emigrant from Marietta, Ohio, who had survived long enough to write from Sacramento in September: "The hardships of the overland route to California are beyond conception. Care and suspense, pained anxiety, fear of losing animals and leaving one to foot it and pack his 'duds' on his back, begging provisions, fear of being left in the mountains to starve and freeze to death, and a thousand other things which no one thinks of until on the way, are things of which

I may write and you may read, but they are nothing to the *reality.*"

Whether they came by sea or land, then, the trip to California was for most of the forty-niners a desperate adventure, one that took an incredible toll of their physical, mental, and financial resources. "One prime wonder of the California gold rush," historian David Lavender has written, "is that so many people survived it." Having survived it, what the ninety thousand or more found waiting at the end of their painful journeying was enough to wither any man's dream.

The problem was simple enough: too many people and not enough gold. The loose surface gold, whose gleaming accessibility had given rise to the great rush in the first place, had been so thoroughly picked over by early 1849 that there simply was not enough to go around by the time intoxicated easterners could make it to the new Golconda. Their bitterness, understandably enough, was profound. "The greater part that you read in relation to this country," one disappointed miner wrote as early as September, 1849, "is *false;* and this everyone . . . will testify. The gold is here, but no man ever *dug* a dollar who did not earn it—the gold digging is a lottery sure enough. Some men make a fortune in a short time, but others in ten years would not make a cent. Of those who will leave here, the proportion will be scarcely one in five who will leave with any money. . . ."

And another remembered that "sudden disappointment on reaching the mines not only did sink the heart but sometimes the minds of the gold seekers. The abrupt dashing of expectations—the sudden wrecking of gorgeous visions that possessed and illumined the imagination—were as falling resurrectionless like Lucifer from gilded Heaven into the gulf of dark despair."

Still, the dream was hard to abandon, and at least forty thousand stubborn hopefuls made their way to the mining region, which spread throughout the lumpy, rolling foothills of the Sierra Nevada, from the Feather River in the north to the Merced in the south, an area virtually crawling with miners, who went from one tangled ravine to another, one river and creek bed to another, convinced that treasure lay just over the next hogback ridge; they were wanderers with the light of tomorrow in their eyes. They sought wealth that

Digging, digging, digging—placer mining was largely a matter of rock, dirt, water, and sweat; noteworthy in this view of about 1851 is the presence of at least four black men, who sweated side by side with whites for wages.

could be picked up, in Mark Twain's phrase, "with a long-handled shovel," but what most of them found was little more gold than could keep them in grub for a day at a time—and this obtained only after back-breaking effort.

"This gold digging is no child's play," one wrote in his journal, "but down right hard labor, and a man to make anything must work harder than any day laborer in the States." Another gave a graphic picture of the marginal nature of the whole business: "My diggings were about eighteen inches of bedrock. I managed to crevice and dig out about a dozen pans full per day from which about an ounce was daily realized. Out of this it required about $10 per day to supply my food, which was usually beef or pickled pork, hard bread, and coffee. By extra economy I sometimes managed to subsist on $8 per day."

Since the price of gold had been fixed at sixteen dollars the ounce, the chances of a man making a profit of more than five or six dollars a day were pretty anemic—and while this was as much as twice the salary

he could expect to make as a laborer in the States, it was hardly enough to justify the dreams of Golconda that had led him west.

The civilization these wanderers erected was as ephemeral as the wisps of dream. Bustling little camps popped up like mushrooms at every real or imagined "strike," cheapjack municipalities whose existence had all the geographic relevance of a village erected in *Gulliver's Travels*, as noted by one man who had spent five years in the gold country: "What a contrast do these funny little villages present, to the eye of one habituated to the sleepy agricultural towns of other countries; built of all kinds of possible materials, shapes and sizes, and in any spot, no matter how inconvenient, where the first store-keeper chose to pitch himself. Sometimes they are found on a broad flat with no suburb visible, squeezed together as though the land had originally been purchased by the inch, the little streets so crooked and confined, a wheelbarrow could scarcely be made to go through them; sometimes again, they are made up of detached buildings, forming

The miners "toiled and wrestled, and lived a fierce, riotous, wearing, fearfully exciting life," one historian wrote; some of the toil and excitement is suggested in the view above, taken in 1851.

an extended village two or three miles long. . . . Some, too, are quite invisible until you discover them at your feet buried in a deep chasm."

The frequently ludicrous names these towns were given suggests their transient nature—Jimtown, Hangtown, Bedbug, Shinbone Peak, Poker Flat, Murderer's Gulch, Delirium Tremens, Whiskey Diggings, Rough and Ready, You Bet—for they were hostages to uncertain fortune, to be taken no more seriously than the outsized practical jokes typical of men among whom the juices of life ran strong.*

They were at the mercy of more than their own dreams. One of the things some men learned relatively early was that there was more gold to be had from the goldseekers than from the Sierran hills. Not only the rapidly-building metropolises of San Francisco and

Sacramento, but every mining camp scattered through the Mother Lode was a mecca for entrepreneurs with an eye out for the main chance—which, more often than not, meant skinning the miner for all he was worth. More than one observer remarked at the "crowds of lawyers, small tradesmen, mechanics, and others, who swarm in every little camp, even of the most humble description, soliciting the patronage of the public—of whom they often form at least one half."

It was a seller's market par excellence; the simple necessities of life went for fabulous prices, and such amenities as eggs could bring as much as seventy-five cents each. Other appetites possessed by generally womanless, lonely young men far away from home could also be satisfied—and at suitably accelerated prices. Saloons, dance halls, gambling dens, and bordellos were as much a part of the proper mining camp as an assay office or a volunteer fire department. Any man with seemly respect for the laws of supply and demand could amass a comfortable estate, and some of the most permanent fortunes in California history were

*A remarkable number have survived, however—either in bits and pieces or as such nearly-intact relics as Columbia, surely one of the most successful examples of wholesale preservation west of Williamsburg, Virginia.

37

Sacramento, which quickly evolved from Sutter's ambitious little fort to a major service center for the mines (and ultimate.

built on a mercantile foundation—of one kind or another.

For such as these, and for those few who had come early enough—or coming late, had been lucky enough—to gather sufficient capital to exploit to the full the potential of the state's mineral wealth—the California Gold Rush was a smashing success. For innumerable others, it was little short of personal tragedy, as suggested by the journal entry of one Ananias Rogers, who wrote in despair from the mines in 1852: "I am solitary & alone. Am I never to see my loved ones again? If I had determined to make a permanent residence in this valley [the Sacramento] I might now have been well off . . . but my whole anxiety was to make a sudden

raise and return to my family. This I undertook to do by mining. This is certainly the most uncertain of any business in the world. . . . Indeed I do not know what to do. Oh that I could once more be with my family. Alas, I fear this may never be. Oh me, I am weak in body & I fear worse in mind. . . ."

No one knows what happened to Ananias Rogers. It may be that he did make his way back to his family. If so, he returned, like thousands of others (twenty-three thousand in 1852 alone), broken in spirit and perhaps in body. They had arrived in California young; most of them returned, like men from the agonies of war, sobered and perhaps matured by the follies of greed that had led them west. Those who re-

apital of the state), wallowed above in the "great inundation" of January, 1850.

mained—by choice or simply because they could not afford to return — found themselves victimized by geology. The bulk of the gold remaining after the early placer regions had been worked over (and there was a great deal of it) was at the bottom of rivers whose courses had to be changed to make it available, imbedded in hills that had to be washed away with powerful streams of water, or locked in quartz veins in the earth, where only deep mining could get it out—all processes that required a considerable capital investment, sophisticated technology, and an extensive labor force.

The American Everyman had none of these, and many were forced to compromise their dreams by join-

ing the working classes, employed by mining companies whose owners resided in the red plush luxury of San Francisco, or as itinerant laborers for farmers who had staked out sweeping vistas of farmland in the coastal and interior valleys, or as clerks for merchants who had been canny enough to keep their hands off the shovel and their eyes on the till.

Others continued to wander the pockets and crannies of the west for years, refusing to give up their hopes and, in their "prospecting," giving birth to a name and a tradition. And others, we will never know how many, were driven to suicide or to the slow death of alcoholism and the netherworld of the half-life.

This is a dismal picture, certainly, and one not

Anytown, California, ca. 1852: This unidentified scene was typical of civilization in the Sierra Nevada foothills.

wholly representative of California life in the early years. Yet it is a picture that has too often been obscured by the electric excitement of the Gold Rush—a kind of lesson in the ironies of something for nothing.

The year 1852 is generally considered to be the "end" of the California Gold Rush. By then, the fact that gold was not exactly lying about on the ground for any fool to pick up had become obvious even in the East. The frantic emigration that had raised California's population from about 14,000 in 1848 to 223,856 in 1852 had begun to taper off by the end of the year, although the period between 1852 and 1860 would still see an average of more than 30,000 people a year enter the state.

In the four years after its discovery, California's mines produced more than $220,000,000 in gold—more than twice the cost of the Mexican War, and more than enough to establish the state as a powerful economic force in the nation. That power would continue. Between 1849 and 1900, production in the state's mines never fell below $11,200,000 per year, bringing its total production to more than $1,300,000,000 in that half century. If she had possessed no other assets but gold, that productivity alone would have guaranteed California a voice in the affairs of the nation at a time when most of the trans-Mississippi West was but little

removed from *terra incognita.*

In fact, California gold changed the course of American history. The slow, steady movement toward the West that had characterized the previous seventy-five years of the nation's life was interrupted violently by a sudden leap to the western edge of the continent. Motives and methods that had typified the Westward Movement were distorted; those who came to California were light-years removed from the kind of pioneers described by Henry Clay in 1842: "Pioneers of a more adventurous character, advancing before the tide of emigration, penetrate into the uninhabited regions of the West. They apply the axe to the forest, which falls before them, or the plough to the prairie, deeply sinking its share in the unbroken wild grasses in which it abounds. They build houses, plant orchards, enclose fields, cultivate the earth, and rear up families around them."

The forty-niners couldn't have cared less about cultivating anything except their own purses. Rank amateurs in the techniques of the Westward Movement, they were not settlers, but gamblers with a single obsession: to strike it rich in California and return to their homes in the East with a stake to take them through the rest of life in ease and luxury. The dream was very nearly a moral imperative; in the eyes of most of them, it would have been a crime against themselves, their families, and their futures to have ignored the lorelei of gold.

They came from all walks of life—and from most of the major countries of the Western world: there were Mexicans, Chileans, Peruvians, Frenchmen, Australians, Russians, and Germans among them, not to mention Chinese—a veritable grab bag from all the recesses of the civilized world. They were young, most of them in their twenties, and a startling number of them in their teens. Most came from solid, if not affluent backgrounds; after all, it took money, quite a bit of money for the time, to get to California. It was an investment in the future, an act of faith similar to that of today's suburbanite, who buys stock on margin and hocks himself to the teeth in the anticipation of rewards to come.

For too many, anticipation ended in the misery of ruined hopes. Yet it doesn't really matter. California gold was real, profoundly real, and it reinforced all the dreams that men had dreamed since Coronado.

In its first few months, San Francisco was the archetype of the ramshackle mining camp, spontaneous, unplanned, and boiling with people—a state of affairs suggested by the illustration above, one of many from Frank Marryat's contemporary narrative of the California Gold Rush, Mountains and Molehills. Bayard Taylor corroborated the view with words in his own El Dorado, or, Adventures in the Path of Empire: "On every side stood buildings of all kinds, begun or half-finished, and the greater part of them were canvas sheds, open in front, and covered with all kinds of signs, in all languages. Great quantities of goods were piled up in the open air, for want of a place to store them. The streets were full of people, hurrying to and fro, and of as diverse and bizarre a character as the houses. . . ."

By 1850, the harbor of San Francisco was a wilderness of masts, and its waterfront was encrusted with barrels, boxes, crates, and deserted ships busily being converted into hotels, warehouses, taverns, and restaurants—a scene documented with great style and loving attention to detail by August Ferran in the painting above.

"The bay was crowded with ships," Vicente Perez Rosales, a Chilean goldseeker, wrote, "all of them deserted. Passengers and crews were raising the unstable population to over 30,000. And so intense was the activity of transient and permanent residents alike, that the city was growing and being transformed as if by magic."

CHAPTER THREE

THE HUMBUG OF HOPE

Fevers and depression, excitements and death

"The roads are lined with mining tools that have been thrown away as they would not pay for bringing back. Some of the men that helped get up the excitement have been hung and others shot. I think all will be killed that do not leave the country and they threaten burning down all the towns on the Missoura."

Hope is as hard to kill as a dimwitted shark. Those who survived the early years of the California experience and stayed on in whatever reduced circumstances quite simply refused to give up the dream. Experience had taught them little, and even the vaguest rumor of a new strike was enough to send men scampering off after one more rainbow's end.

It was not only the dispossessed who were victimized by their own restless seeking; even those who had made it tolerably good in the California mines pulled out after new visions, a phenomenon explained by John S. Hittell in his *History of San Francisco* (1878): "Regions containing extensive placer mines are peculiarly subject to sudden migrations of the miners to districts reported to be richer. The more abundant the gold, the more unsettled the population. They who are doing well, instead of being attached by their prosperity to their claims, are the more ready to move because they have money to spare. They will not wait till the value of the new diggings has been conclusively proved, for

fear that before such proof can be furnished all or nearly all the best claims have been taken up, and then the discovery would be of no benefit to them. They would abandon a good claim for the chance of getting a better one."

Normally, such peregrinations were confined to the slopes of the Sierra Nevada, where miners moved around with all the apparent aimlessness of particles in liquid suspension, an endless saraband which at one time or another populated nearly every accessible pocket of the mountains. But the dream had no geographical limits. In January, 1851, news of a fabulous new strike at Gold Bluff on the beach of the Trinity River in Humboldt County sent hundreds streaming into San Francisco from the mines, ready to book passage on anything that would carry them north; fortunately, proof of the area's limited possibilities was strong enough to discourage most from undertaking the journey.

More attractive were the rumors of gold discoveries in New South Wales, Australia, and in 1852 ships loaded with Californians sailed for Sydney. Two years later, stories published in Panamanian newspapers, which told of rich placers on the headwaters of the Amazon River in eastern Peru, inspired more than a thousand Californians to set off for Callao—where they found nothing.

In 1855, a number of fraudulent letters put together by mercantile and real estate speculators and published

All the hard work in the world was not always enough in the California mines, and many a miner yielded to self-pity and a misty yearning for home and family, as suggested by this Charles Nahl painting.

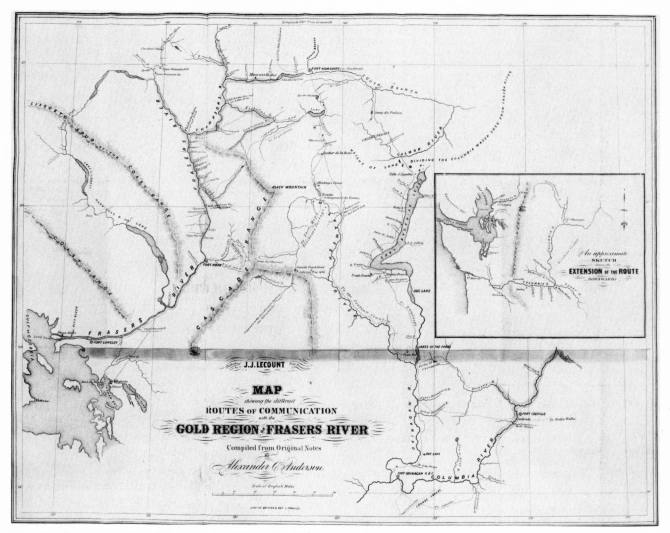

Pursuing dreams into the wilderness of British Columbia was no minor proposition; after a sea voyage into the straits of Juan de Fuca, it involved a laborious land journey up the rivers and across the tangled mountains of the Cascade Range. (Map, 1860)

in the Stockton and Los Angeles papers told of a new strike in the basin of the Kern River in the southern San Joaquin Valley. Five thousand miners went south, and another ten thousand prepared to follow them—until word filtered back that there was possibly enough gold down there to support a hundred men at subsistence levels.

None of these excitements matched the rush to the Fraser River mines of British Columbia in 1858; what the California Gold Rush had been to the United States, the Fraser River rush was to California. Gold had been discovered and worked on the lower reaches of the Fraser River in 1857, and in April, 1858, some

eight hundred ounces of gold dust were sent to the San Francisco mint. This, combined with letters from the area, inspired a genuine rush. Between April 20 and August 9, more than 23,000 men left for the Fraser River on 112 ships. The impact of this migration on the state can be imagined when it is pointed out that, given the respective populations of California and the United States, the equivalent figure in the rush from the East in 1849 would have been more than 1,250,000.

In San Francisco, a reporter wrote in June, 1858, "On every side, at every turn, you hear of Fraser River. Every acquaintance you meet asks whether you are going to Fraser river, or tells how he is going, or would

While the sparks of the Fraser River rush were fading, emigrants to the Colorado fields were using every vehicle at their disposal—from wheelbarrows (left) to handcarts. (Both from **Frank Leslie's Illustrated Newspaper,** *1859)*

go if he could, and enumerates your acquaintances who are going. . . . Here and there you will see fixed up in front of a store, some such sign as this: 'Selling out at cost; going to Fraser river, sure as you're born.' The Coroner of this city complains that the new diggings have put an end to the suicides."

Another added that "None are too poor and none too rich to go. None too young and none too old to go. . . . Many go with money, many go without; some to invest in 'real estate,' that arrant representative of humbug and swindling on this continent; some to see what may turn up . . . some out of curiosity, some to gamble, and some to steal, and unquestionably, some to die."

According to John S. Hittell, writing in 1861, the rush was a kind of combination of desperation and gambler's instinct: "Many of the adventurers had become disgusted with California, had nothing to hope for here, and had nothing to lose; and, of course, it was well enough for them to go. Others were men who had $200 to $1000, with no one to care for (today or tomorrow) save themselves . . . and why should they not go? Take it for granted that they should lose all their money; they would see the country, and would run the chance of making a fortune. . . . It was a bet of $1000 against $20,000. Who can say that the chances were more than twenty to one against the River?"

For whatever reasons, they went; and for a time it seemed that the sudden depopulation would ruin California, which was still suffering the effects of the disastrous panic of 1855. Successful mining camps lost half their populations, good claims went begging and rapidly growing industrial mining found itself without a reliable labor supply for the first time. Real estate values crumbled to as much as 20 percent of their former value, and lots in San Francisco dropped from two thousand dollars a front foot to two hundred. Victoria, British Columbia, was touted as the new metropolis of the West, and some San Francisco merchants actually began planning to move their operations north.

California needn't have worried, for the Fraser River rush soon proved to be another humbug of hope, one more example of too many people after too little gold. As early as June, 1858, one percipient San Francisco merchant had smelled out the truth of the matter, as reported by the Sacramento *Daily Union*: "Some anti-Fraserite, wishing to crack a serious joke at the expense of those who have gone to the new gold mines, has displayed in his shop window at San Francisco a human skeleton, and labelled it 'A Returned Frazer River Miner'; a pair of human skulls, in the same window, are designated 'Heads of Families Returned from Bellingham Bay.' "

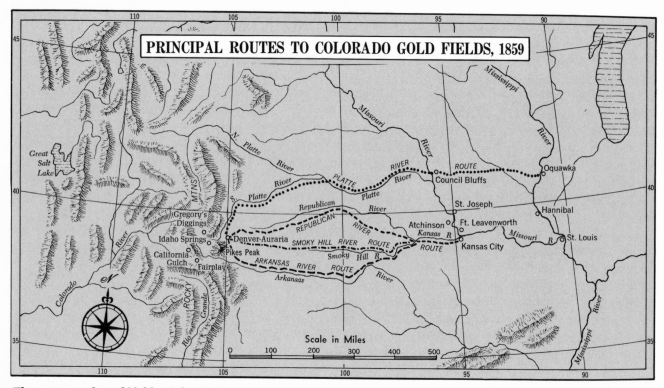

PRINCIPAL ROUTES TO COLORADO GOLD FIELDS, 1859

The routes to the goldfields of the Rocky Mountains, none of them easy, many of them exhausting, some of them deadly.

This grisly jape had an uncomfortable element of truth in it, for the starry-eyed goldseekers of the Fraser River stumbled into a bitter wilderness characteristically ill-equipped and sublimely unaware of the rigors of the country or the labor involved in getting there, as suggested by one observer at Esquinault, one of the debarkation points for the mines: "The scene is beyond description. Imagine hundreds of tents pitched everywhere, and boats being built without being pitched, etc., to travel a distance of ninety miles to reach the Fraser River and then to ascend the same which many hundreds never did, being assailed by natives or lost, crossing the Gulf of Georgia, but the impetus was Gold and to be there first."

What they found when they got there was a disappointment dismally similar to what too many of them had found in California. Not only was the gold much less than had been expected, the Fraser River, in comparison to which the rivers of California were gentle brooks, protected its treasure jealously; not until September could its bars be worked with much

profit, for the late spring melt of the northern mountains kept it at nearly full flood during the summer.

To complicate matters, the Americans were now on British soil and encountered the solid laws of England; inflexible Gold Commissioners wandered through the camps collecting license fees for mining, for the selling of spirits, and for trading. To free-wheeling men accustomed to making up their laws to fit the situation (see Chapter 12), this was a brutal affront. And if the five-dollar license had not been bad enough, the British also insisted that they conform to respectable standards of behavior, a patent impossibility among most miners.

Fortunately for British-American relations, most of those who rushed to the Fraser River in the spring and summer of 1858 were back in California by fall. The relative poverty of the northern mines is indicated by the fact that during the six working months of 1858, some three thousand miners produced only $520,000 in gold, or $170 a head. Those few who remained into the spring of 1859 found the pickings even slimmer. "I am somewhat staggered," one wrote in May, 1859, "by what I learn, for I have become satisfied that along the river the working claims are, with but few exceptions, quite superficial, furnishing 'pay dirt' for a comparatively short duration of time in each locality."

Although it would contribute its share and more to the various strikes which erupted throughout the West over the next five decades, never again would California experience an exodus equivalent to the Fraser River rush of 1858. Perhaps a lesson had been learned.

While Californians were still clamoring for passage to the Fraser River, one of the great bubbles in the mining history of the West was being busily inflated on the other side of the continent in the Territory of Kansas: the manic rush to the Colorado Rockies in 1858 and 1859, second only to the California Gold Rush in its dimensions—if not its productivity. There were a number of ironies involved in the story, not the least of which is the fact that Colorado gold had first been discovered by a band of Cherokee Indians on their way to California in 1849 from the Indian Territory. During the journey, they stopped at Ralston's Creek, a tributary of the Platte River, and did some experimental prospecting. The incident was later related by one who had heard the story from a member of the party: "One of the company waded into the creek, from the bottom of which he obtained a panfull of sand which yielded two or three dollars' worth of gold, with which they returned to camp and proposed

The Colorado rush was rescued from unmitigated disaster by John H. Gregory's strike on the North Fork of Clear Creek in the spring of 1859—and a celebration in tents quickly sprouted. (From Beyond the Mississippi *by Albert D. Richardson, 1867)*

TRAIN OF MINING EMIGRANTS ON THEIR WAY TO THE PIKE'S PEAK GOLD REGIONS.

THE WAGON EMIGRANT.

it all the more pleasant for doing so. These are the right men in the right place, more fit for the work than the white-handed store clerks who come out here expecting to become millionaires in a few months, and then because their expectations are not gratified, have gone back to the cities with lugubrious countenances, cursing the country and the fates that brought them out.

I am not one of those castle-builders who expect to load a wagon with gold in a day or two and start home, and all those who expect to pick it up like pebble stones had better stay where they are, even if they can only earn twenty-five cents a day. But for those who come out expecting and prepared for hard work, this is the country, and to such I would say, "Come, there is room enough for all, and plenty to spare." Let those who intend coming bear in mind this piece of advice. Bring every necessary article that can conveniently be carried, as prices are of course very high here, and will be higher.

It is impossible in the limited space at my command, to give anything like an adequate description of the country, its merits or disadvantages; but no doubt many reports have already been published, and if some are unfavorable, all the better, as they will probably deter some lazy, good-for-nothing loafers and rowdies from coming out, a blessing most devoutly to be wished for. Let honest, working men come here, and they will be heartily welcomed.

sions, we shall first come to those travelling with a wagon and team.

In the sketch which I have sent, one of the horses is rather unruly, an accident that very frequently happens. The major part of the baggage is stowed away in the wagon, so that the journey is comparatively easy.

I have also sent you a sketch of the party taken at the time when, after the day's march is finished, they pitch their camp and rest themselves after the fatigues of the day. The group which I have drawn have brought with them a banjo and a violin, on which they are playing, whilst the others lounging around occasionally shout an accompaniment, not particularly harmonious, but evincing the possession of light hearts and strong lungs, two very desirable things to take to Pike's Peak.

The camping place of this party was very well chosen, having abundance of wood and water close at hand. If proper care be used, the travellers need not be without these important requisites any of the time, the whole country through which they pass being well watered and thickly timbered.

The bundle emigrants come next in order. They generally possess a horse or pony on which they place such baggage as belongs to the common stock; their own personal effects they carry in bundles slung on their shoulders, from which circumstance they derive their name.

The party represented in my drawing were the proud possessors of a skinny pony, on which was piled a heterogeneous assemblage of buckets, tin pans and cooking utensils, making the animal appear like a locomotive tin ware store. The men were all armed with rifles and revolvers, and looked just like the right sort for the mines.

Lower down in the scale are the hand-cart party, which I have also endeavored to depict. The carts which are used in this manner are made with little or no bed, and have a frame both in front and behind, so that all may assist when in a heavy road, or in going up a hill, which was the case when my drawing was taken. The rain was driving sharply in their faces, but they trudged on, with their pipes in their mouths, seemingly caring little for the weather, when they thought of the bright prospects before them.

The last sketch which I shall send you this time is one of the wheelbarrow man, who trusts to his own efforts to reach the land of gold. This was a very pretty little scene; the sparkling of the little rivulet in the foreground lending an additional charm to the landscape.

The voyager himself was one of those *insouciant*, devil-may-care sort of fellows that seem to take life very easily, and find

GIRLS AND OX TEAM ON THE ROAD.

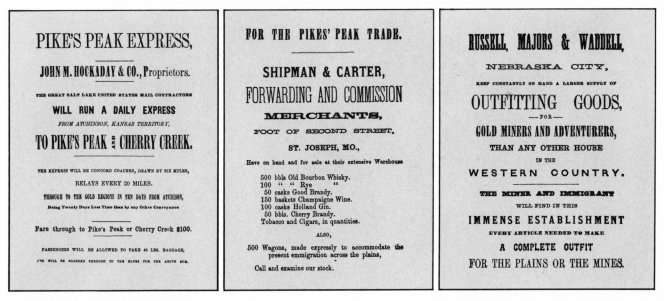

With screaming insistence, a plethora of "guidebooks" announced the glories of Colorado gold—each of them amply subsidized by local merchants, who also managed to include advertisements; above, some flimflam from Parker and Huyett's Miners' Hand-book and Guide to Pike's Peak, 1859.

remaining, but being overruled by a large portion of their companions who had heard such marvelous tales of California, they were obliged to yield . . . ."*

Another irony is the fact that, unlike the California Gold Rush, the rush to the Rockies was in many ways the result of economic and social conditions existing on the eastern seaboard. The depression of 1857, one of the most severe in the country's history, had been particularly damaging to the states of the Old Northwest and the Mississippi Valley. A decade of ruinous optimism—nourished in no little part by the heady influx of California gold—had inspired eastern capital to invest heavily in superbly bloated land, township, and railroad speculations in the trans-Appalachian West; when such enterprises began inevitably to crumble, that capital pulled back, leaving the region to fend for itself. By 1858 most of its inhabitants were ready to believe anything that would promise relief, and when news of gold came to the particularly

crippled merchants of the West's jumping-off points from Lawrence, Kansas, to St. Louis, Missouri, they were more than willing to feed credibility.

Rumors of gold in the Colorado Rockies had persisted sporadically throughout the decade following its discovery by the Cherokee company, but it was not until early 1858 that serious investigation commenced. In that year, one William Green Russell, a veteran of both the Appalachian and California gold fields, organized a party in Georgia and set out for the eastern slopes of the mountains. They arrived at Cherry Creek, near the present site of Denver, and shortly were joined by five other prospecting parties, comprising a total of 104 men. Results were disappointing, and by July all but Russell and a dozen others had returned.

Near the end of the month, the remaining prospectors struck a pocket on the South Platte, of which Cherry Creek was a tributary, and hauled out about one hundred dollars' worth of gold. John Cantrell, a member of the trading organization of Bordeau and Company, passed through their camp and became infatuated with the find. He picked up a small sample of the gold and rode into Kansas City with it, inflating its importance all the way, as reported by the Kansas City *Journal of Commerce* on August 26, 1858: "We

*With all deference to the risks of historical speculation, it is difficult not to wonder what might have happened had they remained in the Rockies that summer; even a minor degree of success in the comparatively rich placers of the area might have been enough to divert a significant number of California-bound goldseekers to the Colorado region, thus altering history—or at least warping it a bit.

The rush to Colorado—like many of the later rushes throughout the West— was a matter of profound national interest; here was news, big news, and it was thoroughly covered by many eastern journals and newspapers.

Of the one hundred thousand who set out across the plains, perhaps fifty thousand actually persevered to the Rockies; some twenty-five thousand of these fled back to the East, but scores of prospecting parties fanned out into the mountains.

were surprised this morning to meet Mons. Bordeau and Company, old mountain traders just in from Pikes Peak. They came in for outfits, tools, etc., for working the newly discovered mines on Cherry Creek, a tributary of the South Platte. They bring several ounces of gold dug up by the trappers of that region, which, in fineness, equals the choicest of California specimens."

The inaccuracies in the paper's story are magnificent: the gold region was a good sixty miles removed from Pikes Peak; the gold had not been discovered on Cherry Creek, but the South Platte; the discoverers were not trappers, but miners by choice; and the specimens of gold were barely a shadow of California's finest. But the newspaper was less interested in the nuances of truth than the imagined implications of the find; it ran the story under the following screaming headline: "THE NEW ELDORADO!!! *Gold in Kansas Territory!!!* The *Pike's Mines! First Arrival of Gold Dust at Kansas City!!!*" Forty years before William Randolph Hearst "invented" the Spanish-American War, the Kansas City

Journal of Commerce understood the mechanics of manufactured news.

Other newspapers picked up and spread the reports, and by September several hundred men had scrambled toward Cherry Creek, setting up housekeeping on opposite banks of the stream in Auraria (whose namesake was in Georgia) and Denver City, two primitive camps later merged into the City of Denver. Swiftly, the available gold in Cherry Creek and the South Platte, never extensive, was worked out; by November, the ground had frozen too solid to be worked, and those who stayed simply dug in for the winter, waiting for spring and the new Golconda—and writing enthusiastic letters back home.

In the meantime, the outfitting towns of the Kansas and Missouri frontiers—among them Council Bluffs, St. Joseph, Kansas City, Independence, Leavenworth, Atchison, and St. Louis—busied themselves through the winter by laying in supplies, promulgating rumors, leaping upon exaggerations and distending them fur-

Auraria (later Denver) in 1859 was an extemporaneous fabrication no more sophisticated (and certainly no more comfortable) than any number of similar municipal fantasies the West would see over the next fifty years.

ther, and generally keeping excitement at a steady pitch. Many contracted for the publication of guidebooks, which—not incidentally—tended to glorify those routes that passed through their particular towns and denigrate those that passed through others.

There were three basic routes: in the north along the Platte River from Council Bluffs or St. Joseph; in the center along the Republican or Smoky Hill rivers from Leavenworth or Atchison; or in the south along the Arkansas from Kansas City or Independence. In nearly all the guidebooks prepared for the spring rush, the deliberate inaccuracies in regard to the various trails were astounding, distances were shrunk by two and three hundred miles; non-existent bridges over rivers were solemnly listed; deserts disappeared; grass grew where it had never grown before; costs plummeted to ridiculous proportions; and at least one maintained that the road along the Platte River was a virtual highway, "without a stone or pebble to jolt the carriage. . . ."

But of all the gross distortions put forward as solid fact by these guidebooks, perhaps none was more insidious than the promotion of the Smoky Hill route from Leavenworth or Atchison, as Ray Allen Billington outlined it in the August, 1967, issue of *The American West:* "No mention was made of the fact that the western portions of this trail were largely unknown, that game and water were almost impossible to find there, and that grass was too scant to sustain any large number of draft animals. Instead, the fifty-niners were assured that the arid stretch between the head of the Republican River and the diggings was only fifty miles wide, and that they would find 'ample supplies of timber, water, and grass, almost the entire distance.' Many an inexperienced greenhorn risked death by accepting such falsehoods as truth. . . ."

The books also mangled the truth when discussing the richness of the mountain placers, as Billington enumerated. "The gold region," one said, "is unlike

*Having survived the rigors and disappointments of gold-hunting, Denver quietly
evolved from a collection of tents to a bustling, if modest, service center in less than a decade.
(From Alfred E. Mathew's* Pencil Sketches of Colorado, 1867)

that of California. In the latter, a few men would make
their piles by striking a good lead; but in the Kansas
gold mines every man can find gold and make good
wages." Another maintained that it was "difficult to
find a shovelful of dirt that does not contain more or
less of the precious metal," and yet another soberly proclaimed that "there is no end to the precious metal.
Nature seems to have turned into a most successful
alchemist by converting the very sands of the streams
into gold." The reason for its abundance was simple
enough, according to many: somewhere in the bowels
of the Rocky Mountains was a solid chunk of gold
weighing hundreds of millions of tons; during preceding eons, erosion had washed bits and pieces of it into
the rivers and streams of the eastern slopes. This curious
echo of California's "Mother Lode" (see Chapter 10)
was accepted as gospel fact by a remarkable number of
the guidebooks—and, unfortunately, many of the goldseekers.

As spring approached, the newspapers sang of gold:
"Oh, the Gold! the Gold!—they say,/ 'Tis brighter than
the day,/ And now 'tis mine, I'm bound to shine,/ And
drive dull care away." More to the point, they sang of
mercantile opportunity, as did the Lawrence *Republican* of March 31, 1859: "If 100,000 men should go to
Pikes Peak this season (which is probable) from all

sections of the Union, it will take the snug little sum
of $2,000,000 to furnish them out at $200 per head,
which is a light estimate."

Such gleeful rubbing-of-the-hands in print was understandable; these towns had helped to create a gold
rush, and they now anticipated reaping the rewards of
their effort. Moreover, that anticipation was justified.
As with the California Gold Rush, estimates vary as to
the number of men who set out for the mountains in
the spring of 1859, but it is generally agreed that the
figure is close to one hundred thousand—and it is reasonable to assume that the outfitters got their two
hundred dollars a head, and more. The goldseekers
came from all over, but most from the states of the Middle West, where depression had driven them to seek the
golden dream. "The number of people in this section
of Iowa who are going to Pikes Peak is astonishing,"
one of them wrote in his diary. "A company of over
sixty will leave Fairfield next week, and nearly every
man you meet is bound for the Peak in a 'few weeks'."

Most traveled in the traditional ox-drawn wagons,
whose covers were emblazoned with sundry glad cries,
chief among them the famous "Pikes Peak or Bust!"
but many who could not afford such luxury went however they could. "We see on the road," a traveler wrote,
"men on foot with packs on their backs—men with

handcarts—men without anything but a blanket and a brazen face—all bound to Pikes Peak." Many attempted to utilize the constant prairie wind for motive power, an enterprise that worked more often in theory than in fact, as reported by a traveler on the Arkansas River: "We overtook today a curiosity in the shape of a wind wagon. It is a four wheeled vehicle, about nine feet across, schooner rigged, a very large sail. The whole weighs three thousand pounds. It plowed right through the mud, but cast anchor in a deep ravine where the wind failed to fill the sail and she stopped. . . ."

Most traveled the generally well-marked and familiar trails to the north and south, but the Republican River–Smoky Hill route was, on paper at least, shorter, and several thousand too impatient to take the longer ways ventured out into the dismal, almost unknown reaches of this trail. For many who did, the journey was a disaster of hunger, thirst, exhaustion, and, too often, death; it gave birth to one more entry in one of the oldest, most macabre traditions of the West—cannibalism, whose ghoulish presence haunts our history.

In early May, 1859, one Daniel Blue stumbled into Denver City; he was the only survivor of a four-man party, which had included his two brothers. For weeks, they had wandered lost and starving in the near-desert country above the Smoky Hill River before the first man died. In a statement issued at Denver City, Blue reported what disposal he and his brothers had made of the dead man: "Before he breathed his last, he authorized and requested us to make use of his mortal remains in the way of nourishment. We, from necessity, did so, although it went hard against our feelings. We lived on his body for about eight days." Shortly afterwards, one of the brothers died, and the remaining two ate him; shortly after that, his last brother succumbed, and Blue lived off the remains long enough to be picked up by a passing stagecoach. One would not care to share his dreams.

By the end of May, the Arkansas and Platte rivers were a bedlam of wagons to rival the days of the California Gold Rush, as one party member breathlessly confided to his journal for May 21. "Today we traveled north eight miles, then came in sight of the Arkansas River, and Jerusalem, what a sight! Wagons—wagons —Pikes Peak wagons. Well! There were a few of them

—I presume three hundred ox-wagons in sight. . . . I went up and spoke to the men; they told me sad news; said there is not gold at the Peak. Some that are going on say they have met three hundred wagons coming back. . . . One man came from the mines and has some gold dust in a quill, and says there is no coarse gold there, a man cannot earn his provisions. We are going to see for ourselves."

"Going to see for ourselves" became the rallying cry for some fifty thousand who refused to let the fact of the matter interfere with their hopes. What they saw in Denver City–Auraria when they got there was enough to make at least twenty-five thousand of them turn tail and run, finally convinced of their folly. Again, it was a problem in numbers: too many men for too little gold. The few placers that had been discovered in 1858 had been worked out almost instantly, and others discovered early in 1859 had been claimed by those lucky enough to be there early—and by May, some of *those* had been worked out. Bitterly, thousands scratched out "Pikes Peak or Bust!" and wrote "Busted, by God!" and returned home, either selling their expensive mining equipment for a tenth of its value or simply littering the trail with it. Some could not afford to return, as evidenced by a plaintive letter of a young man to his father in June: "There is no gold at Pikes Peak. No man can make ten cents a month. I am out of money, and without a chance to make any. . . . If you don't send me some money, I will starve to death."

In an attempt to repair the damage of overblown expectations, Horace Greeley, then in the middle of his transcontinental journey to publicize the need for a Pacific Railroad, joined with his companions, A. D. Richardson and Henry Villard, in issuing a statement from one of the diggings in early June, published in the *Rocky Mountain News*. After outlining various successes and hoped-for successes, the trio added: "We cannot conclude this statement without protesting most earnestly against a renewal of the infatuation which impelled thousands to rush to this region a month or two since, only to turn away before reaching it, or to hurry away immediately after more hastily than they came. Gold mining is a business which requires . . . capital, experience, energy, endurance, and in which the highest qualities do not always command success.

"There may be hundreds of ravines in these mountains as rich in gold as that in which we write, and

Central City, one of the crown jewels of production in "the little kingdom of Gilpin County," was a typically dismal collection of utilitarian architecture in 1864—but no one really cared.

there probably are many, but, up to this hour, we do not know that any such have been discovered. There are said to be five thousand people already in this ravine, and hundreds more pouring into it daily . . . pressing hither under the delusion that gold may be picked up here like pebbles on the sea shore, and that when they arrive here, even though without provisions or money, their fortunes are made. . . . Great disappointment, great suffering, are inevitable."

Great disappointment fed bitterness, which reached

profound dimensions that summer of 1859. In their view—and with considerable justification—the discouraged fifty-niners had been bilked and bilked good by flimflam men, and it was an age when a man's fury usually found physical expression of one kind or another. "The roads are lined with mining tools that have been thrown away as they would not pay for bringing back," one returnee declared, adding that "Some of the men that helped get up the excitement have been hung and others shot. I think all will be killed that do not leave the country and they threaten burning down all the towns on the Missoura." No towns were burned, and so far as we know there is no documented instance of bloody revenge, but those who had participated in the great buildup could not have rested easy in their skins for quite a while after.

D. C. Oakes, one of the guide-book authors, came in for special treatment, and "Hang Byers and D. C. Oakes for starting this damned Pikes Peak hoax" became a favorite bit of doggerel. For reasons best known to himself and his maker, Oakes made the mistake of journeying to the mines that summer, where he escaped lynching by hiding in a wagon; shortly afterwards, he encountered a crude wooden tombstone on which someone had inscribed, "Here lies D. C. Oakes, Dead, Buried, and in Hell"; and he soon learned to avoid Denver City, which was festooned with himself, hung in effigy.

Oakes survived the summer; fate is often kind to the undeserving.

Those who remained in the Rocky Mountain mines in the face of all logic were generally cast in the same green mold as the California miners—albeit somewhat less verbose literarily, since the bulk of them had come from the largely rural sections of the country. They were a rootless, milling breed of amateurs, as Frank Fosset described them in his *Colorado, Its Gold and Silver Mines . . .* (1879): "Probably nineteen-twentieths of these gold-seekers were as ignorant and inexperienced as regards mining as they well could be, and had but a faint idea of the work to be done or the experience to be undergone in this wild rush for wealth."

Unlike the California miners, however, who had been forced to improvise with no mentors save a few veterans of the Appalachian mines, the Rocky Mountain miners were blessed with the presence of a number of "Old Californians"—men not directly from California (those were on their hectoring way to the Fraser River), but those who had joined the rush in 1849, survived it to return home, and had followed the dream once again to the Shining Mountains. Techniques of survival, prospecting, mining, and government were quickly patterned after the California experience, a development that gave the new camps a relative degree of stability in spite of their extemporaneous nature—

and doubtless contributed much toward their survival as a viable mining community, a solid base on which to build.

For there *was* gold in these mountains, not enough to match the California success and certainly not enough to support the bloated expectations of its promoters—but enough to keep the dream alive. Three major strikes beyond Cherry Creek and the South Platte River were made during the early spring of 1859, and it can be said that these three enabled the Colorado rush to transcend the miserable debacle it had threatened to become.

The first, and richest, was made by John H. Gregory. During January, he had set out from Denver City and prospected up North Clear Creek in the foothills of the mountains. At a point later known as Gregory Gulch, he made his first find, but a lack of supplies forced him to retreat to Denver City. Here, he contracted with a local merchant in great secrecy, promising him a share in the enterprise in exchange for enough supplies to return in the spring. Thus "grubstaked," a term which would soon enter the language, he went back up the creek in May, consolidated his find, and quickly sold it for $22,000—a figure he may later have regretted, since this was the Gregory Lode, one of the richest strikes in the region's early history.

The effect of the discovery on the frustrated residents of Denver City and Auraria was described by Henry Villard in *The Past and Present of the Pike's Peak Gold Region* (1860): "A Mr. Bates . . . made his appearance in Auraria with a vial full of gold, representing a value of about eighty dollars, which he claimed to have washed out of thirty-nine pans of dirt, obtained not far from the spot on which Gregory had made his discovery. Mr. Bates being known as a reliable man, his story was at once credited and he and his bottle taken from cabin to cabin. The sight of his gold forthwith produced an intense excitement, and the news of his luck spread like wild-fire and at once moved the hearts of the denizens of the two towns with gladdening sensations.

"Individuals could be heard everywhere on the streets shouting to each other, 'We are all right now,' 'the stuff is here after all,' 'the country is safe,' etc. On the following day an universal exodus took place in the direction of North Clear Creek. Whoever could raise enough provisions for a protracted stay in the moun-

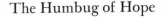

tains, sailed out without delay. Traders locked up their stores; bar-keepers disappeared with their bottles of whiskey, the few mechanics that were busy building houses, abandoned their work, the county judge and sheriff, lawyers and doctors, and even the editor of the *Rocky Mountain News,* joined in the general rush."

By the end of the summer there were more than five thousand crowded into the gulch, and more than one hundred sluices in operation, together with a small stamp mill; shortly afterwards the region featured the hustling little mining towns of Black Hawk, Central City, and Nevadaville.

At about the same time that Gregory was scouting out the possibilities of North Clear Creek, George Jackson was grubbing around on Clear Creek itself, near a group of hot mineral springs (later Idaho Springs). In *The Bonanza West,* historian William S. Greever outlined the mechanics of Jackson's discovery: "The ground was frozen so hard that he had to build a big fire to thaw it, but he took out about $10 worth of gold. He next dumped considerable charcoal in his discovery hole, topped it with dirt, built another large fire over it to help conceal his operations, marked a large fir tree nearby with his axe, cut the top off a small pine seventy-six steps in a westerly direction from his find, and then retreated to civilization."

The eminently cautious Jackson returned with a party of twenty-two in May; they converted their wagons into sluice boxes and in seven days had worked out some $1,900. News of the strike got back to Denver City quickly, and by the end of May Idaho Springs, too, was bustling with activity.

Earlier, but less successful than either of the other two, was a discovery to the north of them, in the country drained by the tributaries of Boulder Creek. The initial discoveries in mid-January had not been so successfully kept under wraps as those in Gregory Gulch and Idaho Springs, and in a few weeks hundreds of refugees from the failures of Denver City and Auraria clambered into this new region of hope, throwing

Black Hawk, an outgrowth of the Gregory Gulch mines of 1859, had become a tight little industrial town by the end of the century, as documented in this scene of 1899.

together a typically helter-skelter town called Gold Hill.

Inspired by the strikes at Gregory Gulch, Idaho Springs and Gold Hill, prospecting parties began filtering into all the crannies of the Front Range, from Boulder County in the north to the San Juan country in the south—a region sprawling across a good two hundred miles of rockbound wilderness, meadows, mountain peaks two and almost three miles high, cascading rivers, gulches, canyons and semi-deserts, much of it totally unexplored, and most of it infinitely more formidable than anything in their experience.

Many of them found their way into South Park, a magnificent valley fifty miles long by forty wide that sits beneath a ring of mountains like the palm of the hand of God. Here, a genuine epidemic of sporadic strikes inspired a flush of camps: Tarryall, Fairplay, Alma, Montgomery, Buckskin Joe, Mosquito, Hamilton, Jefferson, Negro Gulch, and French Gulch.

Most of these were short-lived, if characteristically frenetic, but one that outlasted most of them was California Gulch on the Arkansas River just south of the present town of Leadville. A strike had been made there in April, 1860, by one Abe Lee, who did a quick prospect and shouted to his companions, "By God, I've got all of California in this here pan!" By August there were at least ten thousand hopefuls crammed into this six-mile miniature canyon, some of them washing out hundreds of dollars a day (one of the first to arrive and establish himself in the instant town of Oro City was H. A. W. Tabor, a storekeeper who would come to glory in another twenty years; see Chapter 5).

California Gulch, or Oro City, was typical of the breed, as described by one who was there: "There were a great many tents in the road and on the side of the ridge, and the wagons were backed up, the people living right in the wagons. Some of them were used as hotels; they had their grub under the wagons, piled the dishes there, and the man of the house and his wife would sleep in the wagons nights. They would get some rough boards and make tables where the boarders took their meals, and those who did not want to board did their own cooking. The gamblers would have tables strung along the wayside to take in the cheerful but unwary miner."

In five years, this sub-sub-metropolis was just another ghost camp, a dénouement symptomatic of

mining in Colorado throughout the decade of the 1860s. Whether in simple placer form or lode form—which, as in California, required capital, a labor force, and sophisticated equipment for mining—the gold of the Rockies was insufficient to support a long period of boom comparable to that in California. In 1862, the most productive year during Colorado's first period of mining, only $3,400,000 was taken out of the reluctant mountains, and every year following that until the end of the decade saw a steady decline.

Between 1858 and 1867, the Colorado mines produced $25,000,000—a figure that might seem significant until it is compared to the $502,576,000 which California produced in its first ten years. As early as 1866, the recession in mining activity was obvious to Bayard Taylor, who gave his impressions in Colorado: A Summer Trip (1867): "The deserted mills, the idle wheels, and the empty shafts and drifts for miles along this and the adjoining ravines—the general decrease of population everywhere in the mountains—indicate a period of doubt and transition."

What followed was indeed a period of doubt and transition, but it was also a period of consolidation, a time when all the disparate elements making up the territory's life were shaken down into some kind of workable form. Mining activity began to concentrate back where it had begun—along North Clear Creek, an area that entered a period of steady, if unspectacular gold production. Gradually, placer mining—which had declined to $320,000 in production during 1868—almost disappeared, replaced by the more complicated, methodical system of vein mining, together with more sophisticated methods of milling and processing the particularly refractory ores of the mountains.

It was a time of innovation, of experimentation, of trial and error (for more on this, see Chapter 10), some of it financed by eastern capital faithful that something good might yet come out of the mountains—a harbinger of things to come. The city of Denver gradually absorbed Auraria, and began a slow growth, nourished by embryonic developments in agriculture and husbandry in the surrounding area.

It would be some time before the great silver strikes of the 1870s and the gold strikes of the 1880s and 1890s would enable the region to again play a dominant part in western mining—but when they came, Colorado would be ready for them.

Borrasca was all around, but Denver was a town rapidly taking on the outlines of a city by 1866, as illustrated by this hand-colored lithograph from Harper's Weekly. The mines of the "Little Kingdom of Gilpin County" were producing enough gold to warrant the establishment of a United States Mint in Denver, and Fort Wicked took care of the region's malefactors. Those who survived the assaults of Indians and the weather (somewhat fancifully rendered above, but nonetheless real) found the framework of civilization waiting for them on Larimer Street, as suggested by a Frenchman, Louis Simonin, in 1867: "Denver has numerous buildings, a theatre, a mint, a race track. . . . Everywhere are stores, banks, hotels, saloons. As in all the Union, one partakes freely, several times a day, of the sacramental glass of whiskey. . . ."

Oh the Gold! the Gold!—they say,
'Tis brighter than the day,
And now 'tis mine, I'm bound to shine,
And drive dull care away.

*So sang the newspapers of the Missouri
frontier towns, but for too many of
the fifty thousand who streamed across
the plains in the spring and summer
of 1859, the cry of gold was a humbug
that led only to dry water holes and
death, as documented by this grisly
rendition of a scene altogether
too common to the West's second
great gold rush.*

CHAPTER FOUR

THE BATTLE OF THE COMSTOCK

The mountains of Nevada and the new Zacatecas

"It is as if a wondrous battle raged, in which the combatants were man and earth. Myriads of swarthy, bearded, dust-covered men are piercing into the grim old mountains, ripping them open, thrusting murderous holes through their naked bodies. . . ."

The dream that had been revived by the California experience and given further impetus in the Colorado Rockies was a dream of gold. During the first decade of mining in the American West, it was gold that called men across mountains, inspiring them to pledge their lives, their fortunes, and their sacred honor in quest of something for next to nothing. It was not until silver was discovered in Nevada in 1859 that it occurred to most that there might well be treasure other than that of Midas hidden in the western hills—and even in Nevada miners refused with an almost perverse obstinacy for several years to see that what lay before them was nothing less than the new Zacatecas. The vision of gold was like a glaucoma in the eyes of the dream-seekers, blinding them to the obvious.

Mining activity in the region of what would later become the greatest silver camp in western mining began at a remarkably early date—and, as in the Colorado Rockies, it began as a direct consequence of the California Gold Rush. Early in 1850, a Mormon emigrant train, on its way to California to bastion the stake of the Church in the new Golconda, camped in the Carson Valley for a number of weeks, waiting for the spring thaw to make the great wall of the Sierra Nevada passable. While there, a number of the party did some prospecting along the Carson River and found color in the foot of a ravine that cut far up the southern side of Mount Davidson. They named the ravine Gold Canyon, but when the snows had melted from the mountain passes, they recalled their duty, picked up, and headed west for California—leaving behind them the first outcrops of what would ultimately lead to the richest silver strike in American history.

Those rocky, golden extrusions would not long remain unattended. In August, a group of Sonoran Mexicans drifted into Gold Canyon, doubtless inspired by vague reports dropped in the wake of the Mormon party's travels through the Sierran foothills. They set up shop, and over the next few months were joined by various stragglers, until by the middle of 1851 there were perhaps a hundred miners at work, gradually moving up the canyon toward the shoulder of the mountain, following the thin stream of placer gold to its source.

A scabrous little community called Johntown was erected in typical helter-skelter fashion, populated largely by a collection of singular misfits and reprobates, at least according to the later report of one of the town's inhabitants: "Of the miners, these I particu-

The perambulatory California miner ushered in a new age of prospecting; in the elegant (and more than a little idealized) rendering by Charles Nahl at the left, one of these worthies makes his way to the glories of Washoe.

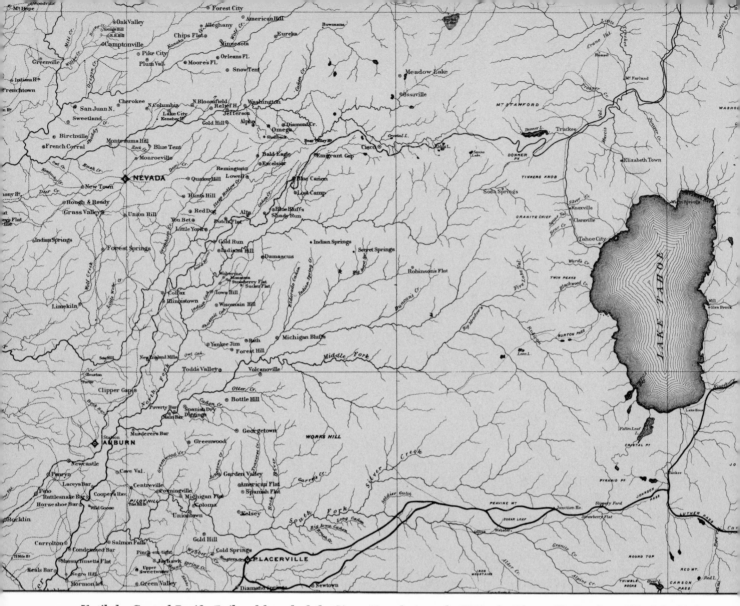

Until the Central Pacific Railroad breached the Sierra Nevada in early 1868, the Placerville Road was Virginia City's (upper right) main link with interior California. (From Eliot Lord's Comstock Mining and Miners, *1882)*

larly remember: Henry P. Comstock, an industrious visionary prospector, though little more than half-witted. James Finney, 'Old Virginia,' frontier hunter and miner, a man of more than ordinary ability in his class, a buffoon and practical joker, a hard drinker when he could get the liquor, and an indifferent worker at anything. Peter Riley, half-witted and 'half-cracked,' lazy and stupid. Joseph Kirby, sober and honest, but indolent. Wm. Sides, who... afterward stabbed to death one John Jessup at Gold Hill. John Berry, 'Uncle Jack Berry,' a great lover of the 'ardent.' Captain Chapman, who was with the troops at Santa Fe during the Mexican War, a large man deficient in courage and in much that goes to make up a man. 'Dutch Baker,' no other name known, a hard drinker

and of little force. Wm. Williams, 'Cherokee Bill,' a dangerous man without one spark of honesty or real manhood."

Such are the materials of history.

In truth, only a peculiarly stubborn hope could have kept men in the canyon during the 1850s, and the residents of Johntown must be given marks for endurance, if nothing else. Both winters and summers were brutal in the extreme, leaving only the spring and autumn months open to mining of any significant scope. Moreover, the winter months made supplies virtually nonobtainable from California. Only John A. ("Snowshoe") Thompson, a redoubtable Norwegian postman–cum–express carrier, cared to traverse the mountain passes during winter with any regularity,

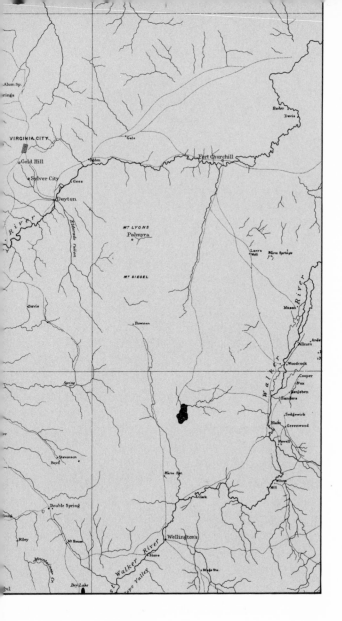

Nevertheless, they hung on, prospecting ever further and further up the steep, rocky walls of the canyon and coming ever closer to a lode whose wealth would not be suspected even when it cluttered the riffles of their Long Toms. For the gold that the miners washed in the canyon was the residue of decomposed outcroppings of the great silver ledges that would come to be known as the Comstock Lode. Eons before, both gold and silver had been deposited in fissures created by mountain faulting; the ore was not distributed evenly, however, and Gold Canyon's outcroppings were principally gold, although accompanied by silver in a form that the miners casually dismissed as "black sand." The higher up the mountain they went, however, the closer they came to the truth.

Two men suspected the truth as early as 1854. Ethan Allan and Hosea Ballou Grosch, two brothers who had come to California during the excitement of 1849 (and enjoyed about the same degree of success as the other hundred thousand), wandered over to Gold Canyon in 1853 and began prospecting. By the end of 1854, they were forced to abandon their efforts, having had no better luck than they had in California. They did have

and he could carry only what he could put on his back.

Until 1857, Mormon farmers in the Carson Valley supplied the miners with enough foodstuffs to carry them through winter, but in that year Brigham Young had to abandon the western portions of Utah Territory to the elements, recalling his colonists for the Mormon "war" with the United States. From then on, whatever the miners could get—and it was little enough—was ruinously expensive. Finally, the richness of the Gold Canyon placers was marginal at best; in *Comstock Mining and Miners* (1882), geologist Eliot Lord estimated that between 1851 and 1857 the average daily take was never more than five dollars, and by 1857 it had dropped to two—hardly wages to inspire visions of sybaritic ease.

John ("Snowshoe") Thompson was a one-man wintertime express line to the miners of Gold Canyon in the late 1850s.

Virginia City, looking west toward Sugar Loaf Canyon about 1880; for a suggestion of how remarkably little the town has changed, compare this view to the modern photograph on page 83.

the glimmer of an idea with profound implications, however, as they wrote to their father early in 1856: "Ever since our return from Utah we have been trying to get a couple of hundred dollars together for the purpose of making a careful examination of a silver lead in Gold Cañon.... Native silver is found in Gold Cañon; it resembles thin sheet-lead broken very fine, and lead the miners suppose it to be...."

In September of 1856, they returned to the canyon and confirmed their hopes with discovery of two silver veins near the head of the canyon. "One of these veins is a perfect monster," they wrote. "We have hopes, almost amounting to a certainty, of veins crossing the Cañon at two other points." By 1857, their excitement was obvious, and justified: "We have followed two shoots down the hill, have a third traced positively, and feel pretty sure that there is a fourth.... We have pounded up some of each variety of rock and set it to work by the Mexican process.... The rock of the vein looks beautiful, is very soft, and will work remarkably easy.... Its colors are violet-blue, indigo-blue, blue-

black, and greenish-black." The ore became even more beautiful when a preliminary assay gave results of $3,500 a ton—which, even if somewhat over-optimistic, would indicate that they had come very close to discovering the great lode itself.

Throughout the summer of 1857, the brothers busied themselves with tracing down their discovery in all its shoots and branches, staking out claims, and supporting themselves as best they could by washing for gold. Their plan was to outline the silver veins as completely as possible, then return to California for the necessary capital to develop them. But luck was no lady. In August, Hosea pierced his foot with a pick; gangrene crept in, and by September he was dead. "I feel very lonely," Ethan wrote his father, "and miss Hosea very much—so much that at times I am strongly tempted to abandon everything and leave the country forever, cowardly as such a course would be. But I shall go on.... By Hosea's death you fall heir to his share in the enterprise. We have, so far, four veins. Three of them promise much."

Ethan remained long enough to work out the cost of his brother's sickness and burial, then set out for California in the middle of November with Richard M. Bucke, a young prospector from Canada. Again, the dismal fortune that had plagued the brothers since their arrival in California nearly ten years before followed Grosch and Bucke into the mountains. At Lake Tahoe (then Bigler Lake) an early winter storm enveloped them. For more than two weeks they wandered lost, hungry, and nearly frozen, until they literally crawled into the mining camp of Last Chance, whose name possessed a fitting irony. Twelve days later Ethan died, and the secret of their silver find died with him. Bucke, whose knowledge of the discovery was limited to the little Ethan had told him, had no heart to carry on. One of his feet was amputated, together with part of the other; he returned to Canada without further chasing the lorelei that had nearly killed him.

The line between pathos and farce is thin enough at best, and in the story of western mining it frequently vaporizes. The pursuit of dreams produces a condition of grand exaggerations, and on the mining frontier life was exercised with a violent conviction; death, in whatever form (and failure can be seen as a kind of death), was never far removed, and the shadow of its ruin enlarged the intensity of existence. The kind of sodden tragedy typified by the fate of the Grosch brothers often served as a stygian backdrop against which were played out dramas of Horatio Alger-like success and Falstaffian excess; in either case, the contrast provided by the possibility of failure gives the story the sharp edges of melodrama—and sometimes of gargantuan humor.

Such qualities are exhibited freely in the history of the ultimate discovery and early development of the Comstock Lode, acted out in the shade of the Grosch brothers' demise. The protagonist of the story was Henry T. P. Comstock, whose superior gift of gall enabled him to implant his name on history and whose monumental and dim-witted prodigality left him with no more than that name to show for his life.

A Canadian by birth, the lanky, rawboned Comstock was typical of a peculiarly western breed of men —a footling species of wanderers with all the stability of quicksilver and an inclination to follow the smell of the west wind at its every freshening. As a fur-trader and trapper, he had drifted through the corridors of the West for years, and in 1856 had finally wafted almost without direction into the little camp of Gold Canyon. Stricken with gold fever, here he remained for an uncommonly long period, working an occasional claim (or, more often, hiring local Indians to work it for him) and spending what little he made with casual laxity. Certainly indolent, and possibly "little more than half-witted," as his townsman described him, he nevertheless possessed a canny instinct for being in the right place at the right time.

For instance, he took up residence in the little stone cabin vacated by the Grosch brothers. Comstock maintained that his squatting was by arrangement with Ethan before his sad journey to California; in exchange for keeping claim-jumpers away, Comstock was to receive a one-quarter share in the Grosch enterprise. This may or may not have been true; what seems fairly certain, however, is that Comstock had not the slightest notion that he was quite literally squatting on a fortune in silver—for all he knew, the Grosch claim was one more placer operation, for it is highly unlikely that Grosch would have revealed the truth to a person of Comstock's wide and unenviable reputation. Grosch may have been unlucky; he was not stupid.

At any rate, Comstock was firmly entrenched near the head of Gold Canyon at precisely that moment in time when four prospectors, led by James ("Old Virginia") Fennimore (alias "Finney"), began investigating the area in the winter of 1858–59. Fennimore, for all his love of the "ardent," had been working in the canyon since 1851 and knew good color when he saw it. He encountered it when he and his companions began digging in a low mound near the head of a small canyon. The four immediately staked out fifty-foot placer claims. A few days later, Comstock, as was his wont, wandered upon the scene and with four other men took up a fifth claim. The embryonic little enterprise was soon christened Gold Hill, and in April work began in earnest.

It was rich in gold, richer than most of the claims the miners had ever seen, producing an average daily return of eight to twenty-five dollars per man. The only trouble with it was the "damned blue stuff" they kept encountering the deeper they went into the earth; it

GOLD AND SILVER IN THE WEST

was hard to dig, heavy, and clogged up their rockers and Long Toms. Needless to say, the "blue stuff" was in fact bloated with silver and far richer than the gold which they pounded and washed out of the earth. Blindly, they had stumbled upon the surface detritus of the south end of the Comstock Lode, a nest of outcroppings eroded by the wind and rain of epochs and covered with a ten-foot or so blanket of gold-rich placer soil washed down from the peaks of the Washoe Range. Had any one of them possessed the relative expertise of the Grosch brothers, he would at least have given the discarded stuff a closer look; but no. As historian Charles H. Shinn put it in *The Story of the Mine:* "Not so was it with these earliest Comstockers, who were mere survivals, mining autochthons of the placer-camp age."

Digging, pounding, and washing, oblivious to the evidence immediately before them, the "autochthons of the placer-camp age" wore away at the earth, and all of Johntown joined them; Gold Hill was the new metropolis of Nevada, a collection of "brush huts and a tent lodging-house among the sage-brush," as one observer described it. Meanwhile, another unknowing assault was undertaken against the Lode, this time on its northern extrusion about a mile over the ridge from Gold Hill, at the head of Six-Mile Canyon. As in Gold Canyon, miners had begun to follow placer gold deposits up this northerly canyon as early as 1857. By May of 1859, two of them, Patrick McLaughlin and Peter O'Riley, had reached its head and in June struck unusually rich color. They set out claims immediately and started washing it as fast as they could carry dirt. Again, they had unwittingly uncovered the top of the great Lode, and, as at Gold Hill, were so blinded by the glitter of gold that they dismissed the "damned blue stuff."

Enter, once again, Henry T. P. Comstock, opportunist extraordinary. Having hired a couple of Indians to work his Gold Hill claim, Comstock had time on his hands and spent it rambling about the hills. One day, he encountered O'Riley and McLaughlin hard at work, glanced into their rocker and saw its bottom winking with gold. He jumped off his horse and ran his fingers around the treasure flecked edges of the hole they were working, then got to his feet and proceeded to inform

the two vague Irishmen that they were working a claim that by all that was right and holy belonged to him. Months before, he told the alleged trespassers, he had staked out a claim to 160 acres for use as a ranch; it so happened that their claim was on his property. That the "ranch" Comstock spoke of was capable of supporting little more than sagebrush and lichens was a point of logic that escaped the two Irishmen, and Comstock was able to bluster his way into equal shares for himself and a friend.

Furthermore, Comstock went on to tell them, the very stream they were using to wash their claim came from a spring which he, Penrod, and James Fennimore owned. That assertion was worth another one hundred feet of the claim. O'Riley and McLaughlin went back to work, and Comstock, perhaps whistling cheerfully to himself, rode off to find "Old Virginia," from whom he purchased his share in the spring for, legend has it, a bottle of whiskey and the horse he rode. It turned out to be an expensive horse, Fennimore later realized to his drunken regret.

So, through sheer nerve and bombast, Comstock had parlayed his way into ownership of claims that effectively bracketed the north and south ends of the Lode —although neither he nor anyone else yet realized what they had. His own account of his operations has all the innocent charm common to many barefaced lies: "I had owned the greater part of Gold Hill; had given Sandy Bowers, Joe Plato, William Knight, and others their claims there. At Ophir [the northern diggings], O'Riley and McLaughlin were working for me. I caved the cut in and went after my party to form a company. With my party I opened the lead and called it Comstock lode." About the only truth in the statement is that the lode eventually *was* blessed with his name.

Still, the truth evaded the bleary gaze of the Gold Hill and Ophir miners. "When will these stupid people find out their own good fortune?" Charles H. Shinn asked rhetorically in *The Story of the Mine.* He then went on to answer his own question: "Not until it is crammed down their throats, like a dose of quinine. That is already evident to anyone who has followed the amusing career of this Peterkin family of stumbling prospectors, whose Dunciad of woes regarding troublesome silver float all the way up the gulches from Johntown has been almost beyond belief." The "stupid people" never did discover their good fortune for

70

A view of Gold Hill long after the great lode of the Comstock had eclipsed its brief moment in the sun; this photograph, taken sometime in the 1880s, looks south from the divide that separated the two towns.

themselves; the knowledge had to be imposed on them by outsiders.

In the latter half of June, 1859, a rancher on the Truckee River Meadows by the name of B. A. Harrison and a local trader, J. F. Stone, became intrigued by the possibilities of the ore which the miners had been discarding as worthless. Following up a hunch, they sent two sacks of it across the mountains to California for analysis by experienced assayers, J. J. Ott in Nevada City and Melville Atwood in Grass Valley. Both assays showed the ore to be tremendously rich. Atwood later claimed that his sample revealed a value per ton of $3,000 in silver and $876 in gold. Some

doubt has been cast by later historians on the accuracy of that estimate, but there never was any doubt that the "damned blue stuff" was in fact the stuff of which dreams were made.

Judge James Walsh, who had helped to arrange the Grass Valley analysis, was one of the few men informed of the results on the evening of June 27. Like the rest, he agreed to keep the news quiet until the insiders had a chance to buy in on the potentially stupendous discovery; there his group loyalty ended. Before daylight the next day, he and a companion, Joseph Woodward, were galloping wildly over the mountains toward Nevada and the Ophir diggings, where they promptly purchased interests in the new mine before the stunned "discoverers" could learn how rich they really were.

Walsh and Woodward then returned to Grass Valley and went out of their way to proclaim the splendiferous possibilities of the Comstock Lode, shrewdly calculating that the greater the excitement, the more valuable would become their shares in the enterprise—a reasonable enough speculation, as it turned out. These were respected men whose opinions carried weight; on the strength of their announcement, enough able-bodied men started an immediate scramble over the mountains to constitute a rush.

One of the first to arrive was George Hearst, a California mine speculator and developer who had been one of those allowed within the ring of secrecy around the Nevada City assay. Not far behind Walsh and Woodward, Hearst rode into the Ophir diggings, arranged to buy a one-sixth interest, then returned to Nevada City to accumulate enough money to settle the purchase. After wheeling and dealing his way into co-partnerships, he went back across the mountains, constructed a pair of crude arrastras, and before the end of the year had crushed some thirty-eight tons of ore. By muleback, the ore was hauled across the mountains that winter to Sacramento, and from there to San Francisco for smelting.

The finished ore gave Hearst and his associates a clear profit of $91,000, and the dull gleam of silver bars inflamed the imagination of San Francisco, as narrated in the redoubtable prose of J. Ross Browne: "But softly, good friends. What rumor is this? Whence come these silvery strains wafted to our ears from the passes of the Sierra Nevada? . . . As I live, it is a cry of Silver! Silver in Washoe! Not gold now, you silly men of Gold Bluff; you Kern Riverites; you daring explorers of British Columbia! But SILVER—solid, pure SILVER! Beds of it ten thousand feet deep! Acres of it, miles of it! Hundreds of millions of dollars poking their backs up out of the earth ready to be pocketed!"

Browne's orotund report was only a little exaggerated. It had been a long time since San Francisco had encountered rumors of treasure substantial enough to justify her enthusiasm, and an eager stream of her citizens almost immediately set out for the new mines, establishing the city's stake in the riches of Washoe at an early date.

In the meantime, what of the Comstock's "discoverers"? What of those hardy souls who had stubbornly hacked at the mountains of Nevada in a quest for gold while their narrow imaginations simply would

The career of Adolph Sutro stands as a testament to how far gall, determination, and a profound ego could take a man in the latter half of the nineteenth century. Sutro had arrived on the Comstock in 1860 and set up business with a stamp mill in the Carson Valley. Even in the early 1860s, it was recognized that the Comstock's biggest problem was in the drainage of its deep mines; among various solutions offered was one by Sutro, who proposed in 1865 that a tunnel nearly four miles in length be rammed from Eagle Valley through the mountains and up into the heart of the Comstock mines at a depth of 1,650 feet. This tunnel, Sutro maintained, would not only drain the mines of excess water, but would provide ventilation, ready escape in case of fire, and an easy route for shipment of ore to the mills in the Carson Valley. Although he surely was sincere about the aspects of safety involved, Sutro also had sugarplum visions of controlling the milling industry with operations at the mouth of the tunnel; in fact, he went out of his way to say so out loud.

Sutro persuaded the Nevada legislature to give him a franchise for the project, and "Ralston's Ring" (see page 79) expressed interest—at least until Sutro's blatant predictions of undermining the Ring's control got under the skin of Ralston and Sharon, who switched from support to opposition. Undaunted, Sutro carried his conviction to the halls of Congress. "The most important and productive mines which the world can show are on the eve of almost absolute ruin and abandonment," he wrote in a promotional brochure of 1868, "an interest upon which the fortunes of an entire state

not admit the existence of silver? Most received the full fruits of their stupidity. Dreamers all, they nonetheless lacked the principal virtue of the true visionary: blind optimism. Even when the truth had been "crammed down their throats, like a dose of quinine," they could not believe the full extent of their fortunes and settled for short-term gains by selling out to those of more muscular foresight—at prices that were but a fraction of what they might have realized by holding on to and developing their claims. (In all fairness to the memory of these fiscal incompetents, it should be pointed out that the prices for which they sold out their interests were in most cases more money than any of them had ever seen or had any reasonable expectation of seeing; to a man accustomed to living on four or five dollars a day, the opportunity to accumulate several thousand in one impressive chunk must have been irresistible.)

James Fennimore, even after being bilked by Comstock, sold out his fifty-foot claim in Gold Hill for fifty dollars a foot, and all of the original holders of rich Gold Hill claims did likewise. At the northern, or Ophir end, McLaughlin sold his claim for $3,500 and was ultimately buried at public expense. Penrod

held out until the end of 1859, but sold out then for $8,500. Of the original Ophir owners, only O'Riley refused to sell for any length of time, and even then the $40,000 he ultimately received was far below his claim's real value; moreover, he frittered away the money in stock speculations and ultimately died in an insane asylum.

Even Henry T. P. Comstock, he who had flimflammed his way to the threshold of fortune, succumbed to the call of the quick dollar. Two months after the lode had been discovered for what it was, he sold off his claims for a measly $11,000—congratulating himself, predictably, on the fact that he had pulled the wool over the eyes of another greedy Californian. Like most of the others, he lived to regret it, and spent the rest of his life in a vain attempt to re-create that brief moment of glory on the slopes of Mount Davidson. He finally killed himself in Bozeman, Montana.

One wonders whether James Fennimore ever really regretted anything. He spent most of his days in a fine alcoholic mist and died from a fall off his horse in 1861, carousing to the end. Like Comstock, however, he did leave his name as a kind of legacy. The town that had sprung like a mushroom around the diggings

are depending, one which supports more than one hundred thousand people; an interest which furnishes the life-blood of commerce and industry, and which helps to pay the *national debt*—will go to careless ruin if no immediate steps are taken to remedy the threatening evil. *Will the American Nation, the most intelligent, powerful, and liberal one on earth, quietly look on and not come to the rescue?*"

Well, yes, as a matter of fact, it would. Sutro went to England, where financing continued to evade him, then back to the United States, where a vigorous stock subscription campaign finally netted him enough to start the tunnel. It was not completed until 1878, at a cost of more than two million dollars, and the timing could hardly have been worse: the gutted and poorly managed mines of the Comstock were failing, and not even the solution of the drainage problem could save them. No great mills sprouted at the mouth of the tunnel, and although it continued to drain the lode into the 1940s, it was a financial disaster.

And Sutro? He may have been a visionary, but he was no fool. In 1880, before the future could clearly be seen, he unloaded his stock and escaped to San Francisco with a profit in excess of one million dollars; he became a patron of the arts and sciences, and ultimately San Francisco's first—and last—millionaire populist mayor.

at the northern end of the lode during the summer months of 1859 had been christened variously by the names of Pleasant Hill Camp and Ophir, but neither of them seemed to stick.

The town received its final name in a singularly appropriate fashion—at least according to one of those legends one always hopes is true. One evening in August, 1859, so the story goes, "Old Virginia" Fennimore stumbled out of the town's saloon with a bottle and a few of the boys. Nearing his cabin, he tripped, breaking the bottle and spilling most of its contents on the ground. In a rare moment of religious inspiration, he sprinkled the area around him with the remainder of the whiskey and proclaimed, "I baptize this ground Virginia Town!" A glad cry of assent was voiced by his fellows, and together they trooped back to the tavern to celebrate the event.

"Town" became "City," and Virginia City it would remain. Whiskey has been put to worse uses.

The news of silver whistled through San Francisco that spring of 1860, "Borne on the wings of the wind from the Sierra Nevada," J. Ross Browne said, "wafted through every street, lane, and alley...whirling around the drinking saloons, eddying over the counters of the banking offices, scattering up the dust among the Front Street merchants, arousing the slumbering inmates of the Custom-House — what man of enterprise could resist it?"

A good many could resist it, tempered as they were by the experience of ten years' disappointment, but a good many could not; at least ten thousand, and possibly more, joined the rush to Washoe that spring, enough to make Placerville Road, which crossed the mountains from Placerville through Johnson Pass, just south of Lake Tahoe, a moving welter of humanity, as described by Browne: "An almost continuous string of Washoeites stretched 'like a great snake dragging its slow length along' as far as the eye could reach. . . . Irishmen, wheeling their blankets, provisions, and mining implements on wheel-barrows; American, French, and German foot passengers, leading their heavily-laden horses, or carrying their packs on their backs, and their picks and shovels slung across their shoulders; Mexicans, driving long trains of pack-mules, and swearing fearfully, as usual, to keep them in order;

The city where silver was a working dream—and fo

dapper-looking gentlemen, apparently from San Francisco, mounted on fancy horses; women, in men's clothes, mounted on mules or 'burros'; Pike County specimens, seated on piles of furniture and goods in great lumbering wagons; whiskey-peddlers, with their bar-fixtures and whiskey on mule-back, stopping now and then to quench the thirst of the toiling multitude; organ-grinders, carrying their organs; drovers, riding, raving, and tearing away frantically through the brush after droves of self-willed cattle designed for the shambles; in short, every imaginable class, and every possible species of industry, was represented in this moving pageant . . . all stark mad for silver."

What they found when they got there would have stricken uncertainty into the heart of a Pacific Street crimp: "Frame shanties, pitched together as if by accident; tents of canvas, of blankets, of brush, of potato-sacks and old shirts, with empty whiskey-barrels for chimneys; smokey hovels of mud and stone; coyote

holes in the mountain side forcibly seized and held by men; pits and shafts with smoke issuing from every crevice; piles of goods and rubbish on craggy points, in the hollows, on the rocks, in the mud, in the snow, everywhere, scattered broadcast in pell-mell confusion, as if the clouds had suddenly burst overhead and rained down the dregs of all the flimsy, rackety, filthy little hovels and rubbish of merchandise that had ever undergone the process of evaporation from the earth since the days of Noah. The intervals of space, which may or may not have been streets, were dotted with human beings of such sort, variety, and numbers, that the famous anthills of Africa were nothing in the comparison."

This clotted, dismal scene must have inspired hundreds to head home immediately, and nearly half of those who had come across the mountains in the spring and summer of 1860 had returned by the end of the year; the census report for that year gave 6,857 as the total population of the entire region of Nevada, perhaps 90 percent of which was concentrated in Virginia City and its immediate environs. Even for most of those who remained, there was one more level of disappointment, that theme which runs through the narrative of western mining rushes like the dark muttering of a Greek chorus.

Those sanguine miners with picks and long-handled shovels slung over their shoulders, which J. Ross Browne described, were soldiers of sublime ignorance—refugees from the placer camps of California, or the gold fields of the Fraser River, or simply rank greenhorns. They were operating on the assumption that a man could get at the Comstock treasure with little more than simple equipment and a willingness to work; the latter was an admirable virtue, but in the case of the Comstock totally irrelevant. The ores, which had finally been uncovered, were great bodies of recalcitrant rock which seamed their way deep into the fissures of the

Some of the entrepreneurial legacies of Ralston are sketched in this memorial tribute following his concluding swim in the Bay (see page 80).

earth. It was going to take money as well as muscle to get it out, to crush it, refine it, and reduce it to its pristine form. Money was the one thing these would-be tycoons did not have. But they did have hope, and a typical western eye for speculation, and so they set to staking out claims right and left, hoping against hope that they would stumble on one more glittering off-shoot of the great lode, sell their claim at an inflated price, and return to California with a pocketful of dreams. "Nobody had any money," J. Ross Browne said, "yet everybody was a millionaire in silver claims. Nobody had any credit, yet everybody bought thousands of feet of glittering ore. . . . All was silver under-

ground, and deeds and mortgages on top; silver, silver everywhere, but scarce a dollar in coin."

During the twenty years of the Comstock's most productive life, nearly seventeen thousand such claims were staked out, but with few exceptions only those who concentrated on the acquisition of town lots (always a generally profitable enterprise in a mining town of any significance) ended up with more than a handful of dirt to mark their efforts. The ore bodies, scattered in huge, pocket-like formations, were not evenly distributed, and only a few claims staked by those who had been early enough and lucky enough paid off for their owners. But Virginia City had been born in speculation, and in speculation it would live for the rest of its natural existence; it was a town ruled by paper, for all the crude reality of the rock carved out of the innards of the mountains.

Even for those with the necessary money, the Comstock did not relinquish its treasure that easily; the technology of silver mining in the United States was all but nonexistent in the early 1860s, and the Virginia City mines presented some special problems that only time and trial and error could overcome. The very width of the ore bodies was one such problem; getting them out of the earth created such huge caverns that special timbering had to be devised to keep the weight of the mountains off the shoulders of the men; the answer was the "Deidensheimer square-set" method invented by a German engineer.

Another problem was translating crude ore into finished bullion; during the first months of mining, many companies actually sent their ore to England, via San Francicso, for reduction, a bitterly expensive proposition even with the profit margin supplied by

uncommonly rich ore. Again, the Comstock came up with its own solution in the relatively efficient reduction system called the "Washoe Pan Process." (For a more complete discussion of the technological evolution of the Comstock mines, see Chapter 10.)

Quickly, Virginia City took on the outlines of an industrial town, complete with factories (the mines and mills), a large labor force (at first dominated by the detritus from the rush of 1860, then added to by experienced industrial miners from all over the country and the world), and many other trappings more familiar to the urbanized East than the barren mountain slopes of the far West. The evolution was clear as early as 1863, when the ubiquitous J. Ross Browne revisited the Comstock: "Descending the slope of the ridge that divides Gold Hill from Virginia City a strange scene attracts the eye. He who gazes upon it for the first time is apt to doubt if it be real. Perhaps there is not another spot on the face of the globe that presents a scene so weird and desolate in its natural aspect, yet so replete with busy life, so animate with

Ralston's Washoe representative, William Sharon, displayed all the charitable instincts of a shark—and did Ralston in.

James G. Fair—one of the four Irish Comstock Kings— had Sharon's generous qualities, but not his allegiance.

Mining on the Comstock involved temperature changes that would have tested the durability of steel; the topless miners above are preparing to descend, the fully clothed ones have just arrived at the surface.

human interest.

"It is as if a wondrous battle raged, in which the combatants were men and earth. Myriads of swarthy, bearded, dust-covered men are piercing into the grim old mountains, ripping them open, thrusting murderous holes through their naked bodies; piling up engines to cut out their vital arteries; stamping and crushing up with infernal machines their disemboweled fragments, and holding fiendish revels amid the chaos of destruction. . . ."

It was a battle, a battle against the primordial element of rock. Some might say that it was a singularly one-sided struggle, with the odds heavily in favor of man and his rapidly growing technological sophistication; it might even more suitably be characterized as rape. But on the Comstock, nature had a weapon that at least assured it of a holding action, if not victory: the fickle placement of her ore bodies, a phenomenon that would from time to time strike fear into the corporate hearts who ruled the Comstock. The first four years of the camp's history were a time of bonanza (rich ore). Between the beginning of 1860

and the end of 1863, the Virginia City mines produced more than twenty-two million dollars worth of gold and silver bullion. Stock values rose accordingly to stunning heights: certificates in the Gould & Curry Mine were going for $6,300 per "foot" in the middle of 1863; this was the richest single mine in the district, but others showed a similiar increase.

A year later, its value had dropped to $900, and while the ore production for the entire year of 1864 reached the startling total of $15,795,585, it was clear to all that the Comstock mines had encountered their first period of borrasca (barren rock). No new ore bodies had been found, and the mines were quickly exhausting those they already held. By 1870, annual production had dropped to $8,319,698; in five years, the production had been cut almost precisely in half. Bankruptcies abounded, hundreds deserted the city, and mine superintendents reflected on the will-o'-the-wisp of job security—and desperately sank exploratory shafts in all directions, seeking the elusive ore.

Late in 1870, the Crown Point and Belcher mines were successful in finding bonanza, and the entire district took on new hope. It took on more in 1873, when reports of a rich find began to drift up from the depths of the Consolidated Virginia mine. For two years, the owners of the mine had patiently delved and explored at depths that reached 1,167 feet, and by the end of 1874 it was clear that their persistence had paid off in the discovery of a body of ore "absolutely immense, and beyond all comparison superior in every respect to anything ever before seen on the Comstock lode," according to the *Mining and Scientific Press* of San Francisco. The effect on the Consolidated Virginia mine was spectacular: in July of 1870, its shares could have been purchased for one dollar apiece; early in 1875 they were selling for $700.

This was the "Big Bonanza," whose discovery catapulted the Comstock into the period of its greatest productivity. In 1875, production leaped to $26,023,036 and increased dramatically over the next two years to a climax in 1877 of $37,062,252. Those with the grim determination to hang on in the face of all logic had discovered that the wages of battle on the Comstock were well worth the price of patience.

It was a battle on yet another level, an outsized struggle for power between men of large appetites and sometimes ruthless conviction—ruthless even in an age in which such men were emerging as the giants of American industry and forging the machinery of civilization into a form compatible with their sinewy conceptions of life. On the Comstock, the struggle involved three principal groups of men. The first has been characterized as the "bank crowd," spearheaded by William C. Ralston, who had come to San Francisco in 1854 and in ten years had welded together the largest financial institution in California: the Bank of California. Always seeking new opportunities for expansion and investment, Ralston sent William Sharon to Virginia City as the bank's agent and branch manager. When the first period of borrasca began to assault the Comstock, Sharon saw their opportunity: he began to loan large amounts of money at ridiculously low rates (often as low as 1.5 percent), most of it going to the many crippled mills in the district. When the continued depression made it impossible for these mills to pay off the loans, Sharon methodically foreclosed; in a short time, the Bank of California owned most of the mills processing the ores of the Comstock.

To further its hold, the bank also acquired substantial interests in the principal mines, built the Virginia & Truckee Railroad to carry ore from the mines to the mills on the Carson River, bought an interest in the water company that served the town, and climaxed its grip with an interest in the company that brought lumber to the town from the slopes of the Sierra Nevada. It was a fortified monopoly on a spectacular scale, and its victims squirmed under the pressure—without being able to do much about it.

By 1870, Ralston's monopoly was producing millions for the bank—and it needed every cent. The completion of the transcontinental railroad in 1869 inundated San Francisco with goods from the East, whose cost undercut local manufacturers and merchants, many of whom had been financed by Ralston in his admirable but altogether overworked conviction that San Francisco must become the leading financial and cultural center in the United States. Ralston borrowed heavily from his Virginia City enterprises to shore up local merchants, but in 1871 a wedge was forced into the Comstock monopoly when he lost control of the Crown Point Mine. This mine, one of those purchased during the period of borrasca, was considered practically worthless early in 1870. But in superintendent, John P. Jones, soon learned better — neglecting to inform Ralston. Instead, he got together with Alvinza Hayward and the two of them quietly bought up a major interest in the mine at two dollars a share. When the mine hit its bonanza late that year, Ralston and the Bank of California were left out in the cold, and Jones and Hayward emerged as the newest giants of the Comstock.

Another fissure was split into the monopoly with the discovery of the Big Bonanza. After careful speculation, James C. Flood and William S. O'Brien, who ran a San Francisco saloon, and James G. Fair and John Mackay, two men with wide experience on the Comstock, bought up a number of unproductive mines, including the Consolidated Virginia, and began exploratory work in 1871. In 1873, they tapped directly into the Big Bonanza, and became forever after immortalized as the Bonanza Four. Not only that, they proceeded to create their own bank, the Bank of Nevada, and further embarrassed Ralston's financial hold on the Comstock.

In a desperate attempt to get a piece of the Big

Bonanza, Ralston sank nearly three million dollars of the bank's money into the purchase of the Ophir Mine, next to the Consolidated Virginia, on the superficially reasonable expectation that it, too, led into the great lode. Except that it didn't, and when Ralston's friend and representative William Sharon learned that the mine was worthless, he quickly dumped his own shares on the market, forcing the price down. Ralston was left with three million dollars worth of stock which he could not sell for what he had paid for it. A run on the Bank of California followed, and it was forced to close. Owing an astonishing list of creditors some five million dollars, Ralston strolled down to the Bay one afternoon for his customary swim and was never seen alive again.

For Ralston, the wages of power had been death.

Between 1859 and 1882, the last truly productive year, the Comstock mines produced $292,726,310 in gold and silver, making it one of the richest single bonanzas in the history of the mining West. Its money, most of it controlled and manipulated from San Francisco, made that city one of the principal mining exchanges in the world and nourished a growth already made remarkable by the California gold mines. Comstock gold and silver helped to finance the Civil War, gave further impetus to the need for a Pacific Railroad, made multimillionaires of a handful of men whose exploits in spending brought a new dimension to the practice of conspicuous consumption, and invested financial centers around the world with a predilection to speculate in western mining stocks.

Perhaps more significantly, the Comstock Lode was the first large-scale example of industrial mining to inhabit the West. Its mines and mills were great factories teeming with employees and ridden with the pounding clatter of machinery. Techniques and practices—both financial and mechanical—forged in the experience of the Virginia City mines contributed to the development of deep mining throughout the country and the world. Further, it created a class of skilled laborers who would furnish much of the manpower for industrial mining in areas scattered from the Coeur d'Alene of Idaho to Cripple Creek, Colorado. In twenty years, then, the Comstock Lode probably gave more to the evolution of the industry than any previous or

following excitement, with the notable exception of the California Gold Rush itself.

Twenty years. Typically, the demise of the Comstock was as swift as it was unmistakable. The Big Bonanza was depleted quickly by the mine owners, whose policy always was to get as much ore as possible out of the ground as fast as possible. After 1877, the year that the mines produced more than thirty-seven million dollars, production dropped to a little over twenty million in 1878, less than eight million in 1879, and less than five million in 1880. In the middle of the 1880s, a brief revival was inspired by new methods of refining ores previously considered worthless, and between 1884 and 1895 the Consolidated Virginia Mine managed to extract about sixteen and one-half million dollars. The repeal of the Sherman Silver Purchase Act of 1890, which had subsidized the silver mining industry by guaranteeing government purchase of 4.5 million ounces of silver annually, came as a nearly final blow in 1893. Mine after mine was abandoned to the subterranean waters, miners flocked to all the points of the compass, capitalists took their money elsewhere, and Virginia City was depopulated to a level only a little above that of a ghost town.

But she had put on a grand show while she lasted, and those who had known her in better days remembered her big. James "Kettle Belly" Brown, who had been the city's fire chief during the 1870s, produced a fitting elegy for the Big Bonanza during a newspaper interview in San Francisco in 1893: "Where would the Palace Hotel be, I'd like to ask, if it hadn't of been for the bullion of the Comstock Lode? Where would the Nevada Bank get off, and what would become of the Flood Building? Wasn't the Mills Building put with profits from the Virginia and Truckee Railroad, and didn't the Comstock furnish all the ore and most all the freight to give those profits? What made Sutro Heights? The Comstock. What built those lordly palaces of architectural splendor on Nob Hill? The Comstock. Who put the postal cable lines across the continent and under the ocean? The Comstock. What gave Uncle Sam his piles of gold to buy ammunition and hard tack when the ark of the nation was buffeted by the war billows of the greatest rebellion ever known in history? The Comstock!"

OH, VIRGINIA!

It has been more than a century now since "Old Virginia" Fennimore dribbled his whiskey in the dirt street of a mining camp and christened it Virginia City. The mines that fed the coffers of San Francisco nabobs have long since closed, leaving only great piles of waste rock and tailings to mark the demise of an era whose silver shook the markets of the world. But the town would not die, and there are still those who will maintain that someday silver will again rise, the mines will be reopened, and Virginia will re-create the days of its glory. In the meantime, there are always the tourists. . . .

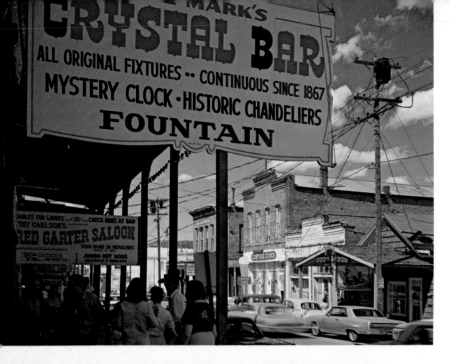

They come by the thousands every year, in jeans and slacks and wild-printed shirts, with cameras dangling from their necks like scapulars in some peculiar religion. They come with money, remarkable amounts of money, and the town has devised a wonderful array of means by which they are separated from it: by tours of mines and "Silver King" mansions; by postcards and posters and photographs; by ash trays, polo shirts, belts, and scarves emblazoned with Comstockian mottoes; by player pianos and peep-show stereopticons; by museums and bars—the Bucket of Blood, the Washoe Club, the Silver Queen; and by slot machines, always slot machines, Nevada's contribution to the technocratic society. Everywhere, signs and billboards proclaim, shout, wheedle, titillate, and demand attention. At night, neon articulates greed with blinks and whorls of rainbow light; from bars and casinos a chaotic babble of voices mixed with caterwauling juke boxes and nickelodeons oozes into C Street and is lost against the looming hulk of Mount Davidson. There are perhaps five hundred people left in Virginia City now, and tourism is the trade of most of them; one wonders how closely they resemble the community that John Taylor Waldorf remembered in 1924: "We shall always hold close and deep our memories of Virginia, the town of our early joys, the town of friends who never forget, the town that we shall recall with smiles and sighs and tears so long as a stick or stone remains and the sagebrush grows at the foot of the dumps. . . ."

CHAPTER FIVE

ACROSS THE GREAT DIVIDE

The diaspora of miners, booms, and busts

"The miners . . . were like quicksilver. A mass of them dropped in any locality, broke up into individual globules, and ran off after any atom of gold in their vicinity. They stayed nowhere longer than the gold attracted them."

In the last forty years of the nineteenth century, the warps and tangles of the intermontane West saw an absolute confusion of mining. All the yeasty dreams that had been released by the explosion of the California Gold Rush and fattened by the experience of the Comstock Lode were turned loose on the mountains, forests, and river plains of a region extending from southern Canada, eastern Washington and Oregon, Montana, Idaho, and Wyoming to southern Colorado —an infestation of astonishing energy and longevity.

It began hardly before the heat of the California Gold Rush had cooled to an ember. As early as July of 1850, expeditions had set out for the Spokane and Yakima rivers of Washington, and while results there fell short of desire, minor placer discoveries were made somewhat later in Fort Colville in the northeastern corner of the territory. In Oregon, placer discoveries in the Rogue River Valley in 1851 sent hundreds streaming across the Cascades, and in 1853 a thousand miners were at work south of Coos Bay. Some quartz mines were uncovered in Jackson County in 1859, but

the veins soon pinched out. Oregon's first discovery of any lasting significance did not come until the autumn of 1861, when rich placers were discovered on the Powder River and John Day River in the northeastern part of the state.

By the summer of 1862, more than a thousand miners were scrabbling after this new hope, with predictable results: not much for the lucky, nothing for the luckless. Still, it was enough to fire expectation, and for the next decade Oregon would play a steady, if minor part in the story of gold and silver in the West, as gold quartz discoveries were made near Baker City in 1863 —with the yield from the Virtue Mine going as high as $1,300 a ton—as hydraulic mining in Jackson and Josephine counties prospered for a time, and as silver ledges were discovered in the Rogue River Valley and the Bohemia district of Douglas County in the latter 1860s.

The result of all this activity was relatively anemic; between 1850 and 1880, all the gold and silver mines of Oregon and Washington probably did not put twenty million dollars together between them. But the fact that mining continued at all is a reflection of the persistence of the dream, a conviction that if one tried hard enough and long enough the hills—some hills, somewhere—would finally release the treasure. And so they kept trying by the hundreds and by the thousands, crawling into all the corners of the Far West. "The miners," H. H. Bancroft wrote in his history of the

As in most of the mining West, placer operations in Idaho quickly evolved from simplicity to industry, as shown in this scene of hydraulic mining outside Idaho City, painted by Mrs. Jonas Brown in about 1864.

Northwest, "were like quicksilver. A mass of them dropped in any locality, broke up into individual globules, and ran off after any atom of gold in their vicinity. They stayed nowhere longer than the gold attracted them." And out of this forty-year clutter of mining activity emerged a few regions whose frequently startling productivity was sufficient to justify all the years of scrabbling after the main chance: in Idaho, the gold placers of the Boise Basin and the silver mines of Ruby City, Atlanta, and the Coeur d'Alenes; in Montana, the placers and lode mines of Virginia City, Helena, and Butte (where the dream was transmuted into copper); and in Colorado, the silver mines of Leadville and the gold mines of Cripple Creek.

Idaho's first experience with the mysteries of gold-hunting took place early in 1860, when a trader to the Nez Percé Indians discovered enough gold on the Lapwai Reservation to inspire him to return with a prospecting party in October. The party encamped through the winter on Orofino Creek, a tributary of the Clearwater River in the north central section of the state, and panned a quantity of gold as soon as the weather permitted. In March two members hauled some eight hundred dollars in gold dust to Walla Walla, Washington. Their arrival inspired a quick rush, and by August the region boasted a population of more than seven thousand and a typically ramshackle community named Orofino. Good claims were paying as much as ten dollars a day per man, but as usual there was too little gold for too many men, and prospecting parties fanned out into the surrounding country, striking color here and there and setting up instant towns.

In July a party of hopefuls uncovered gold on the Salmon River, about 110 miles east of Lewiston, and by the end of the year the new placers had attracted enough miners for the establishment of the community of Florence, which prospered magnificently, if transiently, as the new center of Idaho mining. Once again the overflow of miners spilled into the surrounding area, but in 1862 most headed straight for yet another sunburst of opportunity: the placers of the Boise Basin, on various northern tributaries of the Snake River.

Here gold had been discovered as the result of myth-chasing. In 1845, a persistent rumor had it, a party of

emigrants on their way to Oregon had stopped somewhere between the Snake River and The Dalles of Oregon and panned a significant amount of gold before moving on. This legendary discovery had taken on the name of the Blue Bucket Diggings, and for several years prospectors had been looking for its remains. In August 1862, one more party went looking; they found no ghosts, but they did strike gold on what became Grimes Creek, and by fall several hundred miners had scuttled into the area, smelling out this latest Golconda. Those who arrived early enough found the digging good, if already crowded, as one of them reported for the Lewiston *Golden Age*, Idaho's first newspaper: "We immediately sank a hole to bed-rock; the prospects were not very flattering until we reached it, and then the first shovelful made our eyes stick out, for the real stuff was there in all its beauty. We panned out three pan-fulls of dirt, and the proceeds were $11. That satisfied us, and so we filled the hole up with water and dirt, and tried to get more ground, but it was no go, for before we finished prospecting the men poured in so fast that the ground was all taken up."

It was not quite another California, but the Boise Basin region was Idaho's best hope. From Boise on the west to West Bannock (later Idaho City) on the east, town after town popped into existence that fall of 1862, and miners busied themselves through the winter with the construction of ditches and sluices, getting ready for the spring melt and the first long mining season. Miners around West Bannock alone had some eighty miles of ditches dug by spring, and with the first water they set to washing frantically and continued throughout the summer and fall; the Basin produced at least four million dollars that first season. The region boomed; by September, West Bannock had a population of 6,267, surpassing Portland, Oregon, as the largest city in the Pacific Northwest, and Boise had reached nearly a thousand.

Placer mining is an operation profoundly dependent upon the ready accessibility of water, and in the region of the Snake River plains, water is an unreliable commodity at best, itself dependent for its volume on the depth of winter snowfall in the mountains. When the "wet" season ended in the late fall of 1863—when the streams, creeks, and trickles had ceased their flow—the miners settled down to wait once again for the spring melt in 1864. What followed was an uncom-

Most of the major (and many of the minor) placer mining operations in the Pacific Northwest are shown on this rare hand-drawn map, executed by Mrs. F. F. Victor, one of H. H. Bancroft's many amanuenses.

The travails of crossing the plains to the mines of Montana in the middle 1860s are documented with flair, if little expertise, in this primitive scene; for many, it was uncomfortably close to truth.

monly mild winter; the snowpack fell below average, and by spring the miners knew they were facing an unusually short working season. They tackled the problem with characteristic energy, setting up shifts to work around the clock beneath the flickering light of great fires.

Such efforts smacked of industry, and in truth the placer mines of the Boise Basin had already taken on such outlines. The better claims, most of them staked out by the arrivals of 1862 and early 1863, had become little gold-finding factories, complete with networks of ditches and flumes, numerous sluice boxes and rockers —and some with hydraulicking equipment to blast away whole hillsides with a jet of water—and a clutch of anywhere from fifteen to thirty hired hands to do the work at wages that went as high as seven dollars a day. Another industrial element was added by the fact that as early as the summer of 1864 some lode mining was

being done in the area (some of it with the backing of George Hearst, he who had parlayed his way into a fortune on the Comstock), with extensive underground workings and a number of stamp mills to process the ore.

Although few lode mines paid out for their owners, it was clear by the middle of 1864 that the Boise Basin was no place for a vagabond with high hopes of fortune, and once again prospectors spilled out of the area, some bound for the recently-discovered placers in Kootenai, British Columbia, others for the new gold fields of Montana, and still others into the semi-desert region south and west of the northern bend of the Snake River, called the Owyhee Basin.

Gold placers had been discovered here in the spring of 1863 on Jordans Creek, but they were shallow and worked out quickly. However, in the fall of the year, silver-bearing quartz ledges were discovered, and assays of the ore placed its value at $2,000 in gold and $7,000 in silver—more than twice the richness of the wealthiest

One of the earliest residences of Boise City, a town born of the fever of gold in 1862, nourished by the presence of an army fort, and given final solidity by agricultural growth.

lodes of the Comstock. This was enough to bring capital in, and by the end of 1864 several mines had been established, chief among them the Orofino and Morningstar; a number of mills utilizing the Comstock's "Washoe Pan Process" had been built; and two communities, Silver City and Ruby City, had been erected to service the mines. Although various legal entanglements prevented the mines from producing as well as they might have, they still managed to process some five million dollars in ore by the end of 1869.

Similar silver camps would be established at Bannock and Atlanta, which between them ultimately produced nearly twenty million dollars before being worked out early in the twentieth century, but it was more than twenty years after the Owyhee strike of 1863 before Idaho saw her first—and last—true bonanza. In 1882, gold placers were discovered on tributaries of the Coeur d'Alene River in the far northern panhandle of the state. A rush quickly developed when the discoveries became general knowledge in the fall of 1883 and as

quickly evaporated when these placers, like those of the Boise Basin, evolved into minor industrial operations, leaving but a handful of stubborn prospectors in the town of Murray. One of them was Noah S. Kellogg, a part-time carpenter and full-time goldseeker who wandered out into the mountains one day in 1885 and above Milo Gulch stumbled upon a large vein of silver intermixed with lead and zinc—a mixture given the name of "galena."

Warren T. Stoll, a lawyer with a moribund practice going in Murray, recalled the aftermath: "The news of Kellogg's great discovery was out quickly. Its effect on Murray was that of a spark in a powder magazine.... Claims were deserted. Mining operations in the Pritchard Creek watershed halted. Men rushed down from the hills. Burros and pack horses were loaded with outfits. Galena was the theme of every conversation. Within twenty-four hours half the population had left for Milo Gulch, a rabble racing over a mountain course to a rich finish." It *was* a rich finish: "Never have I seen a

Sluice mining in the 1870s in Jerusalem Canyon, not far from the scrabbling metropolis of Bannock, Montana Territory.

galena to compare with that! One blow of a pick, and its broken fragments glittered with a white silver light. The rock was richly flecked. I was swept off my feet with the marvelous lode depth and width before me...."

He was not alone in being swept off his feet, but again it was those who arrived earliest who managed to monopolize the best claims on the ledge, which ran at roughly the same level on opposite sides of Milo Gulch along two ridges that ultimately came to a point. High on these ridges were sunk the Coeur d'Alene's two richest mines, the Bunker Hill on one side and the Sullivan on the other; below them soon hunkered the town of Wardner, crammed between the ridges like meat in a sandwich, and below that, Kellogg.

Others soon joined them, and by 1890 the Coeur d'Alene district was clustered with a series of dismal little industrial suburbs with a total population of nearly four thousand souls—most of them employed as laborers in other men's mines, mines owned, as often as not, by distant corporations. Industrial mining had come to

Idaho on a unprecedented scale, a condition of affairs amply reflected by the labor troubles that haunted the region throughout the 1890s (see Chapter II), and by the fact that in the first sixty years after its discovery, the Coeur d'Alene district produced more than one billion dollars in silver, lead, and zinc.

In thirty years, then, Idaho had seen the full course of evolution on the mining frontier: from a period when a man could hope to fulfill the most expansive of his visions with little more than his own muscle and luck, to one in which the eight-hour day and a living wage described the boundaries of his dreams. By then, it was an old story.

The role of the "Old Californian" ("Old" no matter what his age) in the development of the mining frontier should be fairly obvious by now. It was "Old Californians" who had instructed the hopeless greenhorns of the Pikes Peak Rush of 1859; it was a pair of "Old Californians"—the Grosch brothers—who had first suspected the existence of the Comstock Lode and "Old Californians" who had bought in on the project early enough to control it; it was "Old Californians" who made up a good portion of those who claimed and developed the Boise Basin placers and an "Old Californian"—George Hearst—who encouraged lode development in the Idaho gold fields; the "Old Californian" was as much a part of the mining frontier as cheap whiskey and overpriced beer.

It is fitting, then, that the first authenticated discovery of gold in Montana was made by a trio of "Old Californians"—James and Granville Stuart and Reece Anderson. Returning unsuccessfully from California in 1858, and stricken with the helplessly perambulatory instincts of prospectors, the three wandered into the Deer Lodge Valley of southwestern Montana in May. On what later became Gold Creek, they did some prospecting, sank a five-foot hole, and took out about ten cents worth of gold. It was not much to show for that amount of work, and an attack by hostile Blackfeet Indians drove them to shelter at Fort Bridger. Still convinced that something good could come of the area, the Stuart brothers returned to Gold Creek in 1860 and remained long enough to be on hand when a group of Idaho-bound miners discovered relatively rich placers on Grasshopper Creek in the summer of 1862.

Some five hundred miners congregated near Grasshopper Creek that fall and winter, and the town of Bannock leaped into existence to serve them. By spring, however, the surrounding placers had already begun to show signs of being worked out, and a well-armed prospecting party was organized to investigate country to the east held by recalcitrant Crow Indians. They left on April 9 and returned to Bannock on June 24, having encountered little more than Indian attacks. But a group of six men who had hoped to rendezvous with the main party, and who had been captured and released by Indians, stopped off on their way back and did some prospecting at Alder Gulch, about seventy-five miles east of Bannock. The results were promising, to say the least; one pan alone produced more than five dollars.

Barney Hughes, one of the party, was sworn to secrecy and immediately dispatched to Bannock for supplies. Hughes kept his mouth shut, but he must have worn the smug look of a man who has just paid off his creditors, for when he left Bannock more than four hundred men trailed along behind him. After several miles of glancing nervously over his shoulder at the ragtag army behind him, Hughes called the expedition to a halt and announced that he would go no further unless he and his partners were each guaranteed two hundred feet of ground. The others agreed willingly enough, and after a suitable period of celebration, they made camp. Hughes and a few of his friends managed to steal off in the night in order to arrive early enough to stake out claims close to the original discovery, but they left an easy trail and the others soon followed.

The town of Virginia City had been laid out by the end of June, and by the end of summer it had been joined by others strung along the whole length of the creek which trickled down Alder Gulch. "There are three points or cities on the creek," a trader wrote in September, 1863, "Nevada, Virginia and Summit—the whole length of the Claims are 15 miles. Some do not pay much, some very rich. The population on the Creek is about 4,000. The houses, stores etc., the same in appearance as at Bannock, but here we have a mining city in full blast—stores, saloons, gaming houses, and streets crammed full—dust everywhere plentifull—and the price of everything at the utmost stretch.... The U.S. Marshal estimates the population in and

Looking down the ramshackle industrial camp of Milo Gulch in the Coeur d'Alene, shortly after the discovery of silver in galena form.

around Virginia diggings at 12,000."

Predictably, there were far too many men in this elongated little metropolis to be supported by the available gold, and the boom had hardly started before unsuccessful miners began an ant-like scuttle after rumors, as recalled by Granville Stuart in his *Forty Years on the Frontier:* "A large number of idle men were about town and it required no more than one man with an imaginative mind to start half the population off on a wild goose chase. Somebody would say that somebody said that somebody had found a good thing and without further inquiry a hundred or more men would start out for the reported diggings."

Most of the abortive expeditions that resulted from this air of hysteria produced little or nothing, but some—notably Confederate Gulch south of present-day Helena, which in less than ten years yielded ten million dollars in gold—paid off handsomely. This and other successes helped establish a pattern of frenetic development that would create more than five hundred gold-producing gulches throughout Montana by the end of

The main street of Helena, Montana, (Last Chance Gulch) sometime between 1865 and 1868, showing the characteristic display of dust and optimism.

the 1870s.

One of the most successful was Last Chance Gulch. In July of 1864 three discouraged miners—refugees from the California gold fields and just about every other mining region in the West—struck color in a gulch some eighty miles north of Virginia City. Not happy with the richness of the prospect, they wandered off, and did not return until September, deciding to give the gulch one last chance before they gave up the dream altogether. It was a wise decision, for their second attempt gave the place a name and launched one more rush.

By the spring of 1864 the Gulch had a thousand inhabitants and a new name: Helena. It flourished quickly and by 1866 had entered its name in the rough-and-tumble lexicon of typical mining towns; one resident described it as "a mighty 'rough hole,'" and another found it to be "not so large a place as I thought it was—but it is the *busiest* place I ever saw." Unlike the majority of mining camps in Montana, Helena survived the inevitable decline of its mines, principally because it was ideally situated as a central point on the trade route between Fort Benton on the upper Missouri and the towns of the western interior of the state.

Altogether, the gold placers of Montana's gulches produced an astonishing amount of treasure over the years. By 1900, Alder Gulch alone had accounted for more than $85,000,000 and Last Chance another $30,000,000. Extensive hydraulic and dredge mining activities helped to account for such figures, as did the development of lodes; vein mining began in many areas as early as 1864, and while it was hampered by the ignorance and impatience of men more accustomed to the crude efficiency of placer mining than the more demanding techniques of lode operations, it contributed its share to the total. It has been estimated that between 1862 and 1950, Montana's mines produced some $390,000,000 in gold, and while some historians have questioned the reliability of these figures, it seems reasonable to assume that the total was well above three hundred million.

Those are spectral figures, but they pale when cast in the shade of Montana's true bonanza—copper (although for a time it seemed that silver might dominate). In 1875, silver deposits had been discovered in a washed-out gold placer region just south of Butte, and over the next several years mines and mills in the area produced the modest but adequate amount of twenty-five dollars in silver per ton, together with some gold. In 1881, the Anaconda Mine, operating as a nominally successful silver development, was taken over by Marcus Daly, who immediately suspected that he had on

Taken at about the same time as the photograph on the opposite page, this scene of Helena is softened somewhat by the presence of a couple of nervous but strong-jawed local belles.

his hands something more than just another silver mine. He needed development money to confirm his suspicions, however, and he turned to George Hearst, who was still busily erecting an empire on the bones of other men's mines.

Together with his partners Lloyd Tevis and James B. Haggin, Hearst took over the mine in exchange for giving Daly a one-fourth interest in whatever developed. What developed was copper; in May, 1883, workers reached the six-hundred-foot level and a copper vein, mixed with gold and silver, that varied in width from fifty to one hundred feet. By the end of 1884, the Anaconda was producing enough copper to influence prices on the world market, additional mines and smelters were developed in the area, and Butte had become one of the major industrial mining centers in the United States. By 1950, the Butte copper mines had produced nearly two billion dollars in ore.

Compared to the productivity of Idaho and Montana in the latter half of the 1860s, Colorado was a disaster area. By the end of 1866, most of the mining camps that had been hastily thrown together during the mania of 1859 and 1860 were moribund and crumbling; machinery lay scattered in rusting piles through-

out the mountains; washes, gulches, creeks, and other placer regions were deserted, and ambitious lode mining shafts were as empty as the bottom of a dry well. Only in the "little Kingdom of Gilpin County" did mining of any consequence continue during the last half of the decade, and even there annual production was more often measured in hundreds of thousands than in several millions, as recorded in each of the other two states.

At the end of the decade, things began to pick up, a shift that was attributable in no small part to a quick spurt of railroad development in the last years of the 1860s. The Union Pacific Railroad, slapping down track with sometimes astonishing speed on its way to a rendezvous with the Central Pacific at Promontory, Utah, reached Cheyenne, Wyoming, in the fall of 1867; a group of Colorado investors, following an instinct for the obvious, got together and began construction of the Denver Pacific Railroad from Denver to Cheyenne; it was completed in the summer of 1870, giving Colorado its first railroad link with the markets of Chicago and the East. In that same year, the Kansas Pacific completed its line from Kansas City to Denver.

In a little over ten years, then, travel time between the Missouri and Mississippi river towns and the Rocky Mountain frontier had been reduced from a matter of

The clamoring hysteria of Leadville in the flush of its first major boom is documented by this woodcut from Frank Leslie's Illustrated Newspaper, *April 12, 1879.*

weeks to a matter of days; prices for all commodities, previously astronomical because of the difficulty of wagon freightage over six hundred miles of the Great Plains, fell dramatically, as did the cost of passenger transportation; even labor costs were slashed—in short, the arrival of the railroad helped to lift an economic shroud from the territory's shoulders. The completion of a line from Denver to Golden and then to Black Hawk in 1872 also gave the economy a boost, lowering the costs of transporting ores from the Gilpin County mines to Denver smelters and forcing an initial wedge into the interior of the mountains.

The effect of all this railroad building was felt almost immediately. Mines that had been abandoned for years were reopened and operated profitably; deteriorating mill machinery was cleaned up and put back to

work, new mills constructed, and smelters to process the more complicated ores were gradually developed. (All of this activity, of course, was in the area of lode mining, for by 1870 Colorado's placers, never very extensive, had been depleted to a point approaching annihilation, a fact even the incurably optimistic Coloradoans were ready to admit.) Even more significant to this sudden renascence in mining was a return to wide prospecting through the mountains, leading to the discovery in the early 1870s of a number of gold and silver lodes of far more than passing consequence, many of them in the southwestern portion of the state, where Summitville, Lake City, Rosita, Silverton, and Ouray came into prominence.

These new discoveries, and others like them, produced well and regularly through the 1880s, finally put-

suspected—when the rush to California Gulch died out. In 1873, an experienced mining investigator by the name of William H. ("Uncle Billy") Stevens arrived at the abandoned gulch and determined that with improved techniques and large-scale operations the placers could still be worked with substantial profits.

"During the winter of 1873–74," David Lavender reported in an article for *The American West* (August, 1967) "he went east and raised $50,000, a capital that might be equated with something like $300,000 in today's currency. This is to say that Uncle Billy Stevens was not engaged, as is sometimes implied, in a picayune backwoods operation." Nor was he so dense as to ignore the intriguing black sand; upon his return in the spring of 1874, he made a field assay of the material and discovered it to be a carbonate ore of lead mixed with silver. Stevens and his partners continued to work the placers, which were producing some twenty thousand dollars a season by then, and quietly spent the next two years investigating their silver lead and staking out claims; but by the summer of 1876 word had leaked out, and others drifted into the camp to see what was up.

Not much, at least for more than another year; the early discoveries were good, but nothing to make the

ting Colorado on a par with the production of Montana and Idaho; still, none of them could have been mistaken for a bonanza—one big discovery that would have lifted Colorado mining from the level of the adequate to the spectacular. Ironically enough, clear evidence of the first of those bonanzas—in a manner similar to the Comstock experience—had been picked up and thrown away by placer miners for years.

During the brief placer days of California Gulch in 1860 and 1861 (see Chapter 3), miners had been irritated by a black sand that clogged the riffles of their rockers. They discarded it as the early Comstockers had discarded the blue sand and clay that had interfered with their work, but there is no record of anyone calling it "that damned black stuff." Whatever, the black rocks and sand were left behind—unanalyzed and un-

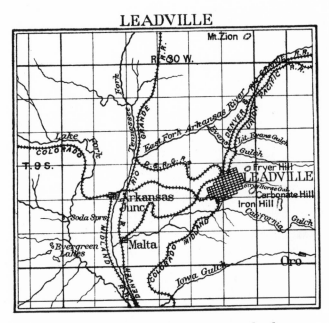

This quick sketch map of the 1880s features the three "hills" that fattened Leadville: Fryer, Carbonate, and Iron.

95

H. A. W. Tabor, the stubborn storekeeper who grubstaked his way to millions—and lost them.

blood race. However, during the winter of 1877–78, as prospectors began fanning out into the hills, the discoveries grew richer and richer in silver, easier to work, and more numerous. In April of 1878, George Fryer left the area of the early workings on Carbonate Hill and began prospecting on another little mountain which came to be known as Fryer Hill; so rich was his find that almost immediately he was able to sell his prospect

Art imitating reality: this photograph of Leadville supplied the inspiration for the woodcut on the preceding two pages.

hole for $50,000. A month later, two prospectors grubstaked by H. A. W. Tabor, a storekeeper in the minuscule village of Leadville, found the Little Pittsburgh Mine on Fryer Hill, and by July it was producing more than eight thousand dollars a week.

In September, one of the discoverers sold out his interest for $98,000; in November, the others sold out for $273,500; and in September, 1879, Tabor, the impecunious grocer who had hung on in the mountains for nearly twenty years, sold his interest for one million dollars (and, in the tradition of the mining frontier, managed to dribble away this and subsequent fortunes on gorgeous spending and fruitless speculation, pinching out the end of his days as a Denver postmaster).

By the end of 1878, the mines around Leadville had produced two million dollars, and the town had experienced its first boom period, as nearly six thousand people streamed in during the summer. As the news of the region's wealth spread through the country, and finally the world, the boom of 1878 was eclipsed by that of the spring and summer of 1879. A journalist dispatched from New York wrote: "All roads leading to the town are alive. Freight wagons coming down loaded with ore, and freight wagons going up loaded with every conceivable thing from mining machinery and railroad iron down to baby-wagons and pepper casters; we saw sixty-two of these wagons in this first day's journey of ten hours. The most interesting thing in the procession . . . was the human element: families—fathers, mothers, with crowds of little children, bedsteads, iron pots, comforters, chairs, tables, cooking-stoves, cradles —wedged into small wagons, toiling slowly up the long hills and across the long stretches of plain all going to Leadville to seek that fortune which had so evidently eluded their efforts hitherto. . . ." An average of one hundred such members of the "human element" arrived at Leadville each day during the spring and summer of 1879.

Among them was the novelist *(Ramona)* and polemicist for the rights of American Indians *(A Century of Dishonor)*, Helen Hunt Jackson, the wife of a mining engineer, who penned for the *Atlantic Monthly* surely the shortest and best description of Leadville in the contortion of boom. The town's houses, she said "are all log cabins, or else plain, unpainted, board shanties.

An 1890s daytime scene in Creede, Colorado, the town where there was no night—at least if the popular doggerel of the day could be believed.

Some of the cabins seem to burrow in the ground; others are set up on posts, like roofed bedsteads. Tents, wigwams of boughs, wigwams of bare poles, with a blackened spot in front, where somebody slept last night, but will never sleep in again; cabins wedged in between stumps, cabins built on stumps, cabins with chimneys made of flower-pots or bits of stove pipe . . . cabins half roofed; cabins with sail-cloth roofs; cabins with no roof at all—this represents the architecture of Leadville homes." The town, with its saloons, its assay offices, its mining supply stores, its banks, its bootmakers and saddlemakers, its doctors and lawyers—256 business establishments in all—simply boiled with humanity; "It looked all the time as if there had been a fire and the people were just dispersing, or as if town-meeting were just over. Everybody was talking, nearly everybody gesticulating. All faces looked restless, eager, fierce."

The materials for entrepreneurial success in Creede (as elsewhere) were not extensive: a few barrels of beer, some bottles of whiskey, a tent, and some professional signs would do very nicely.

Downtown Cripple Creek in 1905 spoke eloquently of progress and enterprise—as in the headframe of the Enterprise Gold Mining Company.

At the end of 1879, Leadville's silver-lead production surpassed $9,000,000, and at the end of 1880 reached close to $12,500,000. While suffering the usual vicissitudes of declining production and sundry economic slumps, many of the Leadville mines continued to produce profitable amounts of ore—abetted by lead, zinc, and a little copper—until well past the turn of the century, making it one of the longest-lived silver districts of consequence in the West. It also was one of the earliest, most extensive, and longest-lived industrial complexes in Colorado, for after its brief experience as a typically frenetic mining camp, Leadville and its environs quickly settled down to a dull respectability more often interrupted by labor troubles than by claim-jumping or hairy Saturday-night sprees.

Mining was big business, and the town reflected this sober fact; as early as 1882, a visiting Englishman, expecting to find the town a clamoring bedlam of wild-eyed speculators and painted ladies, remarked in disgust that "Leadville was like some provincial town. The men would not have looked out of place in the street, say, of Reading, while the women in their quiet and somewhat old-fashioned style of dressing reminded me very curiously of rural England. Indeed, I do not

think my anticipations have ever been so completely upset as in Leadville."

While Leadville was enduring its disappointing evolution, other rich, if less than stupendous discoveries, were being made in other parts of the state, chiefly in Aspen, Gunnison, and, just above the headwaters of the Rio Grande, Creede, whose lambent affection for vice and sometimes murderous hijinks under the supervision of the notorious "Soapy" Smith earned a possibly immortal niche for the following couplet: "It's day all day in the daytime / And there is no night in Creede."* But these were transient excitements, however vigorous, short-lived and inconsequential when compared to the boom of Leadville, much less that of Colorado's biggest bonanza: Cripple Creek.

The discovery and ultimate development of Colorado's greatest gold camp was in large part attributable to the grim persistence of one man, Robert Womack—

---

*The couplet apparently was first applied to Leadville in the following form: "It's day all day in the daytime,/And no night in Leadville." It doesn't scan.

High above the crowded mountain bowl—the "Bowl of Gold"—that held the sprawling metropolis of Cripple Creek, a group of hopefuls sinks a prospect shaft on Gold Hill in 1897.

who never managed to cash in on his own press-agentry. Womack, an itinerant cowboy in the employ of a ranch with holdings in a high mountain basin about twenty miles west of Pikes Peak, was, like nearly everyone else in the Rocky Mountains, an incorrigible part-time prospector who whiled away his idle hours in a search for gold and silver. In 1878, he found a stray bit of rock —or "float"—which he determined would assay at about two hundred dollars the ton, and spent the next several years attempting to locate its source.

In time, the search became an obsession, which Womack enthusiastically broadcast in the saloons and barber shops of Colorado Springs, seeking a grubstake that would enable him to expand his investigations; for more than eleven years, all he got for his trouble was the cognomen of "Crazy Bob." It did not help that his mountain basin, watered by a trickle called Cripple Creek, lay under the shadow of Mount Pisgah, a retired volcano, for in 1884 a couple of confidence men got together with merchants in Canon City, salted a mine near Mount McIntyre west of the Cripple Creek basin, and perpetrated what became known as the "Mount Pisgah Hoax," in one of those geographic confusions common to mining rushes.

The memory of this farce was enough to keep Womack without funds until 1889, when he finally talked his way into a grubstake and in October located one of the sources of the float he had found so many years before. He staked out a claim and called it the El Paso Lode. The ore assayed at $250 the ton, but residents of Colorado Springs and its environs remained cynical, and only a few men were inspired to stake out and develop claims; in 1890, the population of the basin— which had become known as "Poverty Gulch"—was only fifteen.

In 1891, Winfield Scott Stratton, a Colorado Springs carpenter with visions of treasure (he had painstakingly educated himself in the geology of mining, a singular achievement among western prospectors), wandered into Poverty Gulch. The persistent yammering of Womack, still convinced that Cripple Creek was a new Golconda, persuaded Stratton to stay, and during the spring and early summer of 1891 he meandered through the district, possibly with a copy of Plattner's *Blowpipe Analysis* in his back pocket, although this fact is not recorded in the reminiscences of Leslie D. Spell, whose father owned a promising hole called the Blue Bell: "One visitor who passed by frequently was

99

W. S. Stratton, the future multimillionaire. He usually carried a small lard pail containing a meagre lunch, and a type of prospector's pick used in those days....

"I, as usual, trailed Mr. Stratton and found it most fascinating to watch him using his magnifying glass as he examined the specimens he found. He would say to the men working the Blue Bell claim: 'You men stick with it. You sure have it here.' At that time ... mother was boarding the men from the Blue Bell. When she would ring the triangle gong to call them to lunch Stratton would refuse her invitation to lunch with the others and insist that he preferred to sit on the wood-pile near the house while eating from his lard pail."

In July, the retiring Stratton staked his first claim, called it the Independence, and began investigative work. Spell and a friend visited the site that month. "Stratton was on top of a small shaft, using a windlass. The shaft was about 35 feet in depth at that time and we could look down into it and see a man working, loading ore into a bucket. When he emptied it there was one rock about the size of a water pail. I remember Stratton saying: 'Now, Tom, that's the gold, that stuff that looks like white iron, but that's gold.' The rock was plastered with the precious stuff!"

In November, Count James Pourtales, a nobleman by birth and an entrepreneur by inclination, came up to Cripple Creek from Colorado Springs, looked around, and returned to announce that he was buying a claim called the Buena Vista for eighty thousand dollars. This was the kind of money to start men thinking, and the cynicism that normally greeted any reference to Poverty Gulch evaporated. Men with capital moved in and began buying claims from many of the original owners—among them Robert Womack, who sold his claim in the El Paso Lode for three hundred dollars. One wants to shake him; after exhibiting so much dog-ged patience for thirteen years, he abandoned his vir-ginal dream for the strumpet call of a quick dollar.

Men follow money, and the spring of 1892 saw Crip-ple Creek's first rush as twenty-five hundred came up into the mountains. A town was laid out, and by April it possessed a startling number of amenities, including the Clarendon Hotel, which had 125 rooms, a billiard room, bar, 100-seat dining room, hot and cold running water, and electric lights. "Crime in our fair city," the marshal of Colorado Springs remarked, "is at an all-time low. All the criminals have moved to Cripple

Creek." Other superbly productive mines were added to the list—principally the Portland, the Cresson, the Vindicator, and the Strong—and to meet their needs, Cripple Creek was surrounded by a network of sub-urbs: Goldfield, Victor, Elkton, Altman, Independ-ence, Anaconda, Gillett, Cameron, Beaver Park, Are-qua, and Lawrence.

By the end of 1896, the district was a thriving little industrial complex that had produced nearly twenty-two million dollars in gold—a vigorous collection of mining factories nourished by outside capital and manned by professional miners, many of them refugees from silver camps throughout the West which had been stricken into bankruptcy by the repeal of the Sherman Silver Purchase Act in 1893. In 1896, the city of Cripple Creek burned down, and the speed with which it was rebuilt—and the form it took in rebuilding—was a monument to industrial enterprise, as suggested by a reporter's description of the town in 1897: "Cripple Creek is a new city, nearly all brick. You enter the hotel and find a spacious rotunda, elegantly appointed offices, coloured bell boys, and rooms well furnished, carpeted, and heated by steam.... Buildings are ele-gant with elaborate carvings, proportionate pillars, capitals of Greek style, shiny brass work. Down in the lower part of town in the gulch near the Florence and Cripple Creek Railroad station, are the machine shops, forges, and from there the town straggles down through the gulch toward Mound City."

By 1900, the population of the district had leaped to fifty thousand, and it was accounting for nearly one-fourth of the entire gold production of the United States. By 1916, it had produced $340,000,000, and until its final decline in the 1960s, it dumped another $150,-000,000 on the market. During the peak years of its pro-duction, the monthly payroll to more than six thou-sand miners exceeded $650,000. Cripple Creek was no mining camp; it was a machine for making gold.

So Colorado had enjoyed its bonanzas. They did not come without costs engendered by the agonies of a so-ciety grown large; Leadville experienced labor strife as early as 1880, and the great Cripple Creek strikes of 1894 and 1904 were some of the bloodiest class conflicts in western history, as miners assaulted the very ma-chine of which they were a part (see Chapter 11). But the bonanzas came, and it was just as well that the state enjoyed them while it could—for they were the last.

MOUNTAIN OF GOLD

Cripple Creek, Colorado, clusters in a mountain-ringed bowl nearly ten thousand feet above the sea—possibly the single most dramatic setting of all the surviving mining towns in the American West. Hunkered down beneath the conical shadow of an extinct volcano called Mount Pisgah, the town possesses a spectacular vista to the southwest across a land wrinkled with mountain ranges like the surface of the sea, culminating in the snow-edged Sangre de Cristo Range fifty miles away. The hills about the town are sprinkled with the now-abandoned machinery of mining, headframes, shaft houses, hoists, and with piles of wasterock and tailings overgrown with grass and shrubs—the detritus of a civilization whose mines were once a roll call of dreams: Mollie Kathleen, Gold King, Half Moon, Tornado, Gold Coin, Independence, Mountain Beauty.

Like Virginia City, Nevada, Cripple Creek today is a town far more dependent on the exploitation of its past than on the great mining ventures that once made its name familiar in stock exchanges scattered from San Francisco to London. The old depot of the narrow-gauge Florence and Cripple Creek Railroad (seen at the left) is now a museum displaying the memorabilia of Cripple Creek's lambent past, and the town's bars, restaurants, and two hotels lean heavily on that past; Cripple Creek, like any number of other towns in the West, has learned that history is a marketable commodity.

Cripple Creek, in common with most of the mining towns of the West, burned down, in 1896. Unlike most other such towns, however, which rebuilt with wood (frequently to their regret), Cripple Creek had the foresight to choose brick, even if it cost more and took longer. It was a wise choice; Cripple Creek survived further onslaughts of fire, and today the red brick buildings that line both sides of Bennett Avenue, the town's main thoroughfare, lend the tiny village a solid charm.

In comparison to Virginia City, which hammers its message home with the subtlety of an eight-pound sledge wielded by a double-jacking miner in a drilling contest, Cripple Creek's appeal to the tourist is positively subdued. Aside from an occasional sign at the approaches to the town proclaiming it "The Greatest Gold Camp in the World" (wrong on two counts: it was not the greatest, and it was never a camp), there is nothing to match the frenetic billboardry of the Comstock town. But there is plenty to do— including mine tours, gimcrackery buying, drinking in one or more of the several little bars, watching the Saturday night melodramas in the Imperial Hotel, or riding the tour cars of the Cripple Creek and Victor Railroad, one of the finest little narrow-gauge lines left in the country.

The logistics of greed could overcome all the logic of geography and climate; above, a couple endures the slush of a storefront tunnel in Breckenridge, Colorado, during the "Big Snow" of 1898.

CHAPTER SIX

THE HOLY WILDERNESS

Custer takes a vacation and a rush is born

"George Hearst has taken our advice and bought himself a new suit of clothes—a black suede, and don't look half as well as he did in his old harness. George is a pretty big man, but he ain't big enough for his new suit. There is slack enough in the back of the coat to carry several million dollars worth of stock, samples from all the bonanzas he owns on the belt, and one of Prof. Jenney's shoes besides...."

The Black Hills of South Dakota come wrinkling up out of the Great Plains like a forest tableland gone wild—nature caught in one of its frequent contortions. Thickly wooded, its red soil sliced into a thousand tangled ravines, gulches, canyons, and creek beds by the erosion of several millennia, it is a dark wilderness country where the sun is an intrusion that comes late and leaves early. From a distance out on the plains, it rises as if it were the edge of another continent; against the drab, yellow-dust color of the plains, the dark green of its forests appears almost black. From within comes an occasional crackling rumble that might be the echo of mountain thunder or gases exploding from burning coal seams; hot springs bubble and gasp. It is a very old country, and speaks with the mystery of age.

This was the Holy Wilderness of the Sioux Indians, a traditional hunting ground and place of sacred rites for generations, deeded to them in perpetuity by the Great Spirit himself—a transaction ratified by the United States government in a treaty of 1868, which guaranteed that the Black Hills would forever be removed from settlement by the white man. It also was a country rich in one of the last major deposits of placer and lode gold in the West. Although a conscientious army managed for several years to maintain an uneasy equilibrium between these conflicting facts, the thrust of history demanded a confrontation—and only one of its results was the Battle of the Little Big Horn.

Years before, the Sioux had discovered gold in the Black Hills but wisely tried to keep its existence a nervous secret. For a long time, secrecy worked; those few trappers and traders who entered the region and learned of the gold had little desire to allow a gold rush to interfere with their enterprises and so kept a tight mouth on the subject. By the middle of the 1860's, however, the backwash of the mining frontier began to lap at the edges of the Holy Wilderness. Rumors of its gold became the subject of conversation at Fort Laramie, Cheyenne, and Yankton, South Dakota; where there were rumors of gold, there were prospectors ready to go find it, and in the spring of 1866 a party of one hundred and fifty men organized for an investigative expedition into the hills. The army, struggling to avoid as much conflict as possible, forbade the party to leave.

The following spring another large party organized, and once again the army refused to let them go. In the fall of the year, yet another party—this one with three

Glittering with the naked triumph of electricity, turn-of-the-century Deadwood celebrated the virtues of industry and enterprise.

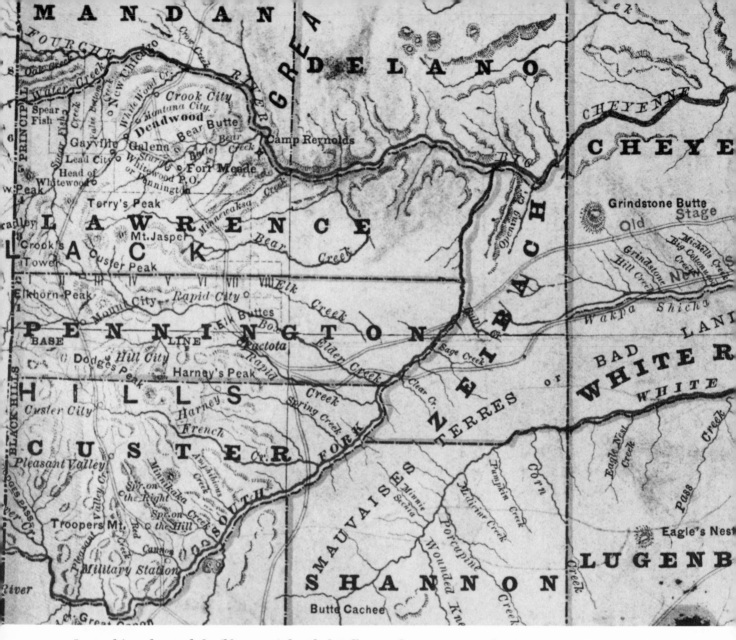

Jammed into the tangled wilderness of the Black Hills near the top center of this 1880 map, the little complex of Deadwood—Lead City huddled in a circle of Indian land.

hundred members—organized at Yankton, but the army threatened to use force to stop them and the party disintegrated. In 1872, the editor of the *Sioux City Times* of Iowa attempted to establish a colony of settlers for the Black Hills, but the army steadfastly refused to permit it.

Interest in what might lie in the Black Hills continued to build, doubtless fired by all the years of prohibition, and in 1874 the army itself decided it was perhaps time to learn the truth. It sent George Armstrong Custer, the Civil War's youngest general, into the region for purposes of exploration. The expedition that the flamboyant Custer put together was of almost ludicrous

dimensions; it included 1,000 soldiers, 1,900 horses and mules, 300 beef cattle, 110 wagons, a battery of three gatling guns, army engineers, experienced gold miners, 60 Indian scouts, a photographer, a cartographer, and a military band.

After a summer of tramping about the Black Hills, panning in streams, hunting elk, collecting petrified shells, snake rattles, and pressed flowers, and finding no use whatever for the three gatling guns, the expedition returned to Fort Abraham Lincoln, and Custer prepared his official report. His report of finding gold was singularly moderate: "While the miner may not in one panful of earth find nuggets of large size or deposits of astonishing richness, to be followed by days and weeks of unrewarded labor, he may reasonably expect in certain localities to realize from every panful of earth a handsome return for his labor. While I am satisfied that gold in satisfactory quantities can be obtained in the Black Hills, yet the hasty examination [hasty? three *months?*] we were forced to make, did not enable us to determine in any satisfactory degree the richness or extent of the gold deposits in that region."

One wonders a little testily even now what Custer's summer vacation cost the government of the United States.

Moderate or not, Custer's report was the first official word on the subject of gold in the Black Hills, and the news was scattered almost instantly from the Chicago *Inter-Ocean* to *Harper's Weekly*. The timing could hardly have been better for the making of a rush. The panic of 1873—which followed two years of hysterical railroad speculation in the West and was immediately inspired by the failure of one of the most expansive of the speculators, Jay Cooke & Co.—left the country in a shaken condition, particularly in the Midwest. What better antidote to depression could there be than a new golden frontier of a dimension to match that of California in 1849—a frontier, moreover, whose distance was measured in days, rather than months?

Even while the army sluggishly continued to refuse entrance into the Black Hills, it was obvious to all that it was only going to be a matter of time before the floodgates would be opened to the new Golconda. Mining companies, in anticipation of that day, began to be organized throughout the cities of the East, including Boston, Brooklyn, New York, Harrisburg, Memphis, Milwaukee, New Orleans, Kansas City, St. Louis—and in the West, San Francisco. As early as the fall of 1874, many such companies made their way to Wyoming and attempted to sneak into the Black Hills through army lines.

Washington was in a typical quandary, caught up in the web of its own solemn guarantees to the Sioux—who tended to take such promises at face value—and assaulted by the demands of thousands of citizens, many of whom were able to vote. It officially wrung its hands over the situation for as long as possible but finally, in the spring of 1875, succumbed to the inevitable and, in truth, just about the only available alternative: in April, a number of Sioux chiefs were

Photographer Matthew Brady caught the flamboyant essence of the young Custer in this Civil War view.

Vacationing in style: the elements of Custer's 1874 expedition into the Black Hills lined up on the prairies.

escorted to Washington and there requested to sell the Black Hills; they balked. In September, the government organized a grand council in Wyoming, attended by nearly twenty thousand Sioux. Again, their efforts to buy the Holy Wilderness came to nothing; many of the Sioux were truculent and at least one stood up to announce to those around him that he would personally kill anyone who signed a treaty with the whites. Legend has it that one chief wanted six hundred million dollars for the Black Hills; the government countered with an offer of six million. Whatever the precise figures, the gap was too wide to be open to negotiation, and the council broke up with nothing resolved.

In December, the army ordered all Indians to return to their sundry reservations by January 31, 1876, or be liable to treatment as actively hostile enemies. Few of them paid any attention to the order, and the army, under the direction of General George Crook, launched a military campaign in the early spring of 1876 and began chasing Indians. In April, a large number of Sioux and Cheyenne gathered under the leadership of Sitting Bull, an uncommonly shrewd tactician, and began countering offense with offense. They fought Crook to a standstill in the Battle of the Rosebud on June 17 and, in an even more dramatic illustration of their new competence, annihilated the Seventh Cavalry

In this impressive four-part panoramic view of 1900, William H. Jackson documented the sheer sweep of Deadwo

under General George Custer at the Battle of the Little Big Horn. . . . Poor Custer; from a summer of light-hearted, if somewhat expensive entertainment, to a sudden summer of death.

After tasting the glories of victory at Rosebud and the Little Big Horn, the Sioux and Cheyenne had done with fighting, at least for this season. After a minor skirmish at Slim Buttes in August, most agreed to return to their reservations, in full confidence that the Department of the Interior would feed them through the winter. So it would, but there was a stipulation: the Sioux would have to give up the Black Hills forever. And on September 26, 1876, at the Red Cloud Agency

of Nebraska, the necessary agreement was signed.

By then, ownership of the Black Hills was a purely academic question.

Throughout the spring of 1875 miners continued to trickle into the hills, despite all the army could do to stop them, and in May the attorney-general of the United States tied its hands completely. In a remarkable reading of the law that forbade trespassing by "foreigners" (i.e., non-Indians) on the lands of the Sioux, the attorney-general declared that it applied only to those born in other countries, not to citizens of the

rough its canyon from south (left) to north (right).

A view of Deadwood's Burlington Depot in 1900; already, the town was beginning to memorialize itself, as a close reading of the blackboard under the drugstore awning will reveal: "Black Hills views on post cards, 25¢ dozen."

United States. Under this ruling, the federal government stepped out from between the Black Hills and the eager goldseekers, and only the fear of Indian attack during the last months of 1875 and the early months of 1876 kept the hills from being inundated instantly.

Not all were kept out by fear of Indian reprisals even during the most tense moments. During the summer of 1875, fifty or more miners had wandered into the area of Deadwood Creek in the northwestern corner of the Black Hills. The creek coursed down the middle of a deep, narrow gulch whose walls were nearly vertical tangles of rock and brush. Three miles away, on the other side of the mountain that divided the watersheds of Deadwood Creek and Gold Run Creek was another gulch, as deep, as tangled, and as thoroughly resistant to human habitation. It was an area of about five square miles altogether, and it was in the middle of this confused jumble that the heart of Black Hills

mining was established. In that summer of 1875, Frank S. Bryant and a party of six others struck the first significant amount of color in Deadwood Gulch, although a claim was not staked out until November. Already, the makings of a primitive little community had been thrown together in the gulch, as a few hardy miners prepared to settle in for the winter.

In the spring of 1876 the rush to the Black Hills officially began, as thousands poured into the mountains from points east, west, and south, bound for the diggings in Deadwood Gulch. Predictably, only those who arrived as early as February were able to locate claims worth the effort of working; Deadwood's placers were rich but limited in extent to a few rich outcroppings and washes, which were taken up quickly. According to the patterns of tradition, disappointed miners then scattered into the gullies and gulches north and south of Deadwood. Among them were the Manuel brothers, Fred and Moses, veterans of gold fields in

George Hearst, the entrepreneur's entrepreneur who muscled the Homestake Mine into a bulwark of his empire.

the water ran through the draw which crossed the lead and I saw some quartz in the bottom and the water running over it. I took a pick and tried to get some out and found it very solid, but I got some out and took it to camp and pounded it up and panned it and found it very rich. Next day Hank Harney consented to come and located what we called the Homestake, the 9th of April, 1876. We started to dig a discovery shaft on the other side of this little draw and the first chunk of quartz weighed about 200 pounds and was the richest ever taken out. We came over next day and ran an open cut and found we had a large deposit of a rich grade ore. We ran a big open cut and saved the best quartz by itself. Afterwards we built a road to Whitewood and bought an ox team and wagon, built an arrastra and hauled the ore over. We ran the arrastra the following winter and took out $5,000."

By fall, the brothers and their partners had added a claim to the Old Abe, next to the Homestake, and that soon started producing ore as rich as that at the original discovery. At the end of the year, the mines were both producing steadily, and a ten-stamp mill had been installed by Moses to pulverize the ore more efficiently than the arrastra. The hills above and below them were a welter of claims and working mines, as prospectors hurried into the area to tap into the great discovery, and a town had been laid out and christened Lead (pronounced to rhyme with "greed") City.*

By the spring of 1877, the entire region from Gold Run Gulch to Deadwood Gulch was a narrow, clamoring hive of humanity that vigorously perpetuated all the grandiloquent traditions of western mining camps; in fact, it can be said that this tiny five-mile region was a sort of condensation of tradition, since crammed into its gulches were enough distinct mining camps to settle a couple of hundred square miles of land anywhere else in the mining frontier: Lead City, Washington, Gayville, Blacktail, Central City, Golden Gate, Anchor City, Oro City, Pluma, and Deadwood. The "capital"

Montana, Utah, Idaho, Nevada, California, Arizona, and Alaska. For nearly ten years they had haunted the mining camps of the West without success and were giving it another try in the Black Hills. After dismissing the possibility of finding a paying claim amid the crowded throngs of Deadwood Gulch, the brothers wandered up to the mouth of Bobtail Gulch and with two partners began prospecting in earnest. Three months later, they found what they had spent nine years searching for.

In 1903, Moses Manuel related the circumstances of their discovery: "Toward spring, in the latter part of March or April, four of us found some rich float quartz. We looked for the lode but the snow was deep and could not find it. When the snow began to melt I wanted to go and hunt it up again but my three partners wouldn't look for it as they did not think it was worth anything. I kept looking every day for nearly a week, and finally the snow melted on the hill and

*So named because of the lead, or well-defined quartz vein trapped between two walls of rock, discovered by the Manuel brothers. The term "laid out," incidentally, is used somewhat loosely here. In such an environment, no town could have been laid out in the ordinary sense; rather, it was arbitrarily jammed into the gulch in a kind of sublime defiance of topography.

By the middle of the 1880s, the deep mines around Lead City (above) had long since surpassed in importance the brief excitement of placer gold.

of this little megalopolitan complex was Deadwood, whose population by the spring of 1877 had reached ten thousand. A reporter for *Frank Leslie's Illustrated Newspaper* essayed a sardonic description of the city in April: "Deadwood is a city of a single street, and a most singular street it is. The buildings which grace its sides are a curiosity in modern architecture, and their light construction is a standing insult to every wind that blows. Paint is a luxury only indulged in by the aristocracy. . . . Wells are dug in the middle of the street, all sorts of building material occupies them and every manner of filth is thrown into them. The city is honeycombed by shafts run down into the bowels of the earth from every yard. A keen-eyed, money-grabbing set of men makes up the population, but they are far from the bloodthirsty scoundrels the average newspaper correspondent would make them out to be.

Shooting is not frequent; fighting is only occasional; and property is perfectly secure."

That last judgment, echoed in a number of sources, casts an odd shadow of contrast to the popular image of the town that has evolved over the past century, one dominated by a litany of shoot-outs, lynchings, brawls, murders, and robberies, and memorialized in names like Calamity Jane, Deadwood Dick, Jack McCall, and his victim "Wild" Bill Hickok, the only gunfighter in the West who would have used a hair-setting gel if it had been available. The names were real enough, and so were many of the checkered events connected with them, but if the reporter for *Leslie's* can be trusted, such people and such antics were being overshadowed by rapid economic and social development as early as April, 1877.

By July of 1878, when mining engineer Louis Janin

The headworks of the Homestake Mine dominated the townscape of Lead City in 1900 much as they do today (for a comparison, see the modern view on pages 4 and 5).

visited Deadwood, that development was even more advanced and visible. "All the conveniences," he wrote, "and even the luxuries of life can be obtained in this section of the Black Hills. . . . It is by no means the rough mining camp that exists in the imagination of many. On the contrary, it is one of the pleasantest of all mining localities I have visited; and in no other district is justice more ably administered, or greater security afforded to life and property."

In *Mining Frontiers of the Far West* (1963), historian Rodman Paul attributed the quick shift from extemporaneity to solid enterprise within a matter of what amounted to months to the maturity of the mining frontier itself. By the middle of the 1870s, that frontier had accumulated a tradition of capitalization, in the lexicon of which "development" was at least as important a word as "strike." Any fool could make a

quick strike, and many did, but only capital could provide the technological sophistication necessary to transform a sudden boom into industrial growth, an axiom revealed true from the quartz mines of California to the galena lodes of the Coeur d'Alene. It was a matter of machinery, specialization, and money.

Deadwood was situated in a singularly hostile environment, crammed into a mountain canyon 240 miles removed from the nearest railroad and served only by stage coaches and freight wagons; its population was the typical collection of restless con men, hard cases, rank amateurs, and harmless drifters common to the mining frontier; its mines were a confused hodgepodge of placer and quartz operations conducted for the most part by men with little more than the most rudimentary knowledge of what was needed.

On the surface, it seemed in 1877 to be a poor candi-

While the Homestake Mine and a handful of similarly ambitious enterprises soon shadowed the Black Hills with industry, less expansive (and successful) operators continued to probe the wilderness well past the turn of the century.

date for the kind of growth described by Janin in 1878. "But mining booms were an old story to the West by now," Paul says. "If there were many tenderfeet who responded to the 'excitement' of 1874–1876, so were there veterans of every economic level and the most diverse ambitions who knew how to seize the opportunity. That is why experienced leadership, men with special talents, and capital for investment appeared so readily once indications of real richness were advertised."

Capital for investment.... Enter, once again, George Hearst.

The figure of George Hearst stands as a kind of antipode to that of the starry-eyed prospector whose wanderings made up so much of the history of the

mining West. Spare, quiet, ambitious, and utterly competent, Hearst made his own mark on the course of the mining frontier, not as a discoverer of mines but an exploiter of them, a developer. The prospector was part of the dream; Hearst was part of the machine that made dream reality. After eight years of unsuccessful development work among the quartz mines of the Sierra Nevada, Hearst had parlayed an inside tip into control of the Comstock's Ophir Mine, one of the lode's richest early producers. The fortune he made off that mine provided him with a kind of grubstake, and from then on there were few major lode-mining operations in the West that did not reveal in greater or lesser degree the hand of George Hearst; with the methodical concentration of a child building a house out of blocks, he constructed a financial empire that would later enable his son, William Randolph, to run a chain of news-

The marginal nature of deep mining on little more than a shoestring and hope in the tangled ravines of the Black Hills is suggested by this scene of about 1890, notable for its primitive conveniences.

papers and invent wars.

An essential ingredient in the formation of that empire was the Homestake Mine of Moses and Fred Manuel. Early in 1877, the San Francisco trio of Hearst, Lloyd Tevis, and James Haggin became interested in lode developments in the Black Hills. They sent out an agent, who reported that the Homestake Mine was a good—perhaps a brilliant—prospect. Late in June, Hearst himself traveled into the Black Hills, took a look at the Manuel operation, and bought it for $70,000 cash. The brothers had already sold the Old Abe Mine for $45,000 and had dispensed with an earlier claim for another $35,000; the total of $150,000 was a reward of respectable proportions for their ten years of searching in the West, but—in character with the nature of "first discoverers" — they had given away a fortune. Hearst returned to San Francisco, and in November

of that year the Homestake Mining Company was incorporated in California at a capitalization of one hundred thousand shares at one hundred dollars per share.

By then Hearst was back in Lead City, where he would remain for the next two years putting the company's holdings on a working basis. It was a remarkable performance, one of the most telling illustrations of the mechanics of corporate mining in the history of the West. The first order of business was a stamp mill to crush the ore, which he instructed his partners to have built in California and shipped to the Black Hills as soon as possible. "We should not have less than one hundred stamps," he noted, "and that number of stamps cannot work out the mine in twenty-five years. Figure it yourselves, how many tons of ore are there in a pile 1,500 feet long, 30 feet wide, and 100 feet deep?"

A typical monument to mining-town success, the Deadwood Theatre staunchly characterized the brick solidity of Deadwood less than thirty years after the Black Hills had been "rescued" from the Sioux Indians.

Of even more immediate importance was the need to consolidate the Homestake's interests so as to "lock up," so far as possible, the major portion of the lode. This was going to be no small task. The big vein on which the Homestake was located ran a little distance south and about a mile and a half north from its site. Strung up and down this vein and in various adjacent locations were ten major mines, together with an odd number of smaller claims. It would take a great deal of money, some litigation, some bitter contention, and no little time to make it all happen, but Hearst considered it well worth the effort, as he wrote to his partners in May, 1878: "Homestake is opening up beyond expectation and the more we do on it, and the more we examine into the vein or mine, the more we are convinced of its enormous proportions. . . ."

Methodically, Hearst purchased claim after claim until he had a firm grip on much of the width of the vein. In addition, he acquired water rights to a portion of Whitewood Creek, appropriated a number of mill sites, and ordered vast amounts of machinery to be constructed and sent out from San Francisco.

All this activity did not take place in a vacuum, of course; Hearst was after power, and he was not alone. Among other things, some of the claims that Hearst was challenging in his single-minded attempt to control the lode were within the boundaries of the town of Lead City itself, putting it in the somewhat ludicrous position of having to defend its right to the ground on which it stood. At times, the natural contention engendered by these and other conflicts threatened to get out of hand, or so it would seem from at least one letter from Hearst to San Francisco: "As I wrote you, if we succeeded in finding out the fraud and maintain our rights there would be more squealing than ever was heard of before. And it is quite possible that I may get killed, but if I should I can't but lose a few years, and all I ask of you is to see that my wife and child gets all that is due them from all sources and that I am not buried in this place." There was plenty of "squealing" as Hearst inexorably put together his monopoly, but so far as is known, no assassination attempts were ever made on his life.

By the beginning of 1879, the company's fortunes were prospering. Nothing succeeds like success, and gradually even public opinion in Lead City began to shift to the side of Hearst and his operations—in the interests of progress, of course. "What difference," the editor of the *Black Hills Daily Times* wanted to know in March, "does it make whose money puts in such great enterprises . . . only so we get the big mills and the wealth of our country is thus developed? Then why this insane cry against the Californians who have made us what we are? They are our benefactors, and instead of speaking of Mr. Hearst as that 'd——d old Hearst,' he should be honored, and every courtesy extended to him by everyone expecting to live and prosper in the hills." Aside from the slightly ominous tone of the last part of the editor's statement, it was clear that the Homestake's control over the mines and mills of the district had reached a point where continuing to oppose it was fruitless. By the end of the month, he was satisfied that his work was done, and he packed up and returned to San Francisco permanently. Shortly before his departure, the editor of the *Daily Times* penned an uncommonly chummy description of Hearst, which leaves one with an intriguing picture in the mind: "George Hearst has taken our advice and bought himself a new suit of clothes—a black suede, and don't look half as well as he did in his old harness. George is a pretty big man, but he ain't big enough for his new suit. There is slack enough in the back of the coat to carry several million dollars worth of stock, samples from all the bonanzas he owns on the belt, and one of Prof. Jenney's shoes besides. . . ."

Control of Lead City's mines and mills had been rather nicely tucked away, at that. Samuel McMaster, who took over as superintendent of the company's Black Hills operations upon Hearst's departure, was left overseer of a staggeringly complex enterprise, consisting of ten major mines and several smaller ones (as well as a number of additional properties awaiting final claims litigation); six mills, comprising a total of 540 stamps, as well as a major interest in the 100-stamp mill of the DeSmet Mine; offices, stables, blacksmith shops, carpenter's shops, forges, and one tramway; and more than 500 employees, 257 of them in the mines alone—all this in less than two years after Hearst's arrival and less than five after General George Armstrong Custer and his mighty expedition strolled through the wilderness of the Black Hills in the summer of 1874.

What Hearst had left, impressive as it was, stood as a kind of skeleton for future development. By the 1890s, the company employed more than 1,900 men; the shafts of its various mines sank to below a thousand feet and drifts ran for miles in all directions. By 1900 it had produced nearly sixty million dollars in gold, and by 1924 had accounted for approximately 90 percent of the total of more than $230,000,000 taken out of the Black Hills since 1876. To date—and it is one of the oldest operating gold mines in the world—the Homestake Mining Company has produced close to one billion dollars. In 1878, Hearst had written to his partners: "You, nor your children, will never live to see the end of the time when this property will not be worked for a profit." One takes exception to his grammar, but not to his prophecy.

The Homestake was not the only mine in the Black Hills, nor was Lead City its only gold town. Lode mines scattered through all the tangled ravines of the mountains were undergoing a similar evolution from small-time operations to full-scale corporate development—at least those rich enough in possibility to survive the rigors of time. And towns like Custer and Central City continued to grow for a time under the prodding of gold. Yet Lead City and the Homestake stood not only as the culmination of all the frantic hopes that called the thousands into the Hills in 1876 and 1877, they were a monument to the evolution that the mining West had experienced over the previous generation; in an accelerated and almost exaggerated form, they had become in a few short years what every significant mine and mining town in the West would become, given time, energy, and money enough. George Hearst, the *sine qua non* of the western mining promoter and developer, had carried a message from the future into the ancient Holy Wilderness of the Sioux Indians.

CHAPTER SEVEN

GRINGO GOLD AND YANQUI SILVER

Dreams in the desert

"You are already taking our country from us fast enough; we will soon have no place of safety left. If we show you where these yellow stones are, you will come there in thousands and drive us away and kill us."

No one can fully explain the way in which a land can be invested with dreams. It is a process as mysterious as the mechanics of love, death, and the female mind, and fully as hard to describe. So it is with the history of mining in the American Southwest, for from the beginning it was a history crowded with myths and dreams, legends, rumors constructed out of the thinnest of air, and all the other paraphernalia of inflamed imaginations—an exaggeration of the same sort of wishful thinking that cluttered up the rest of the mining frontier in all its times and places. Surely, the visible antiquity of the country must have had something to do with it. It is a land with an infinity of space, so much space that distance ceases to have meaning; the horizon could be the sharp edge of the end of the world.

Scattered through all this space are the geologic upthrusts of mountains, mesas, and hills sticking out of the earth like the bones of an animal half-covered in sand, and sliced into it are canyons of an immensity to stagger the comprehension. If men could see dreams in the impressive but familiar mountain landscape rising along the Continental Divide, it should not be surprising to learn that they saw even more in a land that spoke so eloquently of a time that preceded man —and one that would follow him. His little hopes meant nothing to such an environment; therefore, they had to mean a great deal to man himself. It was need married to geography, and its offspring was myth.

Coronado, following the imperative of *must be* into the vague, mirage-ridden land of the Southwest, was the great ancestor of the region's myth-chasers. No man ever traveled farther through this country in search of ectoplasmic certitudes, and few men found less to reward their travels. But even after the myth of the Seven Cities of Cíbola was shattered at Hawíkuh Pueblo in 1540, Coronado had to keep believing; grimly following every fragment of rumor that came his way, he moved his expedition west through the Moqui pueblos to the Rio Grande, then up its valley to the Taos pueblo, hunched beneath the shadow of its Holy Mountain. Yes, yes, the Indians said all along his route, there were great cities, great wealth—but not here. They were always over the next range, across the next valley, in another country. (Move on, Spaniard, move on.)

So he moved on, all the way through southern Colorado and into Kansas, where the straggling expedition astonished roving bands of Indians but found no more gold than it had found in southern Arizona. After its painful return to the Valley of Mexico in 1542, the

How to make a silver mine in the myth-ridden Southwest: in the Coconino Mine of Supai Canyon, it required Indian labor, a wooden wheelbarrow, and a hole in the side of a cliff; also hope, determination, and sweat—as usual.

With a patient eye, every major mining town and region in the Southwest can be found in this 1881 township map.

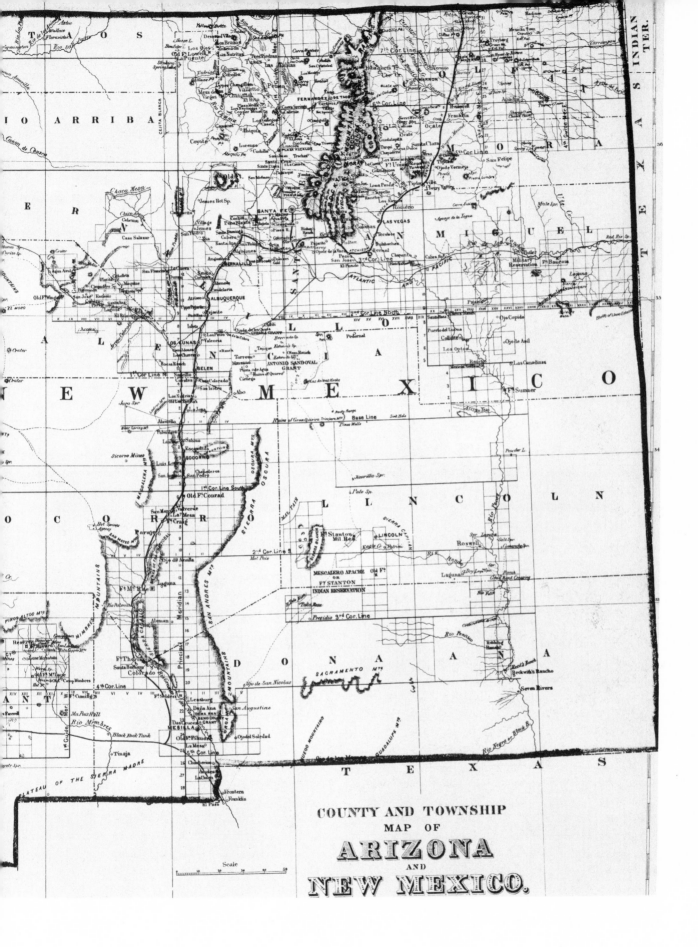

COUNTY AND TOWNSHIP
MAP OF
ARIZONA
AND
NEW MEXICO.

*Relics dredged up in the 1890s from the ancient Spanish **Mina Del Tierra**; today, they are on display in the Museum of New Mexico.*

expedition's chronicler, Pedro de Gastaneda, penned an elegy that embodied all the intensity of the Spanish dream for the New World: "Granted they did not find the riches of which they had been told, they found a place in which to search for them, and the beginning of a good country to settle in, so as to go farther from there. Since they came back from the country which they conquered and abandoned, time has given them a chance to understand the direction and locality in which they were and the borders of the good country they had in their hands, and their hearts weep for having lost so favorable an opportunity."

A place in which to search for them. . . . The first recorded *entrada por minas* into the Southwest after Coronado's dismal effort was by Antonio de Espejo, who wandered all the way to the Bill Williams Fork, west of what is now Prescott, where he found silver deposits so close to the surface of the earth that they could be dug out by hand. But Espejo was ahead of his time; the Bill Williams Fork was a long way from Mexico City, too far for anything to be done with his discovery. In 1604, Juan de Oñate came upon the site

of Espejo's discovery on his way to what he thought was the great "South Sea" (the Pacific Ocean; what he discovered was the Gulf of California), but again the time was not right.

It was not until the Jesuits, and later the Franciscans and Dominicans, spearheaded the thrust of civilization into the Southwest in the seventeenth and eighteenth centuries that mining activity in the region truly began. As the good fathers traveled north from the Valley of Mexico in their search for souls, implanting missions like footsteps throughout Pimería Alta, the edges of Apachería, and Nuevo Mexico, soldiers and citizens followed them, founding presidios and pueblos.

Mission, presidio, and pueblo—what historian W. H. Hutchinson has called "the Spanish tripod of settlement"—comprised the Spanish version of civilization in the New World, and the memory of the riches of Zacatecas hung heavy in the mind of that civilization. Citizens and soldiers alike prospected into the surrounding country, and as early as the middle of the seventeenth century, mining for gold and silver was taking place from Tubac in southern Arizona to Cerillos in northern New Mexico.

We know remarkably little about these mines; neither their extent nor their production has been ascertained with any accuracy by historians. Periodic Indian rebellions, from the Pueblo uprising of New Mexico in 1680 to the Pima Rebellion of Arizona in 1751, had a way of interrupting the existence of any given mining town (as well as its inhabitants), leaving the records scattered and incomplete—and ultimately giving rise to one more tradition of myth-chasing, in the lexicon of which "Lost Spanish Diggings" predominates. We can catch a hint of what such mining was like, however, from a description of the *Mina del Tierra,* a mine near Cerillos, New Mexico, that apparently was started early in the seventeenth century and abandoned during the Indian rebellion of 1680. The writer is Fayette Jones, who visited the site of the unearthed mine in 1904: "The old working consists of an inclined shaft of 150 feet and connects with a somewhat vertical shaft of about 100 feet in depth. Extensive drifts of 300 feet connect with various chambers or stopes; these chambers were formed by stoping or mining out the richer ore bodies.

"The full extent of this old working has never been definitely determined, since the lower depths are covered with water which would have to be pumped out to fully explore the mine. As late as 1870 the remains of an old canoe were still in evidence, which was used for crossing water in the mine or as a carrier for conveying the waste and ore to the main shaft; from this latter point it was carried to the surface on the backs of Indians in rawhide buckets or *tanates*. . . . Many crude and curious relics such as stone hammers and sledges, fragments of pottery, etc., have been taken from both the mine and the dump."*

Some of the mines survived the vicissitudes of both Indian attacks and the shifting political situation, which was climaxed by the establishment of Mexican independence from Spain in 1822, and were still being worked when Americans began to enter the Southwest in the early part of the nineteenth century. Gradually, in reports and isolated shards of information, news of the gold and silver mines of New Mexico and Arizona began to filter back to the United States, arousing an increasing interest.

One of the first such reports was that of James Ohio Pattie, who stumbled into Tepac, Sonora, in 1825: "I traveled through a fine rich country, abounding with cattle [the Santa Cruz Valley], and arrived in the evening at a town called Tepec [Tubac], situated on a small creek near a mountain, in which there is a gold mine worked by the Iago Indians. . . . I remained in this town three days and purchased gold in bars and lumps of the Indians, at the rate of ten dollars per ounce."

Such insubstantial reports — thin to the point of rumor — were supplanted with more reliable communications in the 1830s and 1840s, as American trappers, traders, and finally soldiers entered the tumbling-down country, particularly in the region of Santa Fe and Taos. Of paramount interest were the placers and lode mines of Cerillos in the Ortiz Mountains some twenty miles south of Santa Fe. The gold which had inspired the founding of *Mina del Tierra* by the Spanish in the seventeenth century was rediscovered by Mexicans in 1828 in placer form. Five years later, lode mining developed with the discovery of the Ortiz vein not far from the placers, and in 1839 more placers

*Some of these relics are now on display at the Museum of New Mexico.

were found at the foot of the San Pedro Mountains. These were developments worth more than passing interest to American travelers. In *Commerce of the Prairies* (1844), Josiah Gregg devoted considerable discussion to the mines, and in 1847 Lt. J. J. Abert related a visit to the mines outside Cerillos in his report to the War Department: "We started this morning on a tour of exploration. One-fourth of a mile up the ravine we entered another little town; our way was on all sides full of the precious metals. We saw many miserable-looking wretches, clothed in rags, with an old piece of iron to dig the earth, and some gourds, or horns of the mountain goat, to wash the sand. They sit all day at work, and at evening repair to some *tienda* or store, where they exchange their gold for bread and meat...."

By the time New Mexico and Arizona had been wrested from the Republic of Mexico in 1848, then, the Southwest was a region with a long, if sporadic tradition of gold and silver mining; it remained only for the vaunted technical virtuosity of the progressive American to develop this tradition to the full measure of its potential.

Or so it might have been assumed.

Three factors combined to earn the Southwest a special niche in the history of the mining frontier and dash any chances there were of Americans leaping in and instantly transforming its heretofore soporific development to one of vigorous enterprise. All three had been operating for more than two centuries to limit even Spanish development.

The first was the Indian. In all mining frontiers the Indian was a factor to be dealt with, one way or the other, but rarely had he been a major factor in altering the course of the white man's frantic scrambling; more often a nuisance than a significant problem, those Indians who had placed themselves between the dream-seekers and the dream had been shrugged aside irritably. In Georgia, the Indians had simply been picked up and moved. In California, those few recalcitrant bands who translated their objections into action were hunted down inexorably; it was considered great sport. In Nevada, contention between the silver-seekers of the Comstock and local Indians resulted in the Paiute "War" of 1860, a singularly brief and one-sided conflict which, needless to say, the Indians lost. In Idaho,

the Nez Percé peacefully assented to the invasion of their land and watched it dribble away, piece by piece, as miners scurried over the mountains and creek beds.

In Montana, militant Blackfoot and Crow Indians had forced prospecting parties to strengthen their expeditions with well-armed numbers, but aside from an occasional "depredation," their efforts were about as effective in halting the course of greed as a presidential proclamation would have been. The Eskimo of Alaska, when their turn came (see Chapter 8) would present even less of a problem; being uncivilized, they had little heart for war and could only watch with a kind of bemused puzzlement as the Iron Age assaulted their culture. Even in the Black Hills of South Dakota, the redoubtable Sioux could do little more than fight the briefest kind of holding action. Taken altogether, the Indian's presence throughout most of the landscape in which the mining frontier was exercised could hardly be classed as a "problem."

In the Southwest, it was a problem. To most of the Indians that the white man encountered in his clamor for gold and silver, the act of fighting was a political expression or an exercise in survival; he rarely killed except to defend himself or to make a point. To the Apaches of the Southwest, fighting was a way of life, and death a matter of course. Tough, nomadic, militant, and utterly without scruple when it came to something they wanted, they were a scourge on the Southwest for more than two hundred years, spreading a band of terror among Indians, Mexicans, and Anglos alike from the mountains of New Mexico and southern Colorado to the deserts of Sonora and Chihuahua.

They were marauders by trade and lived off what they could plunder from others. They displayed a particular affection for killing Mexicans, whom they hunted down with the same fierce joy that California's Indian-hunters had exhibited in chasing down Miwoks. Few settlements except the very largest could feel safe from attack at any given moment, and poorly-defended mining camps, from the *reales* of the Spanish and the Mexicans to the sundry ambitious little "cities" of the Americans, were a fond target.

Under such circumstances, mining operations of any scope were imbued with an air of impermanence, a state of affairs suggested by the narrative of Samuel Woodsworth Cozzens, who reported his visit to the Patagonia Mine in the Santa Cruz Mountains just

"Striking it rich!" in the Coconino Mine—at least according to the reversed glass plate notation of photographer Ben Wittick.

Another view of the Coconino Mine; ore clawed out of the recesses of the cliff was laboriously winched up the side of a rock wall, then carried out of the canyon on the backs of mules.

Geronimo, chief of the Apache (or at least some Apache) caught in a characteristically belligerent pose—and looking naked without a rifle.

south of Tubac, Arizona, in 1860: "The ore was yielding from sixty to seventy dollars per ton, which was considered a large paying yield. Since that time, a day's working, or twenty tons of ore, has yielded as high as sixteen hundred dollars, at an actual cost of about four hundred. Notwithstanding these results, the proprietors have never been able to realize much profit from it, on account of the depredations of the Apaches; and shortly after my visit, a band of Apaches drove off all of the company's stock, and murdered the superintendent and many of the miners; since then the mines have been unworked, the valuable machinery useless, many of the buildings destroyed, and desolation and decay have left their sad marks all around." The situation was little better at the Santa Rita Mine some forty miles south of Patagonia: "We found at the mine a Mr. Grosvenor, who was the general manager of affairs there. He had but recently been appointed to the position, and was laboring hard to get things in order. He informed us that the Apaches, within the

past twelve months, had killed his three predecessors in the management of the mines; and within six months Mr. Grosvenor suffered a similar fate."

Such conditions were enough to make any man have second, third, and even fourth thoughts about the prospects of mining in the Southwest, and the presence of the Apaches was a severe retardation to the whole industry. Removing them was a project that had utterly escaped the military competence of the Spanish and Mexicans. Divided haphazardly into roving bands of independent and semi-independent tribes, sub-tribes, and sub-sub-tribes, they were almost impossible to track down. Moreover, they were superior tacticians and masters of skirmish fighting. It took the American Indian-fighting army more than forty years of almost constant effort to subjugate them; it was not until 1890 that Geronimo, the last of a succession of Apache leaders who had given the army a merry chase for its money, was rounded up with his insurgent colleagues and shipped off to Fort Marion, Florida—and by then the mining frontier in the American Southwest had come to an end.

The second factor that hampered the quick development of the Southwest's mining industry was **the problem of transportation.** Arid, broken, hostile, and isolated, the country of the Southwest was barren of all but a few major communication lines. On the west, access could be had via the turgid, thoroughly unreliable, and sometimes deadly currents of the Colorado River; on the east, over the broken trails through west Texas; on the south, over a trail leading north from Chihuahua; and on the north over the well-traveled but nonethless rugged Santa Fe Trail. Shipping loads of ore out along such routes—as well as bringing in heavy machinery for mining, milling, and smelting—was a ruinously time-consuming and expensive matter. The development of stage and mail routes during the 1850s and 1860s helped to ameliorate the problem, but only railroads could have overcome it fully—and it was not until 1879 that the Atchison, Topeka & Santa Fe Railroad reached as far west as Santa Fe, and not until 1882 that the Southern Pacific completed its line from Yuma to El Paso.

The third factor that went to lift the mining frontier of the Southwest out of the standard patterns of evolution was the kind and quality of its ores. With the exception of the Cerillos mines of New Mexico (almost

An 1890 view of the Yavapai County mines near Prescott, Arizona Territory, annotating the foothills of the Sierra Prieta.

completely worked out by the time of the American occupation) and the similar mines on the Colorado River above Yuma, there were almost no placer discoveries to speak of. From the beginning of American occupation, mining in Arizona and New Mexico was dominated by the need for industrial expertise and machinery; its ores were complex, demanding the best skills and technology of the time for profitable development —and that was precisely the kind of orderly, sober enterprise that the presence of marauding bands of Apaches and lengthy, expensive communication lines made all but impossible.

When these facts are taken into consideration, it is not surprising that mining activity in the Southwest was somewhat retarded when compared to other regions of the West; what *is* surprising is that there was any kind of mining at all.

One of the first major mining districts to develop after the American occupation of Arizona, fittingly enough, was also one of its oldest. In 1856, entrepreneur Charles D. Poston organized the Sonora Exploring and Mining Company, which took over development of the Heintzeleman mine, founded some years earlier by a general in the .United States Army of Occupation. It was situated some twenty-five miles south of Tubac in the Cerro Colorado Mountains, which were described by Samuel Cozzens in 1860 as "at once the richest and most barren range in the whole territory." The silver mine itself, he said, "was in successful operation, employing about two hundred men and paying a very handsome profit. . . . At that time the main shaft had reached a depth of one hundred and twenty feet, and the ore seemed to yield far better than it had yet done. The ore at a depth of thirty feet had yielded sixty dollars to the ton, at a depth of sixty feet it yielded nearly two thousand dollars to the ton, and an assay had just

Some sense of the sheer space involved in making enterprise work in the Southwest is suggested by this view of Lake Valley, New Mexico, in the 1890s; in the distance, a locomotive is miniaturized by the landscape.

been made in San Francisco of the ore at a depth of one hundred feet, and found to yield the enormous sum of nine thousand dollars to the ton."* By the time of Cozzens' visit, the Heintzeleman Mine was producing $100,000 annually. Poston, who became *alcalde* of the town of Tubac, which became the service center for the mines in the district, left a tribute to the little pueblo that marks it as one of the most unusual mining towns in existence: "We had no law but love, and no occupation but labor; no government, no taxes, no public debt, no politics. It was a community in a perfect state of nature." Two years later both the town and the mine were abandoned, done in by persistent and deadly raids by the Apache.

In 1864, Poston returned to Tubac and his mine with J. Ross Browne. In *Adventures in the Apache Country* (1869) Browne penned a lament for the mine that stands as a kind of elegy for so much of the mining frontier in a country singularly hostile to it: "Scarcely three years ago the hacienda of the Cerro Colorado presented probably the most striking scene of life and energy in this territory. About a hundred and twenty

*Cozzens, who set down his recollections in *The Marvellous Country* (1873), was better at describing a scene than in recording a fact; among other things, he had Charles Poston killed off by Apaches in 1862, when Mr. Poston did not go to his reward until 1902, unassisted by Indians. The ore that yielded "nine thousand dollars to the ton" must be viewed in the light of suspicion.

peons were in the employ of the company; the works were in active operation; vast piles of ore were cast up daily from the bowels of the earth; wagons were receiving and discharging freights; the puff and whistle of the steam engine resounded over the hills; herds of cattle, horses, mules, and other stock ranged over the valleys.

"At the time of our visit it was silent and desolate—a picture of utter abandonment. The adobe houses were fast falling into ruin; the engines were no longer at work; the rich piles of ore lying in front of the shafts had been sacked and robbed by marauding Mexicans; nothing was to be seen but wreck and ruin, and the few solitary graves on a neighboring hill, which tell the story of violence and sacrifice by which the pathway to civilization has been marked in Arizona."

Sylvester Mowry's Patagonia Mine, just south of the Heintzeleman, was the district's second major development, and it fared a little better—although plagued for most of its life by periodic Indian raids that occasionally closed it down entirely. Worked by Spaniards as early as 1760, it was closed by Apache raids in 1820 and not opened again until Mowry rediscovered it in 1856. In spite of Indians, terrain, and distance, the mine managed to produce more than $1,500,000 during its lifetime—but not without logistical problems peculiar to the Southwest, as suggested by Samuel Cozzens, who visited it in 1860: "At the time of our visit,

Transportation, together with geography and recalcitrant Indians, dictated the course of mining in the "land of ineffable lights"; above, a boiler is hauled across the Galisteo River on the way to the mines of Cerrillos, New Mexico.

the company were engaged in putting in a steam-engine which had been hauled by mules from Port Lavaca, in Texas, a distance of fourteen hundred miles. A boiler weighing nearly six thousand pounds has also been brought in the same way, to the great terror of the Apaches, who not only kept a respectable distance from it, but could not be induced to approach it, believing it to be a huge cannon, brought into the country to accomplish their immediate and entire destruction at one discharge."

The Heintzeleman and Patagonia mines were limited affairs, both in their longevity and in their productivity. Neither inspired anything close to what might be called a rush; indeed, both were very private concerns, operated on an industrial basis — or as much so as the circumstances would permit — and both were rediscoveries of mines that had been worked on and off for years. They were outside the experience of American mining in the West—but part of a tradition common in the Southwest.

More in line with what we have come to expect in the narrative of western mining were the various placer and lode excitements that struck the region in and about the confluence of the Gila and Colorado rivers in the 1850s and 1860s. Gold had been found on the Gila River as early as 1849 by would-be miners on their way to California, but the "certainty" of masses of gold to be found in the Sierra Nevada was too strong

a call for them to resist; they tucked the gold into cans and pockets, and moved on to the new Golconda. In 1858, disappointed but stubborn refugees from the California mining camps stumbled upon this Gila gold and a quick rush developed, only to dribble out in a few years as the comparatively rich, but very shallow placers were worked out. Writing in 1864, J. Ross Browne recounted the course of the Gila excitement, and one reads it with a kind of relief that things could be normal even in Arizona: "Gold was found in the adjacent hills a few years ago, and a grand furor for the 'placers of the Gila' raged through the Territory. At one time over a thousand hardy adventurers were prospecting the gulches and canons in this vicinity. The earth was turned inside out. Rumors of extraordinary discoveries flew on the wings of the wind in every direction. Enterprising men hurried to the spot with barrels of whiskey and billiard tables; Jews came with ready-made clothing and fancy wares; traders crowded in with wagon-loads of pork and beans; and gamblers came with cards and monte-tables. There was everything in Gila City within a few months but a church and a jail, which were accounted barbarisms by the mass of the population.

"When the city was built, bar-rooms and billiard-saloons opened, monte-tables established, and all the accommodations necessary for civilized society placed upon a firm basis, the gold placers gave out. . . . Gila

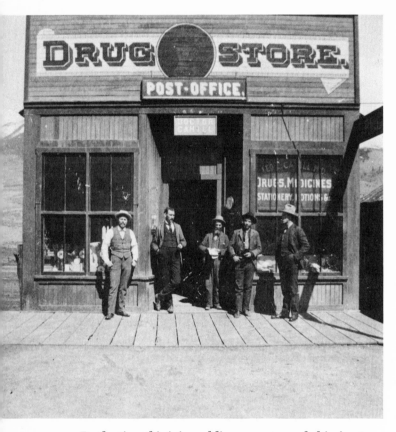

By the time this informal lineup was recorded in front of L. L. Cahill's Drug Store in 1899, Elizabethtown, New Mexico, was foundering in borrasca.

City collapsed. In about the space of a week it existed only in the memory of disappointed speculators. At the time of our visit the promising Metropolis of Arizona consisted of three chimneys and a coyote."

Disappointment on the Gila spewed hundreds of miners out into the surrounding country during the early 1860s, where they followed rumors that had taken on the weight of documented fact; and sometimes there *was* evidence, as Browne reported: "I saw masses of pure gold as large as the palm of my hand brought in by some of these adventurers, who stated that certain Indians had assured them they knew of places in the mountains where the surface of the ground was covered with the same kind of 'heavy yellow stones.' Neither threats nor presents, nor offers of unlimited reward could induce the wily savages to guide the white men to these fabulous regions of wealth. 'Why should we?' said they, 'You are already taking our country from us

fast enough; we will soon have no place of safety left. If we show you where these yellow stones are, you will come there in thousands and drive us away and kill us'."

Indian reluctance or no (and they had their reasons), good placer and even lode deposits were discovered during the 1860s at La Paz, Ehrenberg, Rich Hill, Lynx Creek, Hassayampa, Prescott, and most notably, Wickenburg, where the Vulture Mine became Arizona's single most productive gold mine. But with the exception of an occasional rich lode like the Vulture, these were transient excitements, nothing to compare with developments from Virginia City, Nevada, to Virginia City, Montana. Throughout the 1860s and early 1870s, mining activity in Arizona was still in a retarded condition, at least according to the 1875 report of mining engineer Rossiter Raymond: "At present," he wrote, "only such gold and silver lodes as would elsewhere be considered surprisingly rich can be worked to advantage, and scores of lodes that would pay handsomely in California or Colorado are utterly neglected. . . ." Done in by Indians, geography, and geology, mining in Arizona was in a condition of suspended animation.

Utah, Arizona's neighbor to the north, was faring somewhat better. For one thing, the Indian threat was no particular problem; for another, the California and Colorado gold rushes had created a number of very wealthy men in Salt Lake City—men who had made their money outfitting and supplying goldseekers and who were now willing to invest hard cash in the development of the territory's mineral development; finally, Salt Lake City had a direct connection with the transcontinental railroad at Ogden by 1869, and immediately began sending out a small network of rail connections south and east of the city into newly-developing mining regions in the Bingham Canyon area and the Wasatch Mountains.

Placers had been discovered in Bingham Canyon in 1865 and by the early 1870s may have produced as much as a million dollars; but it was not gold that was being exploited—it was rich silver-lead deposits. Investment-hungry capitalists sent a stream of money south for the discovery and development of more mines, and for the building of mills and smelters, roads and rail lines; still others began erecting little smelting empires on the

*Discussing what may be a dismal
situation outside a hole in the ground
near Cerrillos, New Mexico.*

*Prospecting in the Indian-ridden deserts of the
Southwest was a matter requiring arms and numbers;
above, a group on Whiskey Creek, Arizona.*

outskirts of Salt Lake City itself. By 1871, Utah mining was in a genuine boom period—a rich man's boom, to be sure, but a boom nevertheless, as one silver-lead mine after another popped into existence, each holding forth the promise of wealth that would curl a gentile's ears.

The richest mine of them all, at least on the surface and in the beginning, was the Emma in Cottonwood Canyon, first discovered in 1868. Its owners lacked the money for development, so they conceived of a scheme whereby it was to be sold for fabulous prices in England (see Chapter 13). Unfortunately, the Emma broke through the rich surface ores in 1873, and what lay beneath them was little better than borrasca; her fortunes plummeted, and with them fell the bubble of Utah's abortive boom, for almost all her silver-lead mines proved to be equally shallow. Mining retrenched to a period of more careful development, and new silver discoveries in the southwestern corner of the territory after 1875, coupled with the continued production of a

few of the original mines, enabled the region to produce more than four million dollars a year in silver over the next several years. Besides, her smelting complexes in Salt Lake City were well established, and copper was still waiting to be discovered beneath the gold placers of Bingham Canyon...

While Arizona fumbled along and Utah boomed and retrenched, New Mexico lay in a nearly fallow condition for years. Little mining activity at all took place during the first ten years after American occupation, but in 1860 placer deposits were discovered at Pinos Altos, just north of what would later become Silver City, by a group of "Old Californians" trying out their heretofore dismal luck in the Great American Desert. In December of the year, some quartz deposits of promise were added to the placer mines, and it seemed as if Pinos Altos would enjoy a boom at least superficially

Mogollon, New Mexico, in about 1890—surely one of the least appealing mining towns in the impressive nineteenth-century galaxy of accidental municipalities devoted to greed, not logic.

comparable to that taking place in southern Idaho.

Unfortunately, there were the Apaches, forever with their eyes on promising new opportunities for loot and rapine. They assaulted the mushrooming little development so pitilessly that by the end of 1861 it had been deserted. When the outbreak of the Civil War necessitated withdrawing nearly all troops from New Mexico, the Apaches were left with an almost free hand, and for the next several years mining was confined to relatively small bursts of activity like that which characterized the Morenos district in 1867.

It was not until the middle and late 1870s that mining activity in New Mexico began a rebirth, as prospectors, comforted by the presence of soldiers and spurred on by the hope of railroads, began fanning out into the mountains of the territory, founding camps of varying degrees of success: Burro Mountain, Hachita, San Simon, Tierra Blanca, Ralston, Socorro, Mogollon, Tres Hermanas. . . . One of the richest of the new discoveries was in the southwestern pocket of the territory,

where Silver City soon became a bustling little metropolis in the tradition of mining camps—although not without a shadow, as recalled by James K. Hastings, a boy at the time: "The Mescalero Apache Indians, under Victorio and Geronimo, were raiding at that time, and kept us wondering when they would strike next. Many a rancher was picked off in that day. . . . All food beside range beef . . . had to come from the railroad [at Santa Fe]. While the mail coaches could go there and back in a day, sometimes under heavy guard . . . the 'bull trains,' as they were called, took plenty of time to make the round trip. They were owned and run by Mexicans . . . and these were easily frightened by an Indian scare." (Given the Apache's fondness for killing Mexicans, their fear seems only sensible.)

The railroad, of course, would solve everything; not only that, the country to which it was coming was a veritable mineral paradise, at least according to a railroad dodger of 1880: "The Atchison, Topeka & Santa Fe Railroad has struck the Rio Grande and is pushing down the rich valley flanked by mountains full of rich gold and silver ores. . . . The whistle of the conquering

Copper, the king of the Southwest: a 1900 overview of the Sacramento Pit of Bisbee, Arizona—then, as now, one of the largest open-pit copper mines in the world.

locomotive will soon be heard in the newly discovered mining camps of New Placer, Silver Buttes, Galisteo district, and the famous Cerillos, the mountains around Albuquerque, the rich leads in the mountains back of Socorro, the mines near Belen, and the mines near Fort Craig. . . . Westward lies Silver City, with its mills and mines; then comes Shakespeare, the crowning camp of New Mexico. . . ."

Shakespeare? It was none other than Ralston, founded as a mining camp in the early 1870s with the financial backing of William C. Ralston, whose name it was given. Failing as a miner's delight, the town counted on the railroad; but the railroad passed through Lordsburg to the north instead, and there was failure in a name.

It was not alone as it crumbled into memory; most of the towns created during the flush years of the latter 1870s suffered the fate of Georgetown, described by Fayette Jones in 1904: "The writer and his companion were much distressed by the awful stillness that pervaded the premises. In fact, absolutely nothing was doing, the streets were depopulated and grown up in

weeds. Long rows of buildings casting their ghostly shadows by the lingering sun, impressed us with a feeling of indescribable fear and horror. The once bustling, moving throng of sturdy prospectors and miners who had 'struck it rich,' the incessant clattering of the stamps in the silver mills, and the sharp crack of the mule driver's whip, all have been silenced. . . ."

There simply was not enough gold or silver in New Mexico to sustain a major industry. Modern estimates say that between 1828 and 1956, the state produced only $60,000,000 in gold, and between 1863 and 1956 only $65,000,000 in silver. Her real treasure? To date, New Mexico has produced nearly one billion dollars in copper and nearly three billion in petroleum. Dull perhaps, nothing of which myths are born, but solid, reliable, unromantic.

Arizona survived its moribund period, and in 1876 silver discoveries at Globe launched it into the heady region of boom. It got another boost in that direction in 1877 by further silver discoveries in the southeastern corner of the territory—the Southwest's first (and last) strike that came close to bonanza.

Early in 1877, Ed Schieffelin set out to prospect the Indian-ridden land in Arizona's southern pocket. "All you'll find is your tombstone," a fellow miner told him cynically. When Schieffelin found some ore that looked promising, he staked out a claim and promptly dubbed it Tombstone. He returned to civilization, raised some money to develop his claim further, then returned with his brother. Shortly after making camp, Schieffelin did some more prospecting in the area and came up with a rich find. "You're a lucky cuss," his brother remarked. Having a penchant for names, Schieffelin christened his mine the Lucky Cuss. By the time the matter of names had been settled, others had heard of the new discovery, and new mines were added, chiefly the Tough Nut, the Goodenough, the Contention, the East Side and the West Side. The town of Tombstone was laid out, and by the end of 1879 its population had exceeded one thousand.

It was a common enough mining town, as described in February, 1880 by George Whitwell Parsons in his staccato fashion: "One street of shanties some with canvas roofs. Hard crowd.... Model town. Shooting this A.M. and two fellows in afternoon attempted to go for one another with guns and six shooters—but friends interposed. No law other than miner's and that doesn't sit and deliberate but acts at once. Streets looked oddly enough tonight in Tombstone and reminded me somewhat of that of a frontier oil town. Mingled with the hardy miners tonight. Talk of killing indulged in again tonight. Everyone goes heeled. Jumping claims great cause of trouble...."

The next day, he felt a little more kindly toward the town: "Very lively camp. Fine broad street. Good restaurants. Good square meal four bits. Very reasonable indeed considering. Business good here and signs very encouraging indeed. Money here. Looked at Contention and Tough Nut in distance. Did no visiting.... Saw Scheffelin original discoverer of Tombstone today. Rough looking customer."

By the end of 1880, the population had risen to more than seven thousand, and Tombstone was well on its way to becoming the archetype of the western mining camp, the town whose real and imagined antics have provided fodder for the mills of pulp magazine fiction, novels, movies, and television shows for the past ninety years. The mines themselves were more prosaic. They lasted in full flush for about ten years, then began a steady decline, as did Tombstone, whose population dwindled to less than two thousand and never rose above it. Underground water, encountered at a depth of five hundred feet began to flood the mines by the latter half of the 1880s, as the miners sank ever deeper after the ore, and no economical way of pumping it out was ever found; by 1914, almost all the mines in the district had closed. In its lifetime, Tombstone produced an estimated eighty million dollars in silver; it was not much when compared to the Comstock, the Coeur d'Alene, or Leadville, but it was the closest thing to bonanza in gold or silver that the Southwest would ever know.

The region's true bonanza, of course, was copper. In New Mexico, the Santa Rita mines began producing copper after their silver deposits ran out, and a similar development occurred in Globe in 1882, when Arizona's first great silver strike suddenly became a copper strike. And in 1880 the discovery of rich copper deposits to the southeast of Tombstone led to the founding of Bisbee, one of the richest copper camps in the world—more than a match for the mines of Butte.

Surely there was more.... There *had* to be more. What of all the fine dreams of Coronado, of Oñate, of all the Spanish soldiers, priests, and citizens? What of those stories about Spaniards being buried alive with their gold by vengeful Apaches? What of the rich mines covered with brush and rocks, and never seen again? What of the Lost Spanish Diggings, the Lost Adams Diggings, the Lost Dutchman Mine... all the other lost wonders shrouded in the mists of time and collective memory?

The myths live still in the Southwest, not so many of them perhaps and not held by as many, but they are there. There is hardly a hamlet without its old-timer who will tell you almost before you ask that these hills or those hold a story and a hope, and as he tells you his eyes will sometimes wander to the hills... he once saw a map, a friend of his once knew a man, the old Spanish records say.... The brute reality of more than three centuries of gold and silver mining of modest proportions at best will never be enough in the land of the Southwest to kill myth, the child of need and geography.

TOO TOUGH TO DIE

In a manner reminiscent of Virginia City, Nevada, the mining town of Tombstone, Arizona, has made a good thing of its real and imagined past—and made it at the top of its municipal voice ("The Town Too Tough to Die," civic brochures proclaim aggressively). From the excellent museum in the old Cochise County Courthouse, seen dominating the scene below, to the yellowing Camillus Fly photographs on display in the Crystal Palace Saloon, the town is crawling with history—or what passes for history—most of it for sale, at one price or another.

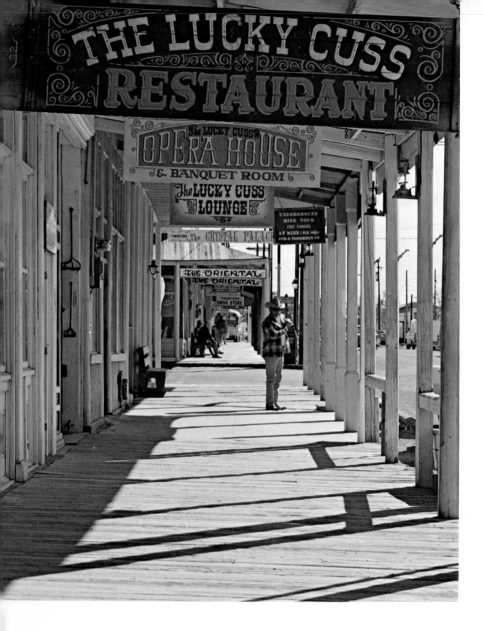

Allen Street, Tombstone's main thoroughfare, is a cornucopia of signboard delights, each of them calculated to so titillate the tourist that he spends his money with the wild abandon of a hairy prospector who has stumbled upon the strike of the century. The Oriental Cafe (sign number six in the series photographed in the scene at the left) has built its historical reputation around the rather dubious distinction of the fact that none other than Wyatt Earp once ran its gaming tables. The Tombstone Epitaph (below, left), founded in 1880, still functions, mixing gee-whiz history with local social news and advertisements. Schieffelin Hall (below, right) stands as the final monument to Tombstone's founder, Ed Schieffelin, and features a dioramic extravaganza narrated by Vincent Price, of all people.

BILLY CLANTON
Tom McLowery
Frank McLowery
MURDERED
on The streets
of
TOMBSTONE
1881

TOM McLOWERY
SHOT 1881

In the days of its somewhat tarnished glory, Tombstone was first and foremost a mining town—the Southwest's closest approach to a genuine bonanza in gold or silver. The adobe ruins of the Tombstone Mining and Milling Company, shown above, attest to that fact, as do the many relics of headframes scattered through the hills. Yet the town's role in the story of gold and silver has been almost smothered in cottony folklore having more to do with the mythos of the cowboy than with bullion. The reason is simple enough: Wyatt Earp and the O. K. Corral, two names that run through the town's remembered history like some kind of demented litany. On the afternoon of October 26, 1881, Wyatt, his two brothers, and John Henry ("Doc") Holliday faced off against the Clanton "gang"; thirty seconds and thirty shots later, three men were dead, finding their final ease in Boothill Cemetery (left). We are never going to be allowed to forget it.

CHAPTER EIGHT

SHOW US THE GOLD!
SHOW US THE GOLD!

Alaska and the last great American gold rush

"In round numbers I shall have $3,000, of which Louis and Stanley get $1,000 each. Deducting Father's one-third and expenses out of the country, I shall have less than I could have made at home playing marbles or shooting craps. . . ."

It was almost precisely fifty years between the first great American gold rush and the last; except for a brief and much less traumatic flourish in Nevada after the turn of the century (see Chapter 9), the rush to California in 1849 and that to Alaska in 1897–1898 effectively bracketed at beginning and end America's heated love affair with the treasures of gold and silver in the West. Appropriately enough, there were a number of similarities between the two—and at least one suggestive difference.

As in the California rush, the goldseekers who made their way to the wilds of Alaska needed money, quite a good deal of money, for supplies, outfits, and transportation. Journeying to Alaska at the end of the nineteenth century was no minor enterprise (nor is it today, for either land or sea travelers). Even for those fortunate enough to be located in the West Coast ports of San Francisco and Seattle, passenger fares on ships bound for Alaska were outrageous during the heat of the rush, sometimes going as high as one thousand dollars for a miserable little bunk aboard a former cod-

fisher; for those who came all the way from the East (and there were a remarkable number of them), the necessary stake could climb to several thousand dollars. Except for those who had been grubstaked by richer, less adventurous individuals, the Alaskan experience was no more a "poor man's gold rush" than the California hysteria had been; it was an investment, and poor people do not ordinarily engage in such speculations.

As in the California rush, the numbers involved were spectacular: at least one hundred thousand crowded onto ships bound for the Alaskan coast during the spring and summer of 1898, and if the proportionate impact on the country at large was less (there were twenty million people in the United States in 1849; seventy-five million in 1898), such figures were nonetheless impressive, far exceeding any other rush following Colorado's in 1859.

As in the California rush, those who made it to the goldfields of Alaska had survived wilderness travails that would have stricken exhaustion into the constitution of a marathon runner; while the journey itself was briefer, rarely taking more than two months, time was more than offset by the brutal hostility of the terrain, which surpassed anything in the frontier experience. Like the forty-niners, the "ninety-eighters" were thoroughly unenthusiastic about settling the country; the paramount idea was to strike it rich as soon as possible and get out. And finally, like the bulk of those who had

The Whitehorse, one of the most stately and beautiful of the steamers that plied the waters of the Yukon River at the turn of the century, sits today in the town of its name, crumbling with neglect.

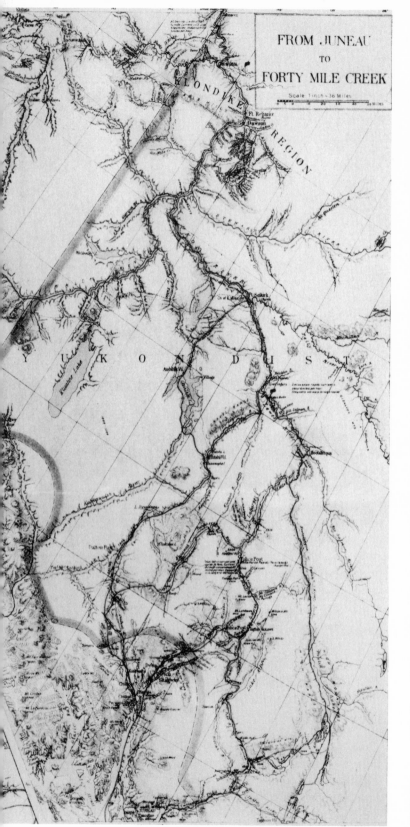

From Juneau in the south to the Klondike region in the north, the gold country of Alaska-Canada was a land of geographic excess.

made it to California, most of the Alaskan goldseekers found only disappointment waiting at the end of their travels, and for much the same reason: too many men for too little gold.

By the winter of 1898, more than eighty thousand had returned to the States; and for most of those who stubbornly refused to let fact interfere with dream, their few months in Alaska were a period of grubbing for survival and little else. Lucky ones made enough to get back home. A few made enough to pay expenses, as did Marshall Bond, who had gone to Alaska months before the great rush of 1898 and who still had not found the end of the rainbow by any means: "In round numbers I shall have $3,000, of which Louis and Stanley get $1,000 each. Deducting Father's one-third and expenses out of the country, I shall have less than I could have made at home playing marbles or shooting craps. The experience has been a bitter one, but instructive, and personally I can accept the result quite philosophically. . . ." This letter, with the figures suitably altered, could have been written by a California miner in 1852.

In one important respect the rush to Alaska in 1898 differed from that to California in 1849, and in that difference can be read much of the history of the previous fifty years. The difference was a matter of kind: of those who rushed to Alaska, a disproportionate number had not the slightest intention of digging after gold, nor would they; the only mining they would do would be in the pockets of the goldseekers. For by the end of the century, periodic exposure to the fever of gold had brought a certain sophistication to the residents of the Far West, and many had learned to their financial advantage that a gold rush was an eminently exploitable phenomenon, an entrepreneur's delight, a way for a man to make a small fortune in everything from canned goods to bartered flesh. As a result of this fiscal evolution, the Alaskan strikes touched off a speculator's rush that was fully a match for the frenzy of the traditional miner's rush.

Among the earliest and most numerous of those who clamored for space on steamers, clipper ships, fishing ships, and lumber schooners in the ports of the West

Juneau, Alaska, at the apogee of its glory, hunkering beneath the marbled slab of a mountain that has all the appearance of a glacier of solid rock.

Coast were lawyers (always lawyers), whiskey dealers, card sharks, pimps, strong-jawed harlots, hardware dealers, real estate speculators, reporters, politicians, photographers, sign painters, notaries public, confidence men, bartenders, barrel makers, carpenters, bankers, and merchants dealing in everything from neat's-foot oil to Dr. Miller's Peptonized Beef Tonic—all of them with not a piece of mining equipment to their names (with the exception of hardware dealers, of course, and these intended to sell the stuff, not use it).

So many of these purveyors of civilization had joined the initial rush to Alaska in 1897 that the hopeful who arrived in that previously untouched wilderness during the great rush in 1898 found them waiting for him, doubtless rubbing their hands in anticipation. By the end of August, 1897—hardly a month after the first news of Alaska gold had reached Seattle—Skagway, the principal gateway to the interior of Alaska, was a town of twelve thousand tents and a hundred wooden business establishments, and Dawson, 550 miles over the northern mountains from Skagway, could be described in September as follows: "The stores and warehouses of the two commercial companies, the saloons and dance halls, and the places of business occupied about two blocks along the river front. This was the center of business and social life of town." In a very real sense, then, the traditional patterns of mining rushes in the West can be said to have been reversed in the fifty years since Sam Brannan raced down the streets of San Francisco shouting "Gold! Gold on the American River!" In Alaska, the miners were preceded by civilization—they did not establish it.

Dawson City, Yukon Territory, where waiting for the mail was an occasion worth documenting and where trading in paper fortunes was a way of life.

William H. Seward, secretary of state during the administrations of Lincoln and Johnson, was an expansionist with vigorous convictions. Shortly after the Civil War, he became enamored of Alaska, then wallowing undeveloped in the control of Russia, and conceived the idea that the United States should purchase it. After three years of dignified haggling, the two countries agreed on a price—$7,200,000—and in 1867 the transaction was completed. Congress and much of the public press sent up an agonized howl, calling it "Seward's Folly" and "Seward's Icebox." Hadn't the country better uses for seven million dollars than buying 586,400 square miles of howling wilderness that even the Russians had written off as hopeless?

Nevertheless, the deed was done, and on October 9, 1867, the official transfer took place in Sitka, situated on Baranof Island in the Alexander Archipelago, some eight hundred miles north of Seattle. It would be difficult to imagine a less promising setting for the beginning of American enterprise. Populated mainly by a collection of Tlingit and Aleut Indians, Sitka was a ramshackle company town, most of whose buildings were owned by the Russian American Fur Company, and distinguished mainly by the Russian Orthodox Cathedral of St. Michael's (destroyed by fire in 1970).

As seen in 1865 by an Englishman, Frederick Whymper, Sitka presented "an original, foreign, and fossilized appearance. . . . Sitka enjoys the unenviable position of being just about the most rainy place in the world. Rain ceases only when there is a good prospect of snow. Warm sunny weather is invariably accompanied by the prevalence of fever and pulmonary complaints, and rheumatism is looked upon as an inevitable concomitant to a residence in the settlement. . . ."

Nevertheless, this was America's first annexation of frontier territory since the acquisition of California and all that went with it in 1848, and Sitka soon attracted a small flurry of emigrants from the West Coast of the United States, principally Seattle and San Francisco. Among these emigrants, inevitably, were gold-seekers. If there had been gold—not much gold, but gold—on the Fraser River and at Kootenai in British Columbia, why should there not be gold in Alaska? It was not all that far from British Columbia, and worth a chance; a man never knew . . .

"Among the civilians on the way to Sitka," a reporter for the *Alta California* wrote in the fall of 1867, "is a California forty-niner, who tells me that if he had invested the fifteen hundred dollars he brought down from the mines in the spring of 1850 . . . he should now be a millionaire. He is now bound for Sitka with an outfit of whiskey and tobacco, the proceeds of which he will invest in lands about that promising town. . . . He has an undoubting faith that in a dozen years Sitka will contain fifty thousand inhabitants."

Faith is a wonderful thing, but non-negotiable. Of the several hundred people who made their way to Sitka in the fall of 1867, less than fifty remained by the spring of 1868. These and about two hundred fifty soldiers stationed in the hamlet comprised practically the sum total of Alaska's non-Indian population—and in a few years Indian troubles in the States forced withdrawal of even the soldiers. Still, it was a beginning. When the weather allowed, and when it appeared that they might not encounter the occasional wrath of Indians, prospectors ventured across the Stephens Passage to the mainland and there began investigating the possibilities of rivers and creeks draining into much of the Panhandle's coast. By 1880, these stubborn individuals had penetrated much of the country from Fort Wrangell in the south to the Taku River in the north—a distance of nearly two hundred miles.

Few discoveries of any consequence were made, however, until August of 1880, when two canoe-borne prospectors, Richard T. Harris and Joseph Juneau, found traces of both placer and quartz gold on what later be-

John Treadwell's little industrial complex on Douglas Island, across the Gastineau Channel from Juneau; in the distance is the channel, and beyond that the ice-mantled slopes of Juneau's mountain.

Jack McQuesten's trading establishment in Circle City in about 1900; the thermometer, which gave him a niche in Alaskan folklore, is not visible.

came Gold Creek. They staked out claims and, by the spring of 1881, were joined by about one hundred others who had followed the news of the strike up from Sitka and Wrangell. A town was laid out, called Juneau, and the miners set to work in earnest, gradually spreading out into the surrounding country as one shallow placer after another was quickly exhausted.

In 1882, industry came to Juneau in the form of John Treadwell, a mining engineer who purchased a lode mine on Douglas Island across the Gastineau Channel from Juneau. The ore from this mine was very poor, but Treadwell was an experienced technician, for the time. He calculated that with enough machinery and up-to-date methods, the lode could be worked at a profit. He organized the Alaska Mill and Mining Company and acquired enough financing to spend more than $400,000 by 1885 on the construction of a 120-stamp mill, sophisticated mining equipment, furnaces, and offices—the whole complex illuminated by electric lights.

In spite of the fact that it took a full ton of raw ore

to produce a chunk of refined gold the size of a button, Treadwell's gamble on the mine paid off—abetted in no little part by the savings realized in the employment of uncommonly cheap labor, first Chinese and later local Indians. At the end of the century, the Alaska Mill and Mining Company's Douglas Island plant was still producing.

Success at Juneau, however limited, kept the dream of gold alive for Alaskan prospectors, and by the middle of the 1880s, individuals and small parties were scattered as far north as Circle City, on the Yukon River near its confluence with the Porcupine. That settlement became a minuscule hub for isolated mining activities on various of the Yukon's tributaries, including Fortymile River, Sixtymile River, and—over in the Yukon Territory of Canada—the Klondike River. By 1896, Circle City had a population of three thousand, a circulating library, an opera house constructed of logs, saloons, gambling houses, and churches—and

"Hootch" Albert, so named because of the vile whiskey he managed to distill from any sort of garbage available.*

Lest it be assumed that Circle City was therefore a pleasant place in which to live, mention should be made of what is probably the town's most famous institution: the "McQuesten Thermometer," a device reportedly invented by the leading trader in the region, Jack McQuesten. It consisted of four small bottles that he kept on a shelf outside his store. One contained mercury, one whiskey, one kerosene, and the fourth bottle, Perry Davis' Painkiller. When the mercury froze, it was inadvisable to stay on the trail overnight; when the whiskey froze, it was best not to leave town; when the kerosene froze, a man shouldn't leave the shelter of his cabin—but when the Painkiller solidified it was worth his life to step away from the fire.

Those Circle City residents not huddled over their fires were usually out in the hills, looking for gold. One such was George Washington Carmack, otherwise known as "Siwash George" because of his affection for the Indians of that name, one of whom he had married. In August 1896, Carmack and his two Indian brothers-in-law, Skookum Jim and Tagish Charlie, discovered rich placer deposits on Rabbit Creek, a tributary of the Klondike River. They immediately staked out four claims—one each for the Indians and two for Carmack —then went down the Yukon River to Fort Cudahy, where they recorded their claims, and from there to the settlement of Fortymile, where they announced their find. Carmack's reliability was questionable at best, and the news was greeted with a certain skepticism by old-time sourdoughs in the town.

Nevertheless, enough miners slipped out of town for Rabbit Creek—soon renamed Bonanza Creek—to stake claims throughout most of its length within two weeks. Circle City residents were even more cynical; it was not until corroborating reports came from respected miners in January 1897 that more than three hundred of them, amid a tremendous clatter of yapping sled dogs and hoarse bellows of "Mush on! Mush on!" set off across the winter mountains for Bonanza Creek. Most of them made it.

*The word "hootch" was a corruption of the name Tlingit Indians of Sitka gave to their native brew: *hoochinoo,* a primitive liquor distilled from molasses which those in a position to know maintained was profound enough to melt rivets. "Hooch," a term common to those Dark Ages called the Prohibition Era, doubtless derived from this Indian name.

During the remainder of the winter and into spring, hundreds of miners sluiced their way through diggings on Bonanza Creek and El Dorado Creek, many of them taking out thousands of dollars a week. Rumors of the discovery slowly drifted into Skagway throughout the winter, and from there to Seattle and San Francisco. They were not given credence at first, the West Coast being altogether familiar with such rumors by now, but by early spring letters began to come in from the mines, and newspapers started publishing them.

Excitement began to mount as the time for the first summer return of Alaskan steamers approached, and when the *Portland* finally docked in Seattle on July 17, her passengers were greeted by the sight of hundreds of spectators crowding the docks and shouting "Show us the gold! Show us the gold!" Obligingly, many passengers held up fat sacks of the stuff and indicated that there was more where that came from. They weren't exaggerating; estimates place the amount of nearly pure gold on board the *Portland* at about two tons—worth more than one million dollars.

The news, instantly flashed across the country by telegraph, spread with a contagion unmatched since the California excitement of 1849. It had been a long time since the nation had taken hold of one subject with such tenacity—not since the Civil War, in fact. It was almost as if the virulence of interest was a kind of gesture toward the vanished frontier. By 1898 the West, to all intents and purposes, had been won, and even if there were enough isolated pockets to undermine Frederick Jackson Turner's contention that the frontier itself had actually "closed," there was no denying the fact that a great adventure had come to an end, an adventure that for nearly a century had given the country a grand excuse for exercising national muscle, for celebrating its existence. Now that was done, and the country turned in upon itself, expanding its manufactures, building its cities, and forging the outlines of an industrial society, with all the problems and frustrations inherent in such a civilization.

And into this progressive, respectable, but somehow unexciting period was thrust news that promised one last adventure, one more chance to try muscle and luck against the wild uncertainties of the American West— and the country responded. Newspapers screamed

"Show us the gold!" they cried. Having seen it, they scrambled in a great fleshy mass for berths aboard anything that would (hopefully) float them to the ragged, inhospitable edges of wilderness Alaska.

headline announcements; magazines immediately dispatched roving correspondents to the West Coast; and young men from Albany, New York, to Harrisburg, Mississippi, gathered in parlors and pool halls and taverns, and excitedly exchanged speculations on whether or not they should band together, pool their resources, obtain a loan from someone, and somehow get to the gold fields of Alaska . . . well, why not? Who knew when such a chance might come their way again? And so they gathered, first by the hundreds, then the

thousands, for the crazy plunge across five thousand miles of land and sea for a country most of them had barely heard of before the summer of 1897.

But that would be the great rush of 1898. Most of those who went to Alaska in 1897 were from areas close enough to West Coast ports to obtain passage before summer ended and weather made travel impossible. Even there, the demand for passage was already cruelly competitive. For the return trip to Alaska from Seattle, the *Portland* instantly increased its fares from $200 to

$1,000—and was getting its price. Ticket scalpers by the dozens bought tickets at $1,000 and resold them for $1,500, even $2,000. Still, hundreds begged passage for Alaska. Ships up and down the coast—lumber schooners, codfishers, freighters, tankers, pleasure yachts, practically anything that would float—sailed into San Francisco, Seattle, and Tacoma, and were pressed into service as passenger vessels for the Alaska run. By the end of summer, tens of thousands had sailed—many of them to claim city lots in Skagway and the fast-booming little town of Dawson, implanted at the site of the great discovery, others to slap together saloons, gambling dens, bordellos, law offices, dentists' offices, and grocery stores in anticipation of the great rush that surely would follow the initial scramble. Many of them actually took to mining.

While the early arrivals spent the winter of 1897–98 consolidating their frontage and laying in supplies, establishments with an interest in seeing to it that this last great gold rush actually got under way made it

Climbing the profound slope of Chilkoot Pass was itself a major feat; hauling the 1,150 pounds of food required by the North West Mounted Police was a task beyond imagination, as suggested by this view of the summit in 1898.

their business to feed the flames of excitement that had been ignited in the summer. Railroads issued trashy little guidebooks that just incidentally mentioned their lines as the cheapest and swiftest routes across the continent. The chambers of commerce in San Francisco, Seattle, and Tacoma advertised their cities and the superior supplies and transportation available in them with glittering adjectives. Shipping lines fabricated promises of luxurious accommodations at deflated prices.

And the newspaper press of the country, celebrating its climactic flush of yellow journalism, leaped on every report of prospects in Alaska and bloated it beyond reason; for example, when the *Excelsior* came into San Francisco from Alaska with half a million dollars in gold on board—a pretty respectable sum—newspapers

promptly inflated the figure to *two* and one-half million. Seattle must be accorded the win in the gold rush trade sweepstakes; its vigorous advertising campaign resulted in business that exceeded twenty-five million dollars; all the other ports of the West Coast could only share five million dollars of the trade among them.

The summer of 1898 was the time of the *cheechakos,* which was what old-time Alaskan prospectors dubbed the thousands of greenhorns who stumbled into Alaska. One hundred thousand of them left West Coast ports for Dawson, and perhaps forty thousand persevered all the way to the town. Among them was Basil Austin, a young adventurer from Detroit who arrived in Seattle in February 1898, well ahead of the general rush. Seat-

151

tle, he noted in his reminiscences published in 1968, "was booming, the streets thronged with would-be miners, the majority dressed in mackinaws embellished by wide belts heavily draped with sixshooters and other hardware. All the hotels, restaurants, theatres and saloons were crowded with men. Aside from the regular steamers, every vessel that would float had been pressed into the Alaskan service."

After securing bunks on board the *Lizzie,* a New Bedford fishing schooner converted to the passenger trade, Austin and his companions saw to the matter of provisions: "Deciding to take at least one year's supply, the amount of each commodity as well as the whole was a complicated problem to work out. We had such questions to solve as: If a man eats a loaf of bread in a day and a half, how many beans are required to last three men one year? Most answers were X. However, the wholesale grocery where we traded had a lot of valuable data which helped us.... The store had everything, even dried potatoes, soup, vegetables, and eggs. The term used for this withered variety of vegetables was, I believe, 'desiccated' which suggested the complete drying up of all moisture, flavor and nutriment. ... Our provisions consisted of flour; beans ... ; rice, oatmeal, corn meal, bacon, salt pork and dried beef, lard, butter in cans and condensed milk. We had heard of the scurvy disease, caused by the lack of fresh vegetables and fruits in the prospectors' diet, so we took a goodly supply of dried fruits, which included apples, pears, peaches, apricots, not forgetting the necessary boarding-house prune.... Then we had to take a sheet iron stove, sleds, and tools for boat building as well as nails, oakum, pitch, and a whipsaw for cutting lumber. A medicine and first aid kit was among other innumerable items. By this time we had accumulated material the bulk of which we were to realize later when called upon to transport it by our own effort."

On February 14, the *Lizzie* set sail for Alaska, carrying about eighty passengers crammed into makeshift bunks in a hold redolent of her years of carrying thoroughly dead codfish: "I congratulated Nels on his forethought, which had provided berths for us so close to the forward hatch, for the air below was getting terrible. No imagination was needed to sense the vapor rising and trailing in our wake from the two hatches, similar to the visible smoke from the twin funnels of a steamer. Not a single ventilator with gaping mouth pushed fresh air below deck, and what little there was wormed its way through the Cook's galley forward absorbing the breath of soup kettles and dish water."

As if the stench were not enough to guarantee an uncomfortable voyage, the *Lizzie* consistently encountered heavy seas, beginning with the first night out: "This first night aboard was not particularly quiet and restful as the noise overhead increased with the wind velocity. At five-thirty a terrific crash on deck aroused us from fitful slumbers.... The crash we had heard resulted from the abrupt removal from the deck of one of the two small but necessary deck structures that had been built on either side. Perhaps Lizzie ... had resented their architectural fitness which did not combine with her more graceful flowing lines. In any event one savage swipe of her boom revenged the insult, leaving only a few shattered cleats hanging by bent nails to mark the site. She had by this bold stroke reduced the toilet capacity of about eighty men a clean fifty per cent."

After twenty-one days of backing and filling, complicated tacking, and fighting off gales, the *Lizzie* finally arrived in Alaska.* For most of the other *cheechakos* who took haphazard passage to Alaska, the voyage held similar travails, and this was just the beginning. Landing at either Dyea or Skagway, they faced a 550-mile trek over either White Pass or Chilkoot Pass, then down the waterway system to Dawson. Neither route had much to recommend it; White Pass was not quite so steep as Chilkoot, but in the summer its trail down to the rivers was a miserable, foot-sucking miasma of mud, a death-trap for men as well as animals. Chilkoot Pass was the living definition of a "narrow defile." Incredibly steep and almost always thick with snow, no matter what the season, it was a lung-stretching, back-breaking climb to the summit and a dangerous, sliding descent down the other side. In both passes, members of the vaunted North West Mounted Police stood ready to collect customs duties and enforce stringent regulations that required each man to carry with him no less than 1,150 pounds of food. Given the nature of the wilderness they were challenging, it was not an un-

---

*Austin and his companions landed at Valdez, north of Skagway, and made their painful way overland from there to the mining camps on the Fortymile River, avoiding Dawson altogether. It was perhaps a wise decision; unlike many others, Austin and his friends eventually managed to make back expenses.

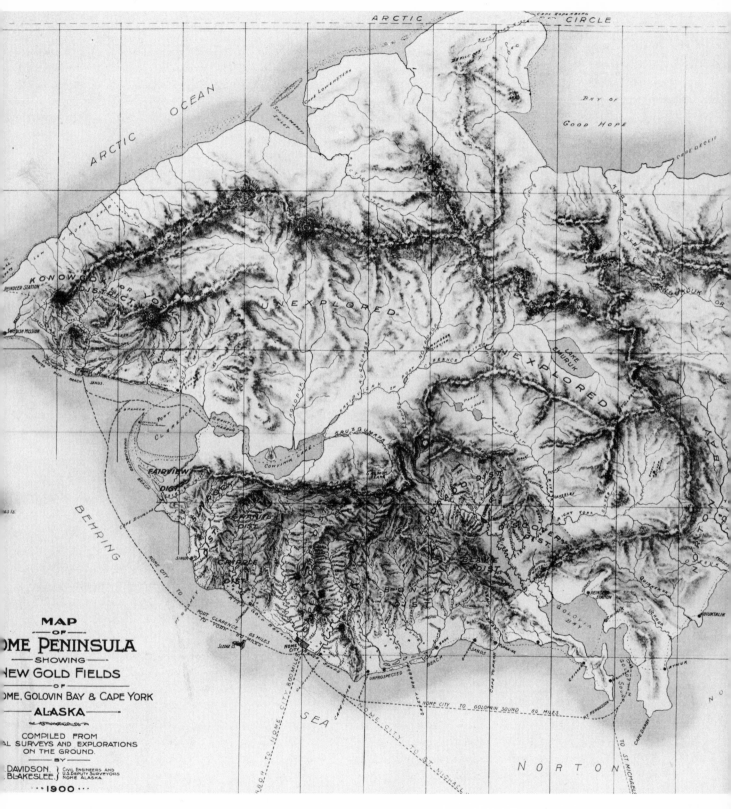

Unexplored—the Seward Peninsula in 1900, Nome at its southwestern tip.

Following the receding dream all the way to the dismal beach of Nome, a lighterful of erstwhile entrepreneurs (and one rocking chair) prepare to disembark and see what they can see.

reasonable stipulation.

Once they made it through the passes, the next requirement was to sit down at the heads of lakes Linde-man and Bennett and put together some kind of float-able craft to take them over the lakes, then down the Lewes River and the Yukon to Dawson. "Every proper Klondike outfit contained the tools, nails, and caulking necessary to construct a boat," historian William Bronson has written, "but few of the adventurers had ever built one. The results were imaginative; sometimes humorous, sometimes tragic. In 1897 more than 200 lives were lost in the rapids down stream." Some hint of the brutal demands involved in the downriver journey is given by the journal of Marshall Bond, who negotiated

the Yukon in September, 1897: "For the *cheechako*, or newcomer, unfamiliar with the country and its conditions, there were many severe and trying tests for his courage all along the inland water route. . . . On September 30 we passed the mouth of White River. It was pouring a vast quantity of ice into the Yukon. The luxury of gliding along the current came to an end by reason of the ice. It was an interminable job getting ashore to camp in the swift and congested current and even more dangerous getting back into the stream again in the morning. Fallen trees, their roots still holding to the bank, stretched out over the river in many places which with the swiftly flowing ice threatened to fill and crush our boats. Clearing these obstacles from

There may have been a less likely environment for the pursuit of dreams, but Nome, on the frigid edge of the Bering Sea, must surely have been the most miserable exercise in canvas towns in the history of the West.

our course was terrifying and sometimes dangerous work and occupied a week before we reached Dawson."

Nearly forty thousand remarkably hardy and incredibly lucky *cheechakos* made it across the mountains and down the tangled rivers to Dawson that spring and summer of 1898. It hardly needs saying that they found nothing but gamblers, whores, and merchants waiting for them. The gold placers of the region, wonderfully rich, had long ago been taken up by those who had been there during the original discovery and by a few who had struggled into the area in 1897. By the time winter began settling in, more than twenty

thousand who had set out with such high hopes had returned to Skagway, and from there home. Of those who remained, another five thousand fled with the coming of spring, having experienced probably the meanest winter in their lives.

Perhaps ten thousand were left in Dawson and its environs by summer of 1899—and many of these went clattering west clear across the territory when word of the newest gold strike reached them: Nome, where it was said a man could make his pile by standing knee-deep in the chill surf and washing the very sands of the beach.

It was true enough, at least for a time. Nome, a freezing, wind-whipped, miserable hamlet placed in violation of all logic on the bitter southwest coast of the Seward Peninsula, had entered the annals of western mining in the summer of 1898, when placer gold deposits of uncommon richness were discovered on tributaries of the Snake River by refugees from the disappointment of Dawson. In those latitudes, winter is an eight-month affair, and before more than two thousand dollars could be washed out of the gulches and creeks of the Snake River, the Bering Sea commenced to freeze.

By then, however, the news had inspired a spurt—one could hardly call it a rush—of miners to the district, and in all violation of tradition, these early arrivals proceeded to make claims in the name of relatives and friends, until some forty individuals had effective control of something like seven thousand acres of potentially rich mineral ground. The action was legal enough, but its morality was another question altogether; it went against the grain of all tradition in mining law as expressed on several frontiers, from California to the Black Hills.

Nonetheless, it was done, and it would have effectively blunted Nome's development had it not been for a remarkable discovery in July of 1899: the sand of Nome's beaches was crawling with gold. It was a prospector's dream come true. The simplest of equipment and effort was all that was required; nature supplied the rest. With a shovel and a rudimentary rocker, a man—or woman—was nicely set up. The "ore" was at his feet, the water needed to wash it a few feet behind him, provided by the Bering Sea.

The combination was irresistible; by the end of the summer, the bleak outpost of Nome had a population of more than seven thousand, and anywhere from a thousand to twenty-five hundred people were scattered up and down the beaches of Nome, energetically washing for gold. It truly was a "poor man's proposition," the last major free placer region in the history of the mining frontier. And, characteristically, it was precisely as brief as it was energetic. By the time the town's population had increased to eighteen thousand in the summer of 1900, much of the influx inspired by the magic sands of her beaches, those beaches had been thoroughly picked over.

Under ordinary circumstances, Nome would have withered in a matter of weeks. Fortunately for her future, men with capital had been spending the last few

months consolidating claims on tributaries of the Snake River. Capital was a necessary ingredient, for unlike the delightfully loose sands of Nome's beaches, the gold in the region outside the town was embedded in the steely grip of the tundra that passed for soil on the Seward Peninsula. Only hydraulic mining of industrial proportions could hope to free it; to this end the region's large mines constructed monstrous ditches to bring water to their claims from the Snake River and its tributaries, set up great sluice systems, and directed powerful jets of water at the reluctant tundra.

It worked; Nome flourished for the next several years, at least in comparison to most of the towns that had been born of the hysteria of 1897 and 1898. In 1905, the town got its first railroad, the Nome and Arctic. It ran fifty miles into the interior, where frustrated Nome goldseekers had established productive mines on the Inmachuck, Niukluk, and Kougarok rivers and their tributaries.

Nome was Alaska's last major mining camp. Others were established on the Seward Peninsula and even deep in the interior along the course of the Yukon River—among them Tanana and Rampart—but the flush days of the rush to Alaska had ended with the establishment of Dawson, and then Nome. For a few, the excitement had been a wonderfully profitable enterprise; in time, the rush to the Dawson region alone may have produced as much as three hundred million dollars. For most, the rush was a financial disaster; tens of thousands returned to the States in 1899 and 1900 in a condition approaching destitution. Yet few of them ever regretted with a full heart the urge that had driven them into that appalling wilderness. It had been a great adventure after all, perhaps the last great national adventure in the history of the United States, and most would remember their participation in it with the warm nostalgia of a Basil Austin, who colored his reminiscence of the Alaskan gold rush with fondness: "There was always pleasure, satisfaction and often excitement in overcoming difficulties, weathering storms, building boats, navigating rivers or crossing divides—and in finding gold. After all the ensuing years I can look back to the adventure with pleasure, getting much satisfaction in the remembrance of those majestic white mountains, the wastes of snow, flaming auroras, roaring rapids and the he-men with hearts as good as the gold they found, or missed. . . ."

The detritus of a vanished civilization rusts aw
in the Talkeetna Mountains, Alas

It would be difficult to conceive of a land more hostile to all the lambent dreams of goldseekers than the tundra and aging mountains of Alaska and northwestern Canada. Not since the time of the California Gold Rush had men entered a wilderness they knew so little of; at the time of the rush to the Yukon, maps of this country featured great blanks marked "unknown territory" or "unexplored region." Most of the blanks did not survive the perambulations of the goldseekers, who pushed into all the nooks and crannies of the land with a persistence matched only by their blind optimism—and left behind the marks of their passing. Above left: the Salty Dawg Saloon in Homer, Alaska, on the tip of the Kenai Peninsula; below, an abandoned cabin near Whitehorse, Yukon Territory, Canada; at right, the "world's tallest log cabin" in Whitehorse.

CHAPTER NINE

DEEP ENOUGH

An ending near its beginnings

"As a result of the earlier ... excitement, prospectors had swarmed over southern Nevada like field mice. Hardly more than wanderers, most of them knew nothing of mineral formation, but now groups of men in eastern cities stood ready to grubstake any man on the scene willing to undertake the search for gold...."

Like any other trade, the profession of mining developed its own jargon over the years, a kind of workingman's shorthand in which much could be said in a few words. One such example out of the miner's lexicon of communication was a phrase that traditionally greeted the end of the day's work: "Well, she's deep enough for today." The phrase was as universal as the miner's affection for rats, whose quick scuttling from the dark crevices of a mine was often warning of an impending cave-in. It could be mumbled in dumb exhaustion by a mucker shoveling in the last of his sixteen tons of rock, or in excitement by a blaster marking his missed shots for the benefit of the next shift and celebrating the nice piece of high grade he had tucked out of sight in his lunch pail. Whatever nuances were applied to it, the meaning of the phrase was clear: it spoke of an ending.

In the deserts of the Great Basin, almost beneath the shadow of the Sierra Nevada where it had all begun, the mining frontier reached the point of "deep enough" with the Nevada booms that punctuated the first ten years of the twentieth century. Compared to the explosion of reckless amateurs into Alaska in 1897 and 1898, the impact of these later strikes appears pallid; yet they were convulsions of respectable significance in their own right; what is more, they were the last. With the not very notable exception of occasional flurries of interest that cropped out from year to year (one centering in the Mojave Desert of Southern California in the 1930s), after 1910 the dream of gold and silver, as the West had known it, entered a decline from which it has never been revived.

Nevada was an appropriate enough stage for such an ending. Mining on a limited scale had started here almost simultaneously with the California Gold Rush, and it was on the slopes of Mount Davidson that the West had experienced its first true bonanza in the ores of the Comstock Lode. Indeed, for more than sixty years mining was not only the principal industry in the region, it was practically the *only* industry, thoroughly overshadowing agriculture and husbandry until well into the twentieth century. No other state in the West was so utterly dependent for so long a time on the fragile, shifting base of a mining economy.

It was mining that brought and held the bulk of Nevada's population; it was mining that built cities; it was mining that inspired railroads; it was mining that made it a state and mining that dictated the course of its politics; and it was mining that placed the state in a

onopah, Nevada, today — a relic of times and places that were.

GOLD AND SILVER IN THE WEST

position its residents were inclined to view as being analogous to that of the American Colonies before the Revolution: a politically impotent borough forced to stand by helplessly while its resources were sucked out and sent off to enrich the destiny of the mother country—in this case, California.*

Nevertheless, while it lasted, mining produced a busy history in Nevada. It populated—for a time, at least—some of the most astonishingly unpleasant pockets of desert wilderness in the Great Basin and produced at least $600,000,000 in bullion (including the

*The degree of Nevada's reliance upon mining as its industrial staple is suggested by what happened to its population after 1910, when the dust of the last boom had settled. Between 1900 and 1910, the state's population almost doubled, from 42,335 to 81,875; but by 1920, it had dropped to 77,407, and over the next twenty years Nevada's rate of increase was far behind that of the country at large, until by 1940 it had added only a little over thirty thousand to the total for 1920.

$300,000,000 removed from the Comstock). From its beginning to its end, it was characterized by two features which contributed much to its liveliness, if little to the economic health of the state: first, a corporate structure that was nourished by outside capital to such an extent that the slightest dip or rise in ore production could cause anxiety or unfettered glee among speculators scattered from San Francisco to New York and even London; second, a degree of transience that was remarkable even on a mining frontier; the exploitive nature of the industry, reflected all over the West, was exaggerated in an environment that offered so little else as an inducement to settle. Whole towns, thrown together in a matter of days, frequently disappeared just as quickly—down to the last piece of lumber in town. "Nowhere in the mining West," historian Rodman Paul has written, "were ghost towns more truly ghostlike than in the Great Basin."

The swift rise of the Virginia City mines in the early 1860s, together with their equally swift consolidation into the hands of a few, sent hundreds of disappointed miners out into the desert to scour the earth in hopes of finding something to match the glory of the Comstock. In 1862 two such prospectors wandered into the region of the Reese River Valley near the center of Nevada. There, on the western slopes of the Toiyabe Range, they encountered ore which looked to them similar to that on the Comstock Lode; and after staking

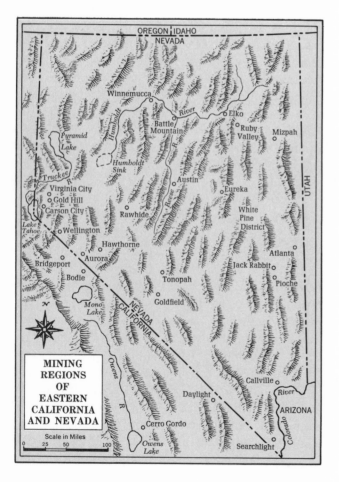

MINING
REGIONS
OF
EASTERN
CALIFORNIA
AND NEVADA

Scale in Miles
0   25   50   100

Ghost: a view of downtown Bodie in the 1920s, stripped of dreams.

out claims, they hauled samples of it back to Virginia City for assaying. Some of it was valued as high as seven hundred dollars a ton, and in 1863 and 1864 enough refugees from the Comstock clambered into the narrow valley for the town of Austin to emerge, with a population approaching six thousand.

The necessary capital for development of the region moved in almost as fast as the population, consolidating mines and putting things on a properly industrial basis, and from 1864 until the mines were finally worked out in the middle of the 1890s, the ups and downs of ore production in the Reese River mines—which eventually reached nearly forty million dollars—jiggled stock figures on the San Francisco Mining Exchange more than four hundred miles away.

An even more telling illustration of the role played by both California and eastern capital in the development of Nevada's early strikes was that of the Bodie region, north of Mono Lake on the eastern side of the Sierra Nevada.* Hardly had the discovery of quartz gold been made in the summer of 1860 before two Californians, James Stark (otherwise an actor) and John W. Tucker (otherwise a jeweler), began buying up claims from the original owners. By the end of 1862, they had been joined by F. K. Bechtel (otherwise a judge), and the three soon owned most of the major gold-producing claims in the young district.

*Although Bodie was legally within the boundaries of California, geographically and emotionally it more properly belonged to Nevada, and so there I have put it.

More capital was needed for full development, however, and early in 1863 the group went to Leland Stanford (otherwise Governor of California), who emerged in March as president of the Bodie Bluff Consolidated Mining Company, which was capitalized at 11,100 shares with a face value of $1,110,000. A further amalgamation took place the following year, when a number of mines and claims that had not been picked up by Stark, Tucker, and Bechtel in 1863, were absorbed, along with the Bodie Buff Consolidated, into the Empire Company of New York, capitalized at $10,000,000.

This was heady stuff for a primitive little mining camp. Unfortunately the district's production did not pay sufficiently for the company to declare a dividend for several years, even though it spent several hundred thousand dollars in exploration and in the construction of ambitious mills in nearby Aurora, described by J. Ross Browne in 1865: "Nothing finer in point of symmetrical proportions, beauty, and finish of the machinery, and capacity for reducing ores by crushing and amalgamation, exists on the eastern slopes of the Sierras."

Nevertheless, it was not until 1877 that the Bodie mines began to pay in quantities sufficient to justify the investments. In that year, the Standard Mine struck a rich vein, and in 1878, the Bodie Mine startled the San Francisco market by uncovering a vein that was assayed at $3,000 a ton (and some particularly high grade went up to $4,000). Activity suddenly blossomed. "There is so much going in mining circles that it is almost impossible to keep pace with developments being made every day," one observer reported in June.

Over the next three years the boom continued, bringing in many investments from San Francisco and New York—all of them doomed to failure, for only the Bodie and Standard mines struck significant amounts of ore approaching bonanza quality, and by 1882, having suddenly produced nearly fourteen million dollars, production began tapering off sharply in even these mines. By the end of year, fifteen mines had been stricken from the San Francisco Exchange. While both the Standard and the Bodie continued to operate well past the turn of the century, the boom days of Bodie were over; the total production during the life of the district has been estimated at $21,000,000, more than half of it supplied by a single mine, the Standard.

Bodie survived nearly twenty years of vicissitudes before it came into its own, an uncommon display of perseverance for a Nevada mining camp. Another such exception was Eureka, in the Diamond Mountains some sixty miles east of Austin. Silver in combination with lead had been discovered here as early as 1864, but the ore was in a form outside the limited experience of the first miners; and after a brief period when the rich and more easily worked deposits gave the district a gentle period of boom, the camp declined, waiting for technology to rescue it.

This came in the form of W. S. Keyes, an experienced engineer and metallurgist, who was hired in 1870 by the Eureka Consolidated Mining Company (a San Francisco corporation, it need hardly be said) to erect smelters capable of handling the recalcitrant ore. He was so successful that by the end of the decade Eureka had become a bustling little industrial metropolis, whose two busy smelters enriched the air with black smoke, sulphur fumes, and the acrid stench of arsenic; in spite of man-made pollution and nature's own desert environment, the town had a population of about six thousand in the middle of the 1880s, together with two daily newspapers, four churches, brick stores and warehouses, a courthouse, its own rail connection with the Central Pacific, and a water shortage.

Facilitated by increasingly sophisticated methods of smelting, Eureka's mines regularly produced more than two million dollars annually through 1882, achieving their best output in 1878, when they processed tonnage valued at $5,316,000. By the middle of the 1880s, flooding in the mines had become a serious problem, and by 1890 an insoluble one; in 1891, both smelters closed, and the town finally dwindled.

The Reese River district, Bodie, and Eureka were the Great Basin's three most successful mining regions outside the Comstock during the nineteenth century. Buttressed by an influx of capital and the technological expertise that sometimes accompanied it, they earned a rightfully important niche in the story of western mining. But they were only three of dozens of camps that were thrust willy-nilly into the mountains and onto the sagebrush flats of Nevada in the forty years after the Comstock. A few of these attained footnote status — among them Pioche, Belmont, Candelaria, Aurora, and Cherry Creek—but most were as ephemeral as Star City in Humboldt County, described by Rossiter W. Raymond in 1868 as once having been "a flourishing town, with two hotels, post office and daily United States mail, a Wells-Fargo express office, a telegraph office . . . and a population of more than 1,000 souls. So sudden has been its decline that the daily mail, the express office, and the telegraph office are all in operation yet, though the entire population consists of a single family, the head of which is mayor, constable, postmaster, express agent, telegraph operator, and, I believe, sole and unanimous voter!" Grubstakes provided by West Coast and eastern speculators gambling one long shot after another on the discovery of a second Comstock—or even a second Bodie—enabled hundreds of prospectors to smell out the land, and with every glimmer of possibility a camp would develop, as much the product of wish-fulfillment as it was of the discovery of gold or silver.

It would be difficult to discover a more poignant example of this process than the camp of Treasure Hill, whose brief, if frenetic, career stands as a kind of summation of forty years of mining in the deserts of Nevada. Silver deposits of minor importance had been discovered and worked since 1865 in the White Pine district south of Eureka, but it was not until the end of 1867, when a local Indian directed miners to the 8,700-foot level of what later became Treasure Hill, that anything of real promise was discovered—and then it passed credibility. What they found very near the surface of the mountain were silver deposits in a

| Hamilton. | | Virginia | United States. | | Treasure City. | | Eberhardt | | Sherman Town. | Lith Brittons Rey |

VIEW OF TREASURE HILL
WHITE PINE, NEV.
Sketched by E.W. PEET.
H. H. BANCROFT & CO. PUBLISHERS
609, Montgomery S! San Francisco.
~ 1869.~

Treasure Hill in the White Pine district of Nevada; the misty, almost Japanese quality
of this 1869 woodcut suggests the superb transience of the "new Silver Land."

startlingly rich, soft form called horn silver, easy to dig and even easier to process. Assays made early in 1868 made headlines in San Francisco: although the average yield per ton was about $130, some samples went as high as $5,000, and one, breaking all known records, was valued at $27,000!

Miners on the Comstock, still wallowing in the depression of its first borrasca, cleared out for Treasure Hill, convinced that history was repeating itself. They were joined by thousands of others from all over Nevada and parts of California, until by the spring of 1868 there may have been as many as ten thousand crowded into the three tiny tent-and-shack hamlets that sprang up within weeks after the discovery. Albert S. Evans, editor of the San Franciso *Alta California,* was among them, and he was moved to describe a visit to the interior of one of the richest claims, the Eberhardt Mine: "The walls were of silver, the roof over our

heads was silver, the very dust which filled our lungs and covered our boots and clothing with a gray coating was fine silver. . . . How much may be back of it Heaven only knows. Astounded, bewildered, and confounded, we picked up a handful of the precious metal and returned to the light of day."

Such gee-whiz reports fed inflamed imaginations, and by the end of 1868 more than twenty-five hundred claims had been filed (by the end of 1869, thirteen thousand would be recorded), and the big-money men in San Francisco, New York, and London were preparing to send their agents to the mines in the spring of the following year.

On February 13, 1869, a note of warning came from an experienced mining engineer, who reported to the *Mining and Scientific Press:* "It is my opinion, after a careful examination of the country, that there is not enough ore in sight, or even in prospect, to keep the

Tonopah cluttering the desert in 1904; the group down in the distant center of the street may be digging another mine, gold being where you find it.

present population in bread and whiskey for the next two years, to say nothing of the thousands who are preparing to come next spring." No one was listening, preferring the more lambent prose of the *Alta California* just five days later: "What a field is here opened for the investigation of the adventurous American people! The gold deposits of California added so many millions to the wealth of the world as to unfix values. . . . What California did with her gold, this new Silver Land is apparently about to do with its silver. . . ."

By the spring of 1869 the district's population had risen to 12,000, and 75 to 100 people were arriving every day. With them came money. A cluster of mills were built, and in April, 170 White Pine mines had been incorporated in California with a face value of $246,-884,000. Production in the mines rose to $1,500,000 by the end of the year, and Hamilton City, the principal town in the district, began planning for such

amenities as schools and churches and street lighting.

And then it was over, or nearly so. By the end of summer it was obvious even to the hopeless optimists on the San Francisco Exchange that the negative report in the *Mining and Scientific Press* had been all too correct: there was just too little ore to support the boom that had developed. Expensive mills lay unused, and weekly and monthly shipments from the mines fell far short of expectations. The hysteria in San Francisco withered to boredom.

The mines continued to produce for another several years, reaching a peak in 1870 of two million dollars, then tailing off to almost nothing by the end of 1875, although an English syndicate managed to keep the Eberhardt Mine going for a number of years after that. Treasure Hill soon fell into a condition approaching disrepair, and today there is little to mark its existence but crumbling stone walls and chimneys cluttering the

Undaunted, as prospectors have a way of being, Butler returned to Cactus Peak and scouted around for even more samples, which he took back to Belmont—this time to a friend of his, Tasker L. Oddie, an equally luckless prospector. Neither of them had enough money for a professional assay, but Oddie knew Walter Gayhart, a young science teacher in Austin who did assaying on the side. Oddie, by now an equal partner with Butler in whatever might come of the project, sent the samples by stagecoach up to Gayhart, offering him half of his half-interest in exchange for a free assay. Gayhart agreed, and when the results came in, Butler and Oddie learned that they were in possession of ore whose best sample had a value of 540 ounces of silver per ton, together with several ounces of gold.

They took in a fourth partner, Wilse Brougher, and among them they came up with twenty-five dollars to finance a more ambitious expedition to the site of the discovery, where they quietly staked claims and began digging along a vein they called the Mizpah. They sacked up two tons of ore, hauled it back to Belmont, shipped it to Austin, from there on the Nevada Central Railroad to the Central Pacific line, and finally east to a mill in Salt Lake City.

By the end of 1900, they had received a check from

By 1904, Tonopah had achieved the final mark of industry necessary to any mining town: a railroad.

landscape of the "new Silver Land."

The last twenty-five years of nineteenth-century mining in Nevada were dominated by such fiascos as Treasure Hill, although none ever generated quite the same degree of excitement. Most of them were like detonations in the night, forgotten by morning. And by the 1890s, there were fewer and fewer of even these, until Nevada lay in a kind of backwash of history. Between 1890 and 1900, the state's population dropped from 47,355 to 42,335—the only state in the nation to suffer a loss in that decade. And so it might have continued, had not an itinerant prospector by the name of James Butler spotted a piece of float beneath Cactus Peak one day in 1900. He gathered a few samples and took them into nearby Belmont for an assay; the assayer considered them nearly worthless.

Dominating the startling clarity of this street scene of Goldfield is the presence of garbage in the street, regarded with studied indifference by passersby, who had more important things to talk about—such as money.

the mill for five hundred dollars, and the secret of their discovery was out. Miners from the long-defunct Belmont district swarmed to the site, founding the town of Tonopah. With few exceptions, they discovered that the four partners had effectively tied up most of the vein. The partners were more than willing, however, to allow leases to be taken on their property—in exchange for the standard 25 percent royalty on any ore produced. By the middle of January, 1901, there were 130 such leases being worked, and for the next ten months, Butler, Oddie, Gayhart, and Brougher had little to do but collect fat royalties from claims that had cost them the grand sum of twenty-five dollars to locate and hold.

In October, Oscar A. Turner, a Grass Valley mining promoter with connections in Philadelphia, arrived in Tonopah and offered the partners $336,000 for their claims. They considered the amount of money needed to properly develop the mines themselves and decided to accept the offer; the sale was consummated at the end of the month, but not before the partners insisted that Turner honor the leases they had issued in Janu-

ary, not due to expire until December 31. To the great relief of the lessees, who were frantically digging as much ore out of the ground as possible, Turner reluctantly agreed, possibly whimpering quietly as all that rich ore disappeared into wagons bound for Belmont, and from there to the railroad at Austin.

At midnight on December 31, the miners—250 of them by now—shot off their guns in celebration and promptly went on a classic binge that lasted well into the next day. Drunken exposure to the hostility of a Nevada winter resulted in a major epidemic of pneumonia, and by January 13, seventeen of them had died — not including Butler, Oddie and Brougher, who lived long enough to become Tonopah institutions.

In January, 1902, the Tonopah Mining Company was incorporated in Montana with a capitalization of one million shares at one dollar the share. By August, the town of Tonopah had a population of three thousand and was beginning to shrug off its air of impermanence; a year later that population had more than doubled, and the town had taken on whatever solidity could be provided in the middle of a desert, as described by Mrs. Hugh Brown in her reminiscence, *Lady in Boomtown*: "Our house was well up on the side of a mountain, and directly opposite was another mountain. Between them, in the canyon and climbing both sides, lay the little rough-board town. Snuggled in among the shacks and dwarfing them were mine shafts with hoists and ore dumps. West of town the desert stretched for miles to the horizon. . . ."

By the end of 1904, Tonopah was a thoroughly industrialized community, dominated by the workings of the Tonopah Mining Company, which held a virtual monopoly on the mines in the district—and with no little profit: in 1904, production was $1,592,285; by the end of 1905, it had jumped to $4,449,487, and it would increase steadily until its peak year of 1918, when $9,311,560 was hauled out of the Tonopah hills.

Even before Tonopah had a chance to settle down and become such a productive little mining town, however, a second strike sent the region into a flutter of activity. "As a result of the earlier Tonopah excitement," Mrs. Brown remembered, "prospectors had swarmed over southern Nevada like field mice. Hardly more than wanderers, most of them knew nothing of mineral formations, but now groups of men in eastern cities stood ready to grubstake any man on the scene willing to undertake the search for gold." Two of these wanderers were Harry Stimler and William Marsh (although they had been grubstaked by Tonopah entrepreneurs—including Jim Butler and George Wingfield, half-owner of an establishment called the Tonopah Club—not eastern capital).

In December, 1902, they discovered promising float gold in the Columbia Mountains about twenty-five miles south of Tonopah, and this attracted a tiny spurt of miners into the area during the spring and summer of 1903. Enough gold of moderate richness was there to keep them working, but it was not until the autumn of the year that the spurt was converted into a genuine rush, when ore paying as high as $150 to the ton was uncovered very near the surface.

Hundreds from Tonopah and other parts of southern Nevada picked up and hauled themselves to the Columbia Mountains, where a quick town developed, called Goldfield — the usual affair of tents and ambitious shacks. The hills themselves were crawling with shallow

The subject of most of Goldfield's talk: George Wingfield's Combination Mine, headworks at the left, dump at the right.

The Florence Mine, in the foreground of this view, and the Jumbo, across the gulch—two competitors of the Combination.

claims and workings, as described by Mrs. Brown: "They really were not mines, hardly more than shallow holes, but already fortunes had been scooped off the surface, loaded into canvas bags, and started off to the smelters in California or Colorado. . . . We saw Mr. Vermilliar, a lawyer from Tonopah, standing guard with a shotgun in a little excavation no bigger than a bathroom, where, with his own hands, he had scooped out $100,000. For weeks, day and night, he stayed there guarding the unprotected mint with an armchair down in the hole, where he could catch forty winks when he thought it was safe. . . ." As in the Tonopah experience, many of the early discoverers simply leased out their claims to those with the wherewithal to begin ambitious development.

One notable exception was Charles Taylor, whose three contiguous claims were considered among the richest in the region. Within weeks after staking out the claims, he had turned around and sold them to Lucien L. Patrick, a promoter with financial backing in Chicago, for $75,000—$5,000 down and the rest in later payments. Patrick combined the three into one

mine, called the Combination, and it soon proved to be one of the three or four most productive in the Goldfield district.

Goldfield boomed impressively throughout 1904 and 1905, until its population topped fifteen thousand. Its mines were still a collection of largely independent enterprises, with nothing approaching the dominance exercised by the Tonopah Mining Company in the northern town. Many of its mines exceeded the richness of those in the Tonopah district, however, including the Combination, the Red Top, the Sandstorm, the Jumbo, the Florence, and the Mohawk, and it was only a matter of time before someone with entrepreneurial instincts considered the utility of consolidation.* That someone was George Wingfield, the Tonopah clubman whose grubstake had helped to finance the discovery of Goldfield's mines. Early on, he had purchased full

*An indication of the richness of these mines is given by the fact that the Mohawk shipped out what is considered the most profitable carload of ore ever recorded: 47½ tons valued at $574,953.39.

A street scene in Rawhide, 1908; beneath the pyramid of people is a stagecoach. Today there is nothing—literally nothing—to mark the existence of one of Nevada's last boomtowns.

control of the Sandstorm from its original claimants, and by 1906 its profits enabled him and his partner, George Nixon, a former bank clerk in Winnemucca, to begin their move. In that year they purchased the Red Top and the Jumbo for one million dollars, gained a controlling interest in the Mohawk, and by November had parlayed their way into control of all of the mines in the district save two, the Florence and the Combination.

Wingfield was particularly interested in buying the Combination, still the potentially richest mine of them all, but Lucien Patrick was not interested — perhaps unwilling to contribute to what was rapidly approaching the outlines of an absolute monopoly. However, Charles A. Botsford, formerly editor of *Century Magazine,* came west on a visit, became close to Patrick, and learned that he was in fact interested in selling—at the right price, which was four million dollars, and to the right person, who just might be Botsford, if he could come up with the $75,000 option money. Botsford couldn't, but he had a friend by the name of J. R. Davis who could; Davis laid down the money and picked up the option—which was then signed over to Wingfield and Nixon, enabling them to purchase the mine in spite of Patrick's reluctance.

Wingfield then incorporated the Goldfield Consolidated Mines Company in Arizona with five million shares of stock at ten dollars per share. In exchange for having relinquished the option, Davis received 100,000 shares of this stock, and for his effective manipulative efforts, editor Botsford received a fee of $75,000. George Nixon became president of the company, a position that would later enable him to maneuver his way into the United States Senate; and Wingfield became its vice-president, which, together with the 250,000 shares of stock he allotted himself in payment for completing the consolidation, made him the richest man in Nevada, and with good reason. In their time, the properties of the Goldfield Consolidated Mining Company produced an estimated eighty million dollars.

This was industry of respectable dimensions; nor was it free of troubles common to enterprises of such scale. Wingfield had hardly consummated his efforts at consolidation before union miners struck the district and maintained a running battle with the company for nearly two years (see Chapter 11)—possibly the most

telling evidence of all that Goldfield, the last frontier camp of significance in the history of the mining West, had been plunged almost instantly into the smarmy industrial agonies of the twentieth century.

As in the Comstock experience, the success of Tonopah and Goldfield inspired a vigorous rash of discoveries and quick booms throughout southern Nevada over the next several years—in Rawhide, Hawthorne, Fairview, Midas, Tuscarora, Rhyolite (Bullfrog), and dozens more. But these were short-lived and relatively inconsequential discoveries when compared to the excitements of Tonopah and Goldfield, much less those of earlier days.* They were almost reflexive booms—the last twitches of life in a dream that had survived more than three hundred years on the North American continent, but had finally come to its ending in the deserts of Nevada.

The dream was born in myth, and while it flourished, it caught and held the imagination of its time and storied our history with the muscular legends of a romance unmatched in American life. After Tonopah and Goldfield, there was little left of it but legend. It was terminated by solid paper realities—consolidation, stock options, dividends, wage disputes and labor battles, efficiency studies, technological evolution, and all the other paraphernalia common to twentieth-century corporate enterprise. Seized in the grip of industry, the dream was no longer a dream but a steadily diminishing set of statistics, with all the romantic connotations of bottle-cap production.

Gold and silver mining continues to the present day, but on so diminutive a scale that it hardly bares comparison to the era of the California Gold Rush, of the Comstock Lode, of Leadville, Cripple Creek, the Black Hills, Alaska, or any one of the other great adventures the dream had generated. It is but the dimmest reflection of a dream that once called men across mountains for a chance at treasure, that inspired them to risk all that they had and were for the one great strike that would startle history and place them on a podium with all the other moneyed gods of an exploitive civilization.

---

*Significantly, the single most important discovery that followed the Tonopah-Goldfield era was at Ely—which soon became the most productive *copper* camp in Nevada's history.

PART TWO:

DREAM AND CIVILIZATION

Nature's first green is gold,
Her hardest hue to hold.
Her early leaf's a flower;
But only so an hour.
Then leaf subsides to leaf.
So Eden sank to grief,
So dawn goes down to day.
Nothing gold can stay.

—ROBERT FROST

In the summer of 1970, after completing some of the picture research for this book in Denver, I took an excursion into the Colorado Rockies to have a look at a few of the local remnants of the mining frontier. One of these was Cripple Creek, which sat in its high mountain basin thoroughly cowed by the darkening threat of a summer storm. It began to rain heavily shortly after my arrival, but the little town still crawled with tourists. A goodly number of them, myself included, went up into the hills for a tour of the Molly Kathleen Mine.

At the full mercy of wind and rain—although protected somewhat by the shabby but surprisingly warm denim jackets provided by the company—we huddled beneath the gray headframe, waiting our turn at the tiny cage which would lower us into the mine. We chatted nervously about the weather, our origins, our trades and professions—anything but face the rather sobering truth: we were about to attach ourselves to the end of an alarmingly thin cable and be lowered,

at the rate of ten feet a second, seven hundred feet beneath the surface of the earth. Finally, the cage rose to the surface, and our guide jammed five of us into a space perhaps three feet to a side; there were embarrassed giggles from the ladies as the guide himself wormed into the cage, pushing us even closer together. He closed the wire gate to the cage, reached up and pulled the bell string that signaled the hoist operator to let us go, and before our eyes had a chance to blink against the light, we had slipped into the earth and absolute darkness.

The cage rattled and bumped against the side of the shaft, but there was no other sound but our breathing; it was a ghostly experience, totally unlike that in a city elevator, which at least gives you a thin, complaining whine to demonstrate its function. For all we knew, the cable had snapped, leaving us in a free fall to the bottom of the mine. Twice we passed open drifts, and sudden images slid past our eyes, subliminal visions of tunnels, equipment, and people impressed on the mind like dioramas that faded almost as quickly as they appeared. Finally, the cage came to a stop in a series of slow jerks that landed us at the seven hundred foot level. I was not the only one who sighed in relief as we stepped out of the cage.

To enter the depths of a hard-rock mine is to discover a kind of empathy for the lives of ants and other burrowing creatures. Like most of the other mines in the Cripple Creek district, the Molly Kathleen was blasted out of rock so solid it needed little or no timbering, and

the earth itself hung over our heads in narrow, twisting tunnels lit by dim electric bulbs. Our guide began a nasal, singsong recitation as he led us through the maze, explaining and demonstrating the meaning of drifts, stopes, and winzes; of veins, ore chutes and fire holes; of waste rock and high grade; of jumbo drills and diamond drills; and at my prodding releasing bits and pieces of his life along the way. He was a wizened, tough little wisp of a man who had worked in the Molly Kathleen for forty years, first as a lowly mucker, and finally as a shift foreman. Then in 1967, the distant powers that controlled the destiny of the mine shut it down. He mumbled something about production costs and the price of gold, but it was obvious he knew little and cared less about such things; he knew only that from a hard-rock miner he had become a shepherd for giggling tourists.

After nearly forty-five minutes, the guide led us into one last tunnel that ended in a chamber perhaps twenty feet square. He raised his little pick and scraped it along one wall of the stope, tracing the line of something we could not see. "This here's the vein they were working out when they closed the mine down. It assayed at about four dollars a pound." He shook his head at the mysteries of higher finance, or whatever it was that had dictated the closing of a mine with such a rich lead to follow, and hacked away at the wall with quick, expert blows from his pick, knocking off a piece about the size of a large grapefruit. We gathered around him as he held it beneath the light of the miner's lamp and

pointed one leathery finger at the deep streaks in it that shone with a dull glimmer. "Them's iron pyrites—fool's gold—mostly," he said, "but there's plenty of gold in there, too. I figure this is worth maybe five bucks." He handed the chunk to me. "Here, keep it. They ain't going to be needing it now, I guess."

That piece of ore sits on my desk as I write this narrative. In its glittering striations can be read much of the history of the mining frontier, from dream to civilization. Men once would have died, and some did, for the sight of such ore, but there is a great deal more than romance to be found in it. To discover rich ore was one thing; to get it out of the earth, reduce it, refine it, and dump it on the markets of the world was quite another. It was a process as complicated as the mechanics of high diplomacy and involved a bewildering variety of technological, social, political, and economic elements whose influence on the shaping of the character of the West has never been fully determined, and probably never will be. Nor did it lack its own elements of color. If the saga of the dream-seekers was one of glittering legends, fabulous strikes, and great nation-shaking rushes, this second narrative was colored with the drama of technological growth, of high finance, of labor strife that approached warfare, and of struggles between men whose only law was the law of power—for after the dream-seekers came the empire-builders, and it was they who leashed the dream and gave it the muscle and direction to change the history of the West, for better or for worse.

CHAPTER TEN

THE GEOLOGY AND TECHNOLOGY OF TREASURE

The essence of gold and silver, distilled and incandescent

"They make openings in various places and go deep into the earth to search for silver and gold. . . . By means of pits which they sink they penetrate for several furlongs not only horizontally but in depth; and, extending their subterranean galleries in different directions . . . from the bowels of the earth they raise the ore which yields their gain. . . ."

The dream was born in stars. Twenty billion years ago, give or take a few billion years, a group of stars constructed the elements of gold and silver within the furnaces of their interiors in a nuclear process which passes comprehension. These stars were part of the great detonation which resulted in the formation of our galaxy, in which a spiral of fiery stardust revolved, contracted, and finally cooled to become the earth. Gold and silver, born in the bowels of stars, were trapped in the gelid interior of the earth.

Then, near the end of what we call the Cretaceous period (perhaps ninety-four million years ago), the interior of the earth began to bubble and flex in a spasm of mountain-building and vulcanism. The great layers of sediment which had been laid down during a period of more than a hundred million years were twisted and wrinkled; enormous batholiths of granite, gneiss, diorite, and monzonite fractured and faulted and jammed up through the surface; volcanoes mush-

roomed to grumble and spurt. Perhaps the most dramatic result of all this upheaval was the formation of the Cordilleran West, and it was here that much of North America's gold and silver was introduced to the surface of the earth.

Responding to internal pressures, hot liquids (magmas), which carried the precious metals in suspension, flowed upward toward the earth's crust, depositing their rich loads in the cracks and fissures of shattered rocks. Such deposits are called veins. Sometimes the deposits were not content to simply sit jammed between walls of rock; if they were in a properly active solution, they set about the business of actually replacing the molecular structure of their host rocks. Such phenomena were called "replacement deposits" and were especially common in limestone, which is unusually susceptible to chemical action.

Whether in veins or in replacement deposits, gold and silver are nearly always found in conjunction with a base material, or gangue, which holds them in place— most often a quartz or porphyry material. Unlike gold, an inert element that stubbornly clings to its own identity under almost all situations (although it occasionally weds with tellurium), silver is highly active and easily succumbs to combination with a number of other materials—including acids and sulphides of baser metals, such as galena, pyrite, or zinc blend.

A great deal of the gold that figured in the history of the mining West was in placer form — loose and

Technology and litter: a gold dredge chews its way across a flood plain, excreting windrows of tailings behind it as it goes.

easily mined. Through eons, veins in such areas as the Sierra Nevada were exposed by time and weather, and began to decompose, dribbling chunks of ore down hillsides and canyon walls. (When still in the form of ore, such pieces were called "float.") The farther it was carried, the more completely the gold was separated from its gangue by abrasion, and ultimately raw gold was transported by streams until its weight brought it to a dead stop on sandbars, gravel banks, or potholes in streambeds. Being inert and durable, the gold simply waited for discovery. Silver, on the other hand, was more inclined to form soluble compounds when exposed and be carried off by erosion without forming placer accumulations.*

Significant gold placers were scattered over a wide spectrum of the Cordilleran West — principally in Alaska, the Boise Basin, southwestern Montana, and the Black Hills—but none matched the sheer bulk of those deposited in the western slopes of the Sierra Nevada. The region of quartz vein deposits extends some 350 miles north from a narrow fringe in the southern end of the range to a belt sixty miles wide in Plumas County. The original depth of these veins has been estimated at nearly seven miles, and by the time man arrived on the scene, almost five miles of that original depth had been eroded away and its free gold spread with prodigal generosity throughout the hills, canyons, gullies, gulches, riverbanks, creekbeds, sandbars, and washes of the Sierra Nevada foothills.

The sheer preponderance of it would seem to justify one early geological theory of the forty-niners, who considered the lay of the land, the configurations of the mountains, the direction of the wind, and their astrological charts—and concluded that the gold had trickled down from the exposed top of a single cosmic pyramid of gold, pure gold, weighing billions and billions of tons, extending God only knew how high, low, wide, and long beneath the thin hide of the mountains. It was a lovely theory, and they called their mountain of gold the Mother Lode: it was as good a place as any to begin fifty years of technological experimentation, innovation, and adjustment, as men attempted to transmute the fulminations of stars into dreams.

*One of the compounds so formed was silver chloride, which often exhibited itself in a dark sand—as in the "damned blue stuff" that plagued the miners of Gold Hill, Nevada, in 1859 (see Chapter 4).

The antiquity of gold-placering startles the imagination. The legend of Jason and the golden fleece—like many legends—had a basis in rather prosaic fact: on the banks of the river Colchis, Jason and his argonauts extracted gold by washing the gravel through sheepskins, whose fleece trapped the gold. Their methods were only a little less primitive than those first brought to the Sierra Nevada by the goldseekers of 1848 and 1849. "No capital is required to obtain this gold," an 1849 guide-book author wrote, "as the laboring man wants nothing but his pick and shovel and tin pan, with which to dig and wash the gravel." This was true—at least for some and at least for a time. The labor involved in such one-man operations was considerable, but the system could hardly have been more simple; and as long as the gravel or sand was justifiably rich in gold, it was a paying proposition. Squatting by the side of a stream, the miner would deposit his sand or gravel in the bottom of a shallow pan about the size and configuration of a large frying pan (some in fact *were* frying pans), then add a quantity of water.

Beginning a slow, steady swirling motion, he would gradually wash out portions of gravel-and-sand-laden water, until only the heaviest material—hopefully including gold—was left in a thin residue, or "drag," in the bottom of the pan. A good average for a hard-working former bank clerk was perhaps fifty such panfuls a day—no mean achievement. An even simpler process was "crevicing," which required little more than a durable pocketknife and a willingness to clamber around canyons looking for chunks of gold lodged in the cracks and crannies of rock.

Almost from the beginning, Yankee impatience dictated operations on a larger scale. For one thing, the more bulk a man could handle in a day, the better his chances were of washing out hundreds, rather than tens of dollars. One of the first innovations was the rocker, or cradle—an ambitious extension of the pan method. The rocker, about the size and shape of a baby's cradle, was fitted with a screen at its upper end to filter off the larger pieces of gravel, a bottom that featured riffles, or cleats, behind which the gold presumably would lodge as it was washed through, and rockers. One man would keep it rocking as another poured in shovelfuls of dirt and water.

Quickly this system evolved into an even more extensive one which involved the sluice. In its most

(Continued on page 185)

EVOLUTION AND REVOLUTION

*In less than a generation, the techniques of mining in the West experienced an evolution
from utter simplicity to a complexity of astonishing dimensions. Placer mining as a
free man's art in 1849 is documented by the illustration above from Frank Marryat's
Mountains and Molehills; hacking, chopping, digging, and washing, these ungifted
amateurs—former law clerks, gentleman farmers, delivery boys, butchers, and
blacksmiths—infested the foothills of the Sierra Nevada like ants, each of them
determined to fill his own pocket, with no more sophisticated equipment than pan,
pick, shovel, sweat, and optimism.*

*On the following two pages, one of the most famous lithographs of the nineteenth century
illustrates the other end of the technological spectrum, as industrial mining clawed
into the recesses of the Comstock Lode in the latter 1870s; here, money—typified by the
mill complexes that annotate the top and bottom of the drawing—and technique—
typified by the rendering of the Deidesheimer "square-set" timbering—had
transformed art into industry.*

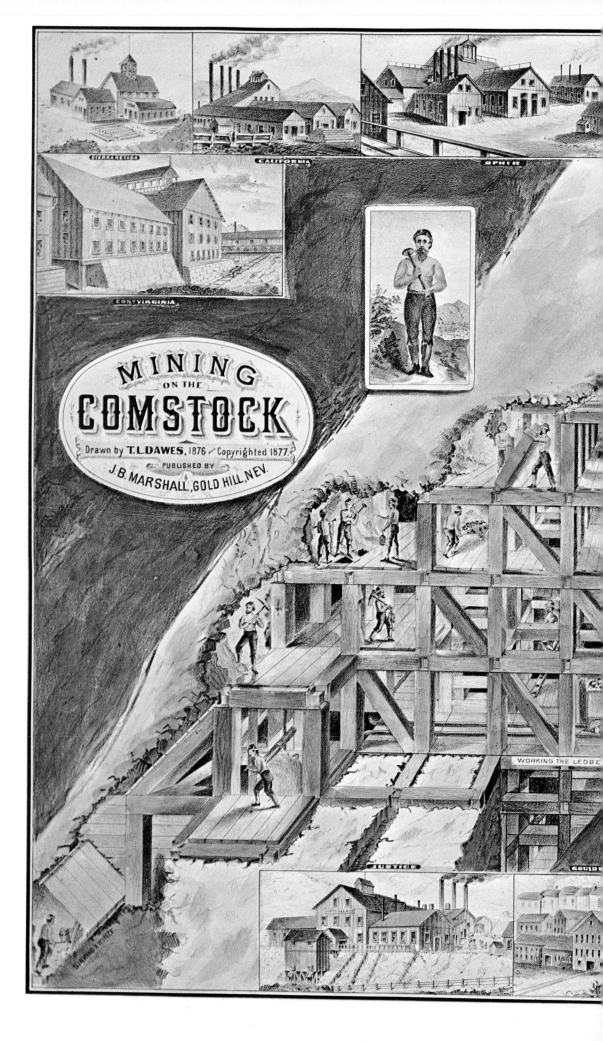

SIERRA NEVADA · CALIFORNIA · OPHIR

CON VIRGINIA

MINING
ON THE
COMSTOCK
Drawn by T.L.DAWES, 1876 and Copyrighted 1877.
PUBLISHED BY
J.B. MARSHALL, GOLD HILL, NEV.

WORKING THE LEDGE

JUSTICE · GOULD

A CALEDONIA & OVERMAN

IMPERIAL EMPIRE

CROWN POINT

BELCHER

TOOLS USED IN THE MINES

TIMBERTRUCK. CAR WATER BARREL.

MEN COOLING OFF.

STATION.

YELLOW JACKET

INCLINE SHAFT

179

In the century since the Comstock Lode began to take on the outlines of industry, the techniques of deep mining have changed remarkably little. They have been refined to a fare-thee-well, however, by the application of machinery and even computerized technology that in many cases has replaced, or at least abetted, the labor of men. Still, the basics remain the same: the ore must be found, blasted out of the earth, hoisted to the surface, milled, refined, and poured into bars, as illustrated by the operations of Homestake's Bulldog Mountain Silver Mine in Creede, Colorado and the Homestake Mine in Lead, South Dakota— the largest still-functioning gold mine in the United States.

Above, left: Miners in a man cage prepare to descend to the Homestake's depths, which have reached a level of 6,800 feet.

Left: In a drift or stope, the drift boss checks out the course of the vein and marks the fire holes for drilling.

Below, left: Light-years removed from the days of "single-jacking" and "double-jacking," drilling is a skilled profession.

In stopes where the vein has widened to cavern-like dimensions, drilling requires the use of "stope jumbos," which look like nothing more than great praying mantises (opposite page, bottom right). Once blasting has lifted the ore out into the floor of the stope, it is loaded up by automatic muckers (above, left) and transported to ore chutes. The rock is then loaded into eight-ton ore cars via automatic chutes (above, right) and hauled by electric-powered tandem trolley locomotives to the shaft station (right), where it is lifted to the surface by massive ore hoists, controlled by a technician dwarfed by all the machinery and surrounded by lights, levers, gauges, and push-buttons (below, right).

At the surface, the ore is introduced into huge crushers (above, left and right) equipped with specialized chain-link feeders that regulate the flow of rock. The crushers reduce the ore to one-half inch size. Then it goes to the rod and ball mill (right) whose mammoth tumblers pound it, beat it, and grind it with water until it is finer than flour.

In the recovery process finely ground ore (pulp) is piped into large vats (left) where it is treated with a very dilute solution of sodium or calcium cyanide, which dissolves the gold.
The gold is recovered from this solution by adding powdered zinc. The resulting precipitate, comprised of zinc and gold, is mixed with suitable fluxes and smelted (below, left). Zinc and other impurities are poured off as slag, leaving only a crude bullion of gold and silver. The gold is "parted" from the silver by further smelting and the injection of chlorine gas, then poured into graphite molds (below, right).

After the bars are cooled, they are weighed, most coming to about 500 troy ounces (or thirty-five pounds). An indication of the tremendously sophisticated and painstaking milling and refining processes required to make a gold mine a paying proposition today is given by the fact that to produce the stack of gold bars shown below (worth about $230,000), approximately 36,000,000 pounds of ore had to be blasted, hoisted, milled, and refined—or about three tons of ore processed for every ounce of gold realized.

primitive form, this was no more than a long ditch, whose bottom was "cleated" with rocks, holes, and gravel rifflebars; more often, however, the sluice was in the form of a "Long Tom," a carpentered affair twenty feet long and about a foot-and-a-half deep. These were built with a taper at one end so that a number of them could be fitted together to increase the chances of trapping most of the gold behind the riffles—a procedure rendered even more efficient by pouring elongated pools of quicksilver behind each cleat. Quicksilver, an ingredient which would play a dominant role in mining all over the West, possessed an uncommon affinity for gold, clutching it from the rushing water in a process called amalgamation.*

After a period of washing, the amalgamated gold was collected from the Tom and the quicksilver vaporized by heating it in an iron retort; later the quicksilver was recovered for use by the addition of a vapor condenser. A sluice operation of respectable dimensions could involve several hundred feet of Long Toms and dozens of men; many such enterprises functioned at some distance from water, as necessary an ingredient as quicksilver, and to supply this need networks of flumes were constructed, many of them by "water companies" whose sole source of income was the rate they charged miners for the use of "their" water. This went against all traditions of "riparian rights" to water, a long-held doctrine which maintained that it was illegal to divert water from a stream for anything but domestic consumption unless it was returned to that stream undiminished—so California promptly revised the concept to meet its needs and came up with what was called "appropriation and beneficial use." This innovation became a touchstone for the entire mining West

*In one of those fortuitous accidents of history, rich cinnabar deposits (from which mercury, or quicksilver, derives) had been discovered just south of San Jose in 1828. For lack of a ready market, these New Almaden Mines lay nearly fallow for twenty years—until supply was confronted by demand with the discovery of gold in 1848. In 1850, the British firm of Barron, Forbes and Company took them over and began enthusiastic development; this was perhaps the first instance of foreign ownership of a mine in the West. Californians resented the fact of British ownership of a western resource, and after a period of legal and emotional hassles, the firm finally sold out to the United States Quicksilver Mining Company. Although later cinnabar discoveries were made at New Idria and in New Mexico, the Almaden mines produced more than half the quicksilver used in mining over the next several decades. Chauvinism has its advantages.

and further laid the foundation for the development of massive irrigation projects in later years.

Those who weren't panning, rocking, or sluicing on sandbars, banks, and dry gullies were river-mining. As the term suggests, this was nothing more or less than washing the gravel of streambeds themselves. By the use of dams and rechanneling ditches, whole sections of riverbed were exposed to the busy shovels of the goldseekers. River-mining was common enough as late as 1851 for it to be maintained with not too much exaggeration that the Sacramento from its source to its mouth had been picked up and moved from its original channel.

Equally ambitious, though somewhat less dramatic, was "coyoting." Since free gold often dribbled down through loose sand and soil until it came to rest against bedrock, the logical assumption was that the richest paydirt could be found by digging down to where it lay. Shafts were sunk as deep as necessary to reach bedrock, then radial tunnels were carved out from the bottom like the spokes on a wagon wheel. The top of the shaft was fitted with a primitive hand winch for hauling up the paydirt for washing.

It should be obvious by now that placering in California quickly evolved beyond the "pick and shovel and tin pan" stage. Sluicing, river mining, and coyoting all required a labor force of sizable dimensions. Often, this necessity was met by the formation of miners' associations or cooperatives, whose members shared equally in the work and profits, if any. Less frequently, such operations were owned by a man or group of men. In whatever structual form, these enterprises had by the early 1850s assumed the configurations of an industry—a far cry from the simple dream of the average forty-niner, who had grandly supposed that a long-handled shovel and an occasional hour or two's labor would fill his pockets with nuggets and his head with visions of sybaritic ease.

The trouble with this supposition was the fact that gold-bearing gravels of a richness to justify one man's efforts were few and far between—and those few had been thoroughly worked over by those who arrived in California in 1848. The answer to the problem was to increase the volume of dirt worked, so that medium- or low-grade deposits could be turned to a profit, and this

The basics of placering: in the foreground, panning and feeding a Long Tom; center, winching up ore from a coyote hole and, to the left, washing in a cradle; in the rear, tunneling; and in the distance, flume-sluicing.

ultimately led to the invention of the most dramatic—and destructive—extension of placering methods: hydraulic mining.

The mechanics of hydraulicking were impressively simple—and effective. Expansive flume systems were constructed to carry water from the upper reaches of rivers and streams; falling at a tremendous rate of speed, this water was directed from the flumes into nozzles, called "monitors," and the resulting lance of water turned against whole hillsides, simply washing them out of existence. The stream of mud was then directed into ground sluices thousands of feet long to extract the gold, and the turgid residue, or "slickens," was channeled into whatever river or stream might be handy.

By the late 1870s, these massive operations dominated the industry of placer mining, with 425 individual companies busily hosing away great sections of the foothills and dumping the silt into various branches of the Sacramento River system. The outcome was predictable. Much of the farmland all along the east side of the upper Sacramento Valley found itself inundated by a sea of muck deposited with each spring flood. The Sacramento itself began to silt up, and even

San Francisco Bay was affected. Riverbeds rose inexorably, adding to the danger of annual flooding, and by 1880, 43,000 acres of farmland in the upper Sacramento Valley had suffered a depreciation of $2,597,634.

Such a cost was too great even for a state born in mining. In 1883 and 1884, under the prodding of screaming farmers, the state legislature and courts finally required that hydraulic mining companies construct holding basins for their muck; the cost was prohibitive and the enterprise died out, leaving a legacy as impressive as it was destructive. In 1891, a corps of government engineers made a survey of the affected area, and estimated that along the Yuba, Bear, and American rivers alone, hydraulic mining had dumped 210,746,100 cubic yards of debris on the river plains.

If hydraulicking made possible the working of low-grade paydirt at a profit, dredging, California's second great contribution to placer mining, made it even more possible. Again, the procedure was simple — simpler even than hydraulicking. A shallow, man-made lake would be created over potentially productive (and necessarily level) land. The dredge itself was a shallow-draft boat hull with an engine that moved it slowly over the lake surface while a bucket-chain kept a con-

Sluicing on the San Juan River, Utah. The wheel at the left dumped water into a flume, which diverted it into the sluice in the foreground. A team of shovelers kept the sluice running with mud—and, hopefully, gold.

stant stream of gravel falling onto mechanically-agitated riffle beds coated with quicksilver. The debris was simply dumped behind the dredge in windrows as it moved forward.

Such were the methods of placer mining as they evolved in California—from pan to dredge. California was the great testing-ground, and techniques forged in its experience were broadcast throughout the mining West wherever placer gold was a significant factor. Massive sluice and hydraulicking operations, for example, were common in the Boise Basin and in southwestern Montana; dredges were transported piecemeal to such out-of-the-way places as the lower reaches of the Colorado River, reassembled, and put to work virtually beneath the walls of the Grand Canyon. Coyoting was a standard practice in the anemic placer fields of Colorado in the early 1860s, and even more so in Alaska, whose rock-solid tundra rendered it safe even without timbering—although hot water had to be poured on the soil constantly in order to make digging possible.

Whatever incidental adjustments might be made to fit the circumstances of any given area, the basics remained the same as those developed in the Sierra Nevadan foothills. California could claim no such distinction in the matter of lode or vein mining, however; here techniques as old as man's exploitation of the earth's innards were the basis of operations from Tubac to Telluride, and owed more to the contributions of the ancient Romans than to the ingenuity of any transplanted Yankee.

This, at any rate, is an assumption suggested by a reading of the account of the Roman chronicler, Diodorus, who described the mines of southern Spain worked by Romans in the second century before the birth of Christ: "They make openings in various places and go deep into the earth to search for silver- and gold-bearing strata. By means of pits which they sink they penetrate for several furlongs not only horizontally but in depth; and, extending their subterranean galleries in different directions, sometimes transverse, sometimes oblique, from the bowels of the earth they raise the ore which yields their gain. . . ." With little or no adjustment to fit the specific case, he could have been describing a gold mine in Colorado in 1895.

Methods developed in the mines of Roman Spain were refined and improved over the centuries in the

187

Hydraulicking near Junction City, California, in 1905. The profound force of the stream of water directed through a monitor has already converted much of this hillside into slickens; in time, it will dissolve it completely.

gold and silver mines of New Spain; in the silver-lead mines of Saxony, Germany; in the coal mines of Wales and the copper and tin mines of Cornwall; and in the coal, tin, iron, and copper mines of America—even, to some extent, in the gold mines of Appalachia. By the time of the West's emergence as a major force in the history of gold and silver mining, then, deep mining was firmly developed in many parts of the world.

The physical configurations of an average mine were relatively simple. Once the location of a vein was determined, access to it was provided by either a horizontal tunnel into the side of a mountain or, more often, by a vertical shaft; in either case, this entrance was called an "adit." Shafts often went to incredible depths. Grass Valley's Empire Mine, begun in 1850 and only recently closed, ultimately went 7,000 feet through the mountains, bottoming out at 1,500 feet below sea level! The shaft's principal function was one of trans-

portation—of both men and materials—and this was facilitated by a hoist engine, which drove a drum around which was wound the necessary length of cable. The cable led from the drum to a large "sheave," or pulley, at the top of a headframe above the open shaft. From the sheave, the cable was attached to a cage, or stacked series of cages.* The shaft served a second function, however: since its bottom (sump) was usually the lowest point in a mine, subterranean waters tended to gather there and could be pumped directly to the surface, most often by the Cornish pump, a huge, steam-powered elaboration on the standard farm-well pump that was capable of lifting as much as four hundred gallons a minute from the deepest mine.

*Among the many useful inventions of Andrew S. Hallidie, who contrived San Francisco's hill-defying cable car, was a steel cable whose construction from many strands of steel wire provided unusual strength and flexibility without consequent bulk; with few exceptions, Hallidie's cable was utilized exclusively in western deep mining.

Along the length of the shaft would be various levels —horizontal tunnels that provided access to regions in the mine where the ore was being worked. From these levels ran "drifts," tunnels so called because they followed, so far as possible, the "drift" of the vein itself. Occasionally, the vein would widen to large proportions, and as the ore was mined out of it, a good-sized chamber called a "stope" was created. Additional underground tunneling included "cross-cuts," short lateral burrowings which connected major workings for purposes of exploration, communication, and ventilation, and "winzes," vertical shafts without connection to the surface. In most mines, nearly every inch of all the levels, drifts, stopes, cross-cuts, and winzes was covered with timbering to reduce the possibility of cave-in. "A large mine," Dan De Quille wrote in describing the Comstock mines, "contains millions on millions of square feet of timber—in it whole forests have found a tomb."

From the surface headworks—which usually included a headframe (sometimes enclosed in a shaft house), a pump house, a hoist house, together with offices, living quarters, shops, change-rooms, and storage yards—to the deepest drift following the twist of a vein into the crevices of the earth, a mine was no more or less than a good-sized community. "In the building of one of these mines," a reporter from the Comstock wrote in *Frank Leslie's Illustrated Newspaper* in 1877, "more care, money, labor, and engineering skill are exercised than in the erection of those congeries of buildings which in the West are dignified by the name of cities."

The business of such underground cities was getting out the ore, and this required removing it from the grip of centuries. Before the era of gunpowder—and later nitroglycerin and dynamite—this was accomplished by nothing more elaborate than brute labor in the form of "cold mining"— simply breaking it out with a combination of muscle and hand tools. Time-consuming and highly inefficient, it was a technique that could only be used with profit to obtain ore of unusual richness by the use of forced labor—conditions present in such areas as Andalusia under the control of the Romans and, even after the invention of gunpowder, in New Spain, where labor was cheaper than explosives. A labor-saving, but no less time-consuming, innovation was developed by Spanish miners, however: fire-setting. This required building a fire against the face of an ore body and keeping it going until the rock was well heated; at the right time, cold water would be thrown against the heated rock and the resulting thermal stress broke free great chunks.

Ever since its invention sometime between 1300 and 1500, attempts had been made to utilize gunpowder in mining, but it was not until the invention of the Bickford fuse in 1831 that it came into general use, since the lack of any reliable setting device shattered as many miners' bodies as ore bodies. After 1831, gunpowder revolutionized mining all over the world, enabling tons of ore to be handled in a fraction of the time needed for cold mining — and with fewer employees, a factor never held lightly by mine owners.

The elements of placering, known even in ancient times, had been considerably sophisticated as long ago as the Middle Ages.

The evolution of the hoist as seen on three frontiers: horsepower in Wyoming, a sputtering donkey engine in New Mexico, and the culmination of a Great Machine and its aristocratic operator in a Colorado mine.

The procedure of blasting began with drilling. Until the use of compressed-air machine drilling became common after 1875, this was accomplished by hand-sledging steel rods into the lode face, creating the necessary holes for the explosive. "Single-jacking" involved a single driller, who held the rod in his left hand and hit it with a four-pound sledge with his right, being careful to turn the rod after each blow so that it did not stick, or "fitcher." "Double-jacking" involved two or three drillers, one of whom held and turned the rod while the others swung syncopatic blows at it with eight-pound sledges, averaging no less than fifty blows a minute.

Seven holes were normally drilled into the lode face, averaging 24 to 36 inches in depth. The first three marked the points of a rough triangle, and were drilled on tangents so as to meet at the apex of a pyramid. Above this was drilled the "reliever" hole, and on each side an "edger" hole. Beneath the triangle, a "lifter" hole was sunk. After the holes were finished and cleaned, the blaster slid powder cartridges into them, tamped the cartridges down with a wooden rod, stemmed the holes with mud or drill cuttings, then called out the traditional "Fire in the hole!" and began lighting carefully measured rat-tails of fuse with a "spitter," or burning length of fuse. The blasts did not occur simultaneously (hopefully, at any rate), but at spaced intervals. The first to go were the three center holes, which created a central cavity. The reliever and edger holes were next, exploding ore into the cavity left by the first three. Finally, the lifter hole simply picked up the already broken ore and lifted it out into the drift for easy handling. The ore was then sorted out from the waste rock and each loaded into its appropriate car by muckers with long-handled shovels.

Loaded cars were trundled out of the drift and down the level, frequently being drawn by mules, whose superior strength made them preferable to human labor and whose superior intelligence made them preferable to horses, which had a way of slamming their heads against the roof of the tunnel at any sudden noise. The cars were then lifted to the surface, where "toplanders" disposed of them—in a "dump" for the waste rock and into ore bins for the profitable rock. From there, the ore was transported to the mills and smelters for processing.

This, in briefest outline, was how lode mines looked

The "patio process," as seen in a mine above Mexico City in 1828. The blindfolded mules are doomed to an early death from mercury poisoning, as are the peons driving them to crush the mix of silver ore.

and functioned from Lead, South Dakota, to the Coeur d'Alene, Idaho — and with suitable adjustments to modern technology, how they look and function today.

Probably the single most important problem deep mining in the West had to face was that of water. Sooner or later, in nearly every mine of significant dimensions a subterranean river began to develop, comprised of surface water that had percolated down to fill whatever underground reservoir it could find, and natural subsurface water, that trickled its way into the mine through faults and fissures in the rock.

In some cases, even the mighty Cornish pump was unable to handle the flow, and steadily rising waters gurgled a death knell for such mining camps as Tombstone, Arizona, and Eureka, Nevada—not to mention Virginia City, where even Adolph Sutro's magnificent tunnel came too late with too little (see Chapter 4). In such cases, nature simply outclassed technology, but in at least one instance the ingenuity of man overcame a difficulty that might have spelled an end to the glory of the Comstock almost before it had a chance to get started.

In 1861, George Hearst and the co-owners of the Ophir Mine encountered a problem totally unfamiliar

to them. At the 175-foot level, the vein they were following widened to as much as sixty-five feet—a delightful turn of events, except that the ore was almost impossible to work. Extremely friable in composition, it was too loose and heavy to be supported by standard timbering; cave-ins were frequent, and miners were reluctant to face the almost constant danger in the cavern-like stopes such mining required. The company sent for Philip Deidesheimer, a German engineer then managing a mine in El Dorado County, California. In a matter of a few weeks, Deidesheimer contrived the "square-set" method of timbering, a device that enabled not only the Ophir but all the other mines in the Comstock to work the great bulges of the lode in relative safety and with stupendous profit.

Simply put, the "square-set" system provided that heavy timbers be mortised and tenoned so that they could be put together to form hollow cubes. Each cube could be locked to another in an endless chain if need be, and could be stacked to the ceiling of a stope of whatever height to form a massive pillar to support it. In some of the larger chambers, which had taken on the configurations of beehives, selected stacks of cubes could be filled with waste rock to give added support.

The interior of a seventy-stamp mill in Mammoth, Arizona. This monster was the logical extension of the California Stamp Mill and was itself only of medium size; many mills went to a hundred or more individual stamps.

The interior of a Virginia City mill in about 1870, showing the mechanics of the Washoe Pan Process. A mixture of silver ore, quicksilver, salt, and copper sulphate was stirred by iron mullers in the center of each pan seen here.

In Colorado, the particularly refractory ores of the mountains demanded refining processes of huge scope and industry, as suggested by this view of the Economic Gold Extraction Company of Cripple Creek in 1904.

Historian Rodman Paul has called Deidesheimer's invention "easily the most important technical development of 1860." Mining experts from all over the world came to gaze in awe at the enormous timber-supported caverns of the Comstock, and returned to put the method into practice elsewhere.

Except for such comparatively startling innovations as the Deidesheimer square-set, the impact of the western experience on the techniques of deep mining was felt largely in the invention and improvement of equipment: air blowers for ventilation, "skips" (ore cars which would automatically dump their loads at the top of the shaft), air compressors for operating machine drills, tramway systems for conveying waste rock to dumps, hoist engines, drills, pumps, and a myriad of similar devices — each contributing to the increased mechanical efficiency of western mining, but in no sense revolutionizing it. Revolution was reserved for the matter of *treating* all the ores mining produced.

In the gold quartz mines of California, the problem of treatment was largely one of mechanics; breaking

the ore up in fine enough form that the gold would be separated from its gangue and amalgamated with quicksilver—a process called "free milling." The simplest method for accomplishing this was the *arrastra,* an ancient device of the Spanish. It consisted of a circular bed of flat rocks enclosed in a retaining wall. Two or more large boulders were placed in it and attached to one end of a horizontal beam whose center was fixed to a pivot beam in the middle of the *arrastra.* Mule or waterwheel power was applied to the opposite end of the horizontal beam and the boulders dragged over broken-up ore and quicksilver; in time—in quite a lot of time—the ore would be pulverized sufficiently for amalgamation to take place. A variation on the *arrastra* was the Chili Mill, which utilized one or two large stone wheels in place of the boulders, providing a more thorough grinding.

Neither device was overly popular with impatient Yankee types, who hadn't the time to sit in the sun watching a couple of mules walk around; this impatience led to the wide use of the stamp mill—a fairly simple contrivance that consisted of a series of two or more vertical iron-headed pestles (or "stems") driven

A shift foreman, mucker, and driller with his assistant—the working core of a deep mine—line up for a formal portrait at the face of a Colorado operation in 1900.

by a camshaft that raised and plunged them into mortars (or "batteries"). The ore was placed in the batteries, mixed with quicksilver, and, after having been crushed, was either cleaned out by hand or flushed out by water and run over the surface or riffle tables and any number of other devices designed to extract as much gold as possible. Californians so improved this device that it came to be known as the California Stamp Mill. By the end of the century, the thundering clatter of mills with as many as a hundred stamps was rattling dishes from Grass Valley to Cripple Creek.

One of the devices developed in conjunction with the California Stamp Mill was a grinding "pan," a kind of mechanical *arrastra* some four or five feet across which put stamped ore through another grinding process to further reduce it and increase the quantity of amalgamated gold. This pan figured prominently in the development of the West's second major contribution to the technology of working gold and silver ores: the "Washoe Pan Process" of the Comstock.

Again, the immediate precedent for the treating of uncomplicated silver ores was established by the Spanish in the *cazo* (kettle) process and the *patio* process. In the *cazo* method, ore that been mixed and ground up with quicksilver in an *arrastra* was placed in a

copper-bottomed vat and boiled with salt and more quicksilver, which speeded the process of amalgamation.

The *patio* process, invented in 1557 by Bartolome Medina of the Pachucan silver mines near Mexico City, was an elaboration on this method that sought to treat ores in greater volume. Ore pulverized in an *arrastra* was spread out in a paved yard, quicksilver and copper sulphate added, and horses or mules driven through the whole mess repeatedly; heat was supplied by the sun. The death rate among animals from mercury poisoning, of course, was 100 percent, and it was not much better among the miserable *peons* who had to keep the animals at a steady trot. Nevertheless, a great deal of ore could be processed in this manner, if one had enough patience—and enough *peons*, horses, and mules.

The Comstockers had animals enough, but neither *peons* nor patience, and they immediately set about putting Spanish methods into a mechanized framework capable of handling a large quantity of ore at maximum speed and efficiency. Almarin B. Paul, a quartz-mining man of some experience in California, set up a 24-stamp mill in Virginia City in the spring of 1860 and began experimenting with variations on the *cazo* and *patio* processes. What he had developed by the end

TRAILS TO EMPIRE . . .

In whatever form they appeared, gold and silver had the disconcerting and inconvenient habit of locating themselves in country that would have challenged the climbing expertise of a mountain ram. This was particularly true of the rock-ribbed cordilleran West, where some of the greatest strikes of the nineteenth century were made in mountain basins nearly two miles high, in canyons and gulches and ravines that were deep, narrow, steep-sided slits in the earth, and on the talus-covered slopes of mountain peaks. All of this simply increased the already profound technological difficulties of translating rock into money, for once the ore was blasted out of the earth, after it was reduced, and after it was refined and finally melted into gleaming bars, it had to somehow be gotten out of the sawtooth country in which it had been found. Moreover, machinery and supplies had to be hauled into the mines; communication with financial centers had to be maintained; passenger service had to be established—in short, there had to be roads. And there were—some of the most heart-stopping roads in the history of man were painfully carved into the sides of mountains (as seen in the view of an ore wagon on the road to Telluride, Colorado, above, and the Ouray and Silverton road, at the right). Sooner or later, the railroad came to most of the major mining regions of the West, but there were areas so formidable that they utterly defied the peculiar western genius of railroad-building, and for years in such spots a steady stream of miners, their families, mine managers, bartenders, gamblers, whores, merchants, and drummers braved such primitive exercises in road-making; most of them survived.

195

In The Big Bonanza, *Dan DeQuille stated
a truism applicable to all western mines of major
dimensions: "A large mine in which are
employed from five hundred to one thousand
men is of itself a considerable village. . . . it
contains millions upon millions of square feet
of timber—in it whole forests have found a
tomb." Mountains surrounding major camps
were literally stripped of timber, which explains
why most comtemporary photographs of these
regions possess a dismal, treeless aspect. At the
right, a tram hauls another log up to the Liberty
Bell Mine above Telluride, Colorado.*

*Members of the "lace-boot, tack-hammer brigade," these engineering students from the Colorado
School of Mines ham it up for the class album in 1900. After a few decades of ill-natured disdain on the
part of old-time "practical" miners, the scientifically-trained mining engineer had come into his own
by the turn of the century. "His hands are soft," an observer reported, "his tongue unused to all the
rough phrases and quaint slang of the diggings, his frame so light that one of those brawny pick-swingers
could hurl him over a cliff with a single hand; but they are glad to see him, and, however much they
may laugh at his greenness in mountain manners, hold in high respect his scientific ability, and wait
with ill-suppressed eagerness for his report. . . ." He was the Renaissance Man of the industry: a
surveyor, mechanic, accountant, carpenter, chemist, and geologist; he was an authority on mining law,
a detective with a nose for fraud, a management executive, and a labor relations expert who sometimes
got shot for his troubles.*

of 1862 became the standard method used by all the mills of the district until the Comstock's decline. After passing through ore breakers and stamps, pulverized ore was dumped into the iron pans developed in California; Paul added heavy iron mullers to grind the ore to a fine powder, introduced quicksilver, salt, and copper sulphate to the mixture, and heated the brew with steam as the mullers stirred it about. After the pans, the mix was carried into an elaborate system of settling basins and other devices designed to separate the silver amalgam from the base rock, and after that, the quicksilver was vaporized.

As complicated as the Washoe Pan Process might sound, it was designed to treat comparatively simple silver ores—ores further enriched by a healthy portion of gold, in itself an uncommon situation. Another fairly simple form of silver was in galena, or silver-lead ore, which was common to such districts as the Coeur d'Alene of Idaho. Since lead has a lower melting point than silver and most other metals, galena was simply heated in smelters until the lead ran off.

Most of the silver—and a good deal of the gold—that existed in central and eastern Nevada, Utah, Montana, Colorado, Arizona, and New Mexico was in forms other than the quartz-and-gold combinations of the Comstock or the silver-lead deposits of the Coeur d'Alene, of Leadville, Colorado, or of Eureka, Nevada. In most cases, it appeared in the form of sulphides, or sulphurets—in other words, in combination with sulphur, together with any number of base metals, including copper, zinc, and lead. To separate gold and silver from such combinations required chemical manipulation of far greater sophistication than existed in California or the Comstock, and, with reason, such ores were called "rebellious." As a ditty of the 1860s put it:

> Our German fathers, working mines,
> First exorcised the devil;
> While we affirm that sulphurets
> Are the sole cause of evil.

To exorcise this particular evil, a number of important chemical processes were devised over the years. In the treatment of gold sulphides, one of the first was chlorination: pulverized and roasted ore was placed in tanks and allowed to steep in chlorine gas, which drew the sulphides from the gold; the gold was then leached out of the mixture with water. With various improvements and refinements, this remained the standard method of treating gold sulphides until the widespread introduction of the cyanide process in the 1890s. Basically, cyanidization recovered gold by leaching pulped ore with a solution of potassium cyanide followed by water, which precipitated* the gold on sheets of zinc or aluminum. Likewise with refinements, this is a method still in use today.

The treatment of silver sulphides, given the devious and recalcitrant nature of silver, were even more complicated and esoteric. At the Santa Rita Mine, near Tubac, Arizona, an Austrian metallurgist by the name of Guido Kustel pioneered the use of lixiviation—the separation of a soluble from an insoluble by washing with a solvent—in the early 1860s, and for decades thereafter it remained the basic method. After it accumulated a number of refinements through the years, the lixiviation process involved the pulverizing, roasting, and chlorination of the silver ore, followed by leaching with water, which drew off much of the base metal. Then sodium hydrosulphite and cuprous-sodium hyposulphite were used to leach the remaining pulp, and the silver was drawn off, or precipitated, by the action of sodium sulphide.

After the turn of the century, the oil flotation process came into wide use. In this method, oil and air were introduced to pulp ore and the whole kept in a steady mix. The colloid action of the oil drew the mineral from the base materials, and air bubbles percolated it to the surface, where the natural tension kept it floating while the residue wastes sank to the bottom of a settling tank.

Complicated to the point of confusion for minds not attuned to the niceties of chemical action, reaction, precipitation, retorting, and transmogrification, such processes as chlorination, cyanidization, leaching, smelting, roasting, and lixiviation nonetheless reflected the increasing sophistication of the milling process, as it evolved from the simple *arrastra* to the multileveled, machinery-crammed mill stinking of spectral chemistry and thundering with the slamming of a hundred stamps—all of this in less than a generation.

---

*That is, separated it out from a solution as a solid by the action of chemical reagents in combination with heat.

CHAPTER ELEVEN

OF MEN AND MACHINES

An exegesis on the sons of sorrowing mothers

"For the mine it is a tragic house,
It is the worst of all prisons—
In bitter stone excavated
In barren depths located. . . .
"We, miners, sons of sorrowing mothers,
Look like men from the wastelands.
In our faces is no blood
As there is in other youth. . . ."

Who was this miner, this "son of a sorrowing mother"? In the beginning, he was Everyman. The West's first "professional" miner was none other than the peripatetic forty-niner, who fumbled his way around the gulches and ravines of the Sierra Nevadan foothills with an ignorance matched only by his enthusiasm. He was a professional by virtue of the fact that he spent all his time—or as much as humanly possible—in the search for gold, and almost in spite of himself he managed to learn something about the techniques of placer gold mining.

What many learned above all else was that it was cold, miserable, disappointing work that paid little more than the price of subsistence, as suggested by a pair of journal entries of Ananias Rogers in November 1849: "Nov. 6. Rain, rain, nothing but rain & mud for this & the most part of the day. I am witness to much suffering. Many of the emigrants are much worse off

than we are. Having no shelter, whilst our tent keeps most of the rain from us, but it is very damp & chilly. Many are troubled with Bloody Flux. . . . 12th. yesterday was fair & Mr. B & self washed for gold as we had only been able to work but 2 days in the past week, and probably made less than 2 ounces. . . ."

As the main chances steadily ran out, such men were forced to abandon their independence and take jobs—as butchers, bakers, candlestick makers, carpenters, barbers, farmhands, or laborers in other men's mines; thus was formed the nucleus of the labor force that would populate the mining frontier. It was a kind of evolution that reproduced itself on almost all branches and shoots of that frontier, and rarely was it a transition easy to take by men who had dreamed otherwise. Samuel Clemens (Mark Twain), who had plunged into prospecting and mining and speculation on the Comstock, soon found himself at work in a stamp mill. He liked it not at all: "There is nothing so aggravating as silver milling. There never was any idle time in that mill. There was always something to do. It is a pity Adam could not have gone straight out of Eden into a quartz mill in order to understand the full force of his doom to 'earn his bread by the sweat of his brow'."

Twain went on to better things—he became a reporter for the *Territorial Enterprise*. Few other men were so lucky. In California, those with no other place to go went to work for major sluice companies and water companies, for hydraulic mining companies, for

The hard-rock miner in a splendid pose, surrounded by the tools of his trade and strengthened by the dignity that comes to men who know precisely who and what they are—and know that they are good at it.

dredging companies, and as hard-rock miners in the quartz mines of the mountains. In Nevada, luckless speculators either crossed the mountains or ended up in a mill, like Twain, or two thousand feet underground. By the time deep mining had begun to dominate much of the Cordilleran West, a solid working class of miners had been concentrated out of such frontier dregs—together with a body of true professionals from Cornwall, in England, an equally large body of strong backs from Ireland, as well as Tyrolean professionals from Italy, Germans from Saxony, mercurial Serbo-Croats from central Europe, and singing Welshmen from the green mists of Wales.

Of them all, the Cornish miner—or "Cousin Jack" —was the aristocrat of the trade. Cornishmen, in fact, were the *only* professional deep miners who made their way to California in 1849, ultimately settling in such lode mining towns as Grass Valley and Nevada City. They were refugees. By the middle of the nineteenth century, the venerable copper and tin mines of Great Britain's Cornwall district in the island's southwestern finger had been thoroughly undercut by copper deposits in America's Old Northwest and by tin deposits in Brazil. The Cornishmen simply followed their trade, first to the lead mines of Wisconsin in the 1830s, then to the copper mines of Michigan in the early 1840s— and finally to the gold mines of California in the late 1840s and early 1850s. And when the Comstock was ready to boom down into the earth, the Cornishmen were there to help make it possible.

For the next forty years, the Cousin Jack was as ubiquitous as the Chinese laundryman in the mining camps of the West, as Wells Drury reported in *An Editor on the Comstock Lode:* "After the decline of the Comstock, many of the Cornish went to Grass Valley and Nevada City . . . some wandered to Australia and South Africa; others went back to Cornwall. . . . Some of the old boys died there, but a majority sought new fields to conquer, scattering in all directions: Butte, Montana; Leadville, Colorado; Tombstone, Arizona; Bodie, California. . . ."

As in all professions, service organizations, clubs, corporations, families, neighborhoods, or governments, the trade of mining developed a rigid system of prejudice. The Americans (that is, anyone whose white, Anglo-Saxon Protestant father had been born in this country) were at the top of the pile—or at least in their own opinion. Next in the pecking order were the Cornish, who looked down upon the immigrant Irish muckers, who in turn looked down upon the Welsh, who in turn looked down upon the Italians, who in turn looked down upon the "Bohunks" or Serbo-Croats. The Serbo-Croats normally had no one else to whom the baton of prejudice could be passed; they tended to sing a good deal. Whatever racial and national antagonisms that might have existed among the deep miners of the West (and some of them—particularly between the Cornish and the Irish—could be bloody and bitter), they were generally agreed upon one basic point: deep mining in the workings of the West was a rotten way to make a living.

"Life at the mines was tough," Frank Crampton, an old hardrock professional, recalled in 1956. "Working conditions . . . wherever one went, were about the same. A mucker had to muck and tram sixteen one-ton cars in an eight-hour shift, or twenty if the shift were ten hours. Two cars an hour was the minimum wherever the stiff mucked and trammed. If there was a trammer to push the ore car, the job of the mucker increased, for it was continuous mucking to fill cars while the trammer took out a loaded car and brought back an empty. Hard-rock stiffs drilled single or double jack, and they drilled a round and shot it before tally, on every shift. In the larger mines there were sometimes 'machine' drills which made it easier in the hard rock, but hand drilling was the preferred method if the hard-rock stiff were a good one."*

Handling the eight-pound sledge in double-jacking required strength, endurance, and precise control; handling the drill itself required all three—together with arctic nerves. George Whitwell Parsons, who journeyed to Tombstone in 1881 — like Mark Twain to

---

*He would have had to be a good one indeed. Although there are on record instances of hand drillers outperforming machine drills, it was only by the sort of herculean effort which broke John Henry's heart, and not the kind of thing a man was likely to display during the course of his daily shift. Actually, the machine drill was preferred by management for its efficiency and despised by the hardrock stiff, who called it a "widowmaker" because of the fine mist of rock dust the early models produced, increasing a man's chances of contracting silicosis—the nemesis of the hard-rock miner. Cornish miners, hidebound traditionalists and masters of hand drilling, particularly disliked the machine drill.

(Continued on page 209)

Verlag v. F.A. Behrens.

THE FOOLS OF '49

They climbed mountains, traversed deserts, waded streams and forded rivers, were poled across the Isthmus of Panama and crammed into leaky tubs and hauled around Cape Horn—and all for the lorelei of gold. They were the West's first "professional" miners, and a less competent lot it would be difficult to find. Still, they were the first, and their counterparts would enliven all the scattered pockets of the West for another generation. Who they were, what they were like, and what they found waiting for them in the golden land of California was documented in a bewildering variety of contemporary paintings and drawings. On this and the following four pages we present a brief composite—a pictorial view of the ancestral miner.

"*You can scarcely form any conception of what a dirty business this gold digging is,*" *a miner wrote in 1850. "A little fat pork, a cup of tea or coffee, and a slice or two of miserable bread form the repast of the miner; a couple of pair of blankets spread upon some rough boards . . . form his bed. . . .*"

"*A Rich Find*" *and* "*Busted,*" *two drawings by a man who obviously knew whereof he spoke, documented the prevailing theme of the miner's life. Another wrote: "I can look back and see the thousand mistakes that I have made, but I can't see ahead. All is misty—darkness and confusion. . . .*"

Some few struck it rich, most made no more than a day's wages, and for the rest—well, there was always the oil of good cheer, as one chronicler noted: "Drinking was the great consolation for those who had not moral strength to bear up under their disappointments. Some men gradually obscured their intellects by increased habits of drinking. . . ."

Despair was not the only theme. "I would not for ten thousand dollars have stayed at Madison and lost what I have seen," one diarist wrote. And another remembered the strong pull of hope: "It seemed that every rock had a yellow tinge. . . . During the night yellow was the prevailing color in my dreams. . . ."

204

A timeless portrait of the ancestral miner: The decrepit-looking individual shown above was probably a young man, appearances to the contrary notwithstanding. "A razor has not been used by any of us since we left St. Joseph," a miner wrote to his family, "and with the help of shears to keep the road open to our mouths . . . we are at the top of fashion." Bayard Taylor pointed out the error of judging a miner by his patina: "It was never safe to presume on a person's character from his dress or appearance. A rough, dirty, sunburnt fellow, with unshaven beard . . . might be a graduate of one of the first colleges in the country, and a man of genuine refinement and taste. . . ."

Rusting mining equipment in Gleason, Arizona.

MACHINES...

The attitudes—if not always the dress and mannerisms—expressed by the California forty-niner were broadcast throughout the mining West wherever there was a chance, however remote, that a rank greenhorn might stumble upon the wealth of Croesus. He was the spiritual kin of the clamoring placer miners of Idaho, of Montana, Wyoming, and Colorado in the 1860s, and even of the Klondike goldseeker in 1898, as he was described by a NorthWest Mounted Police officer: "There is certainly nothing heroic about the ordinary miner; he risks his life for no scientific enterprise; he faces danger to conquer no foe; he desires neither notoriety nor glory; he merely seeks to fill his own pockets." For most, however, the chance to fill their own pockets had long since gone the way of all ephemeral dreams. The great bulk of the miners who populated the West between 1860 and 1910 were working men employed in an industry; their lives were bounded by the howling clatter of machinery, not dreams of yellow gold: of thumping steam engines, sucking pumps, rattling ore cars, whining tramways, pounding stamp mills, and screaming compressed-air drills. The miners left little of themselves to mark their passing, but the industry that defined the limits of their lives is monumented all over the West by a scattering of abandoned relics, the detritus of a machine civilization.

Headframe in the hills above Victor, Colorado.

Washoe in 1863—with an eye out for the main chance, found himself working as a contract miner in another man's mine. After a few days of double-jacking, he was moved to write a somewhat breathless description of it in his journal: "Holding the drill is something not too easily acquired to do it properly. The terribly cramped and strained positions at times and strength required to manage a hole in soft ground enforces a great physical strain and much nerve when the swinger of the heavy sledge hammer has to aim over and draw in to prevent hitting you and sometimes will graze the edge of your moustache in striking a hundred pound blow upon a piece of steel ¾ of an inch in diameter. . . . My poor hands and arms are in a terrible state."

If the work itself was difficult, the conditions under which it was sometimes performed were appalling. "There were few air blowers, or suction fans, in use," Crampton maintained, "and the stiffs worked in lung-choking, eye-smarting powder gas for an hour or two after their shift went on. There was little, and sometimes, no, timbering—men were cheaper and expendable." Ventilation was always a problem, particularly in the deepest mines, and the absence of blowers and adequate timbering was a common drawback—in spite of the fact that fires, cave-ins, and dead miners were singularly unprofitable phenomena. Even in the handful of mines run on a businesslike basis, working conditions were crawling with danger, and most operations scattered across the West were somewhat cheapjack affairs, either poorly supervised or run by quick-buck artists squeezing the last dollar of production out of marginal enterprises—all of which meant increased danger and potential death to the hardrock stiffs who worked them.

The Comstock, as usual, presented problems peculiar to itself. Here the presence of hot subterranean springs in various places and depths of the Lode (some of them reaching temperatures as high as 170 degrees) created a kind of steaming hell, with men working at temperatures that often exceeded 100 degrees. "Tons of ice were sent down daily into the mines," Eliott Lord wrote in *Comstock Mining and Miners*. "The half-fainting men chewed fragments greedily to cool their parched throats, and carried lumps in their clenched hands through the drifts; iced water from the tanks was drank [sic] in extraordinary quantities. In the hotter levels three gallons was a moderate allowance for one

man during a shift of 8 hours; and 95 pounds of ice was the average daily consumption of every miner employed in the hottest workings. . . ."

Disfigurement and death were never far removed in deep mining, and the shadow of their ruin colored every man's life. Bad air, crawling with dust, breathed over too long a time, could and did produce any number of respiratory diseases, including asthma and emphysema—not to mention silicosis, capable of sandpapering a man's lungs away. Pneumonia was equally common, particularly in such areas as the Comstock, which frequently displayed marked extremes of temperature between the depths and the surface; a trip up the shaft in winter, Lord noted, "was like a magical transfer from Guiana to Spitzbergen."

But these were relatively long-term disasters; more immediately apparent were accidents. The ways in which a man could get himself maimed or killed in a deep mine is a catalog of horrors to challenge Dante's tour through the Inferno: premature explosions; falling cages; falling *out* of cages and being reduced to pulp between the side of the fast-moving cage and the shaft timbers; falling into hot water pools and being scalded; being crushed by falling equipment; simple falls into shafts, winzes, and stopes; "overwinding," in which an inattentive hoist operator simply pulled an ascending cage up through the roof of the shaft house and catapulted it through the top of the headframe (unbelievable as it might seem, this was a relatively common happenstance); boiler explosions; being crushed by runaway ore cars; asphyxiation from pockets of dead air and powder gas; heat prostration, and, in mills and smelters, falling into equipment and sundry forms of chemical poisoning were common.

No accidents, however, were quite so dramatic, or quite so feared, as fires and cave-ins. An underground mine, with its network of timbered drifts, shafts, winzes, stopes, and cross-cuts, was a great tinderbox; once fairly started, a fire could burn for days—even weeks—before it could be sealed off to die of suffocation. The fire itself was dreadful enough, but it was the malevolent gases it produced in a confined and poorly ventilated space which killed; most of the thirty-four men who died in the Comstock's famous Yellow Jacket —Crown Point fire of 1869 were snuffed out by a rush

ging with delicate grace, this abandoned mill in Colorado is a monument to dreams.

Himself, the Cousin Jack, the Cornish miner, complete with a fringed beard and trusty dinner pail, which may hold a lovely beef pasty—and maybe a chunk of high grade.

of gas capable of killing almost instantly, a grotesque business that produced tableaus of terror for the eyes of rescuers: "Here the sights which they saw were graven in their memory forever. Dead men were lying on the floor of the level as they fell in the agony of suffocation, with their mouths glued to cracks in the planks or raised over winzes, turning everywhere for one last breath of fresh air. Their faces were flushed and swollen, but the features of well-known friends were not past recognition. . . ."

Such deaths were at least sudden. A cave-in, if it did not bury miners alive, could produce the creeping horror of starvation and madness if rescue did not come in time. Frank Crampton was caught in such a cave-in in a Utah mine in 1907 with twenty Serbo-Croat (Bohunk) miners. For ten days they waited for rescue, as miners on the outside slowly blasted their way through the four hundred feet of caved-in tunnel that had trapped them. What food there was went bad quickly in the stifling, moist air, but there was plenty of water —too much water, constantly dripping from the walls and ceiling of the drift, saturating clothes, shoes, and hair, loosening and wrinkling the skin, tenderizing it so

that the slightest contact with rough surfaces could tear it maddeningly. Communication was kept up with the outside by daily crawls to a compressed-air line, where tapping signals let their rescuers know they were still alive. Crampton kept up his daily crawls to the line even after the last candle went out, leaving them in a darkness so absolute it is beyond imagination.

Soon, those trips ended, terminated by a surreal fear, as Crampton related in his reminiscences: "I have no way of knowing when it happened, but it must have been well along on the ninth day. There was a piercing shriek. . . . After that a few moments of silence . . . then another shriek, and sounds of a man running, the sound of a body falling, or hitting something, and another shriek followed by deep moans. More sounds of running, more shrieks, more sounds as of a body falling or hitting something. All the time the sounds grew dimmer; . . . finally, a scream that pierced the workings as would the whistle of a freight engine. Then silence.

"I waited for more sounds to follow, hoping they might, and yet hoping that none would come. Nothing came. . . . There was not one of us that did not know what had happened. One of the stiffs had come to the limit of strain, and his nerves and mind had broken. He had gotten up, started to run and beaten himself when falling to the floor or against drift walls. . . .

"We gave up going down to signal on the compressed-air line after that; fear pinned all of us to the platforms. I could not have gone even had I wanted to. There was no strength left to go, and my legs were so swollen that the pain was unbearable. I put the bandanna over my mouth and tied it behind my head to help keep from making audible sounds. I wanted to moan, or to cry; it didn't matter which. . . ."

Crampton's agony, and the agony of those with him, came to an end on the fourteenth day: "I was in a dazed and nightmarish doze when the break-through was made. A sudden rush of ice-cold air brought me out of it momentarily, and I could hear voices down the drift, but they did not seem to get nearer. . . . And then I heard sobs, deep-breathing sobs, trying to be held back, but breaking out nonetheless, for the strength to hold them back was gone. Then I was sobbing too, and tears running down and smarting my tender-skinned face. . . ." All but the miner who had gone screaming into the pit of blackness, slamming his helpless body against the unseen rock, eventually recovered. Hundreds of others over the century and more since deep mining began in the West were not so lucky.

Precise figures on the number of those done in or seriously injured by mining accidents in the West are not available, but a hint of the possible scope of the statistics is given in Eliott Lord's *Comstock Mining and Miners*. From newspaper files in Virginia City, Lord compiled a list of those killed or injured in the mines of the Comstock between 1863 and 1880; the figures are sobering: 295 killed and 606 injured. Such numbers would seem to justify the gloom that pervades "Underground in America," a ballad by Lazar Jurich, a Serbo-Croat miner and poet:

> For the mine is a tragic house,
> It is the worst of all prisons—
> In bitter stone excavated
> In barren depths located—
> Where there is no free breath,
> With a machine they give you air.
> By you always burns a lamp,
> And your body struggles with the stone.
> Hands work, never do they stop,
> And your chest sorrowfully heaves,
> For it is full of poisoned smoke
> From gelatin's powder white.
>
> We, miners, sons of sorrowing mothers,
> Look like men from the wastelands.
> In our faces is no blood
> As there is in other youth.
> Many poor souls their dark days shorten,
> Many poor souls with their heads do pay.
> There is no priest or holy man
> To chant the final rites.

The Slavs are a lugubrious people, given to dark striations of despair in their poetry. Most of the West's professional miners looked upon life in the mines a little less bitterly, perhaps, but not without recognizing that they were industrial laborers in a hard trade and were likely to remain so. It was only a matter of time before such men moved from that conclusion to another: that they had a right and a duty to themselves to control at least some part of their working lives. The result was a **generation of violence.**

A "Johnny Celestial" in Georgetown, Colorado, one of the thousands who scattered through the mining camps of the West.

To reduce wages is to drive to despair and death the miner and his family. It cannot and must not be. By the law of ancient Rome a convicted traitor was hurled from the Tarpeian rock. Let the man who in this crisis advocates a reduction of miners' wages be girdled with burning faggots and receive the fate of the Roman felon!" Such was the rhetoric of confrontation in the first open conflict between capital and labor on the mining frontier. The place, appropriately enough, was Virginia City; the time, the summer of 1864; the cause, one that would remain constant over the next forty years: money.

Virginia City miners had from the beginning received the highest wages in the trade: four dollars for a ten-hour day. But when borrasca began to afflict the district by the middle of the 1860s, overextended mine owners reacted in the traditional way of the employer: they sought to pare down on expenses by cutting the daily wage from $4.00 to $3.50. The miners of the district responded characteristically by marching and holding meetings punctuated by the kind of prose exhibited above, tendered by the Hon. Frank Tilford. The mine owners agreed to maintain the four-dollar day for all

This otherwise characteristic line-up of hardrock stiffs and "supers" is given an element of genuine class by the presence of the cook, whose food may or may not have been as attractive as his appearance.

underground workers, then quietly set about blacklisting members of the "Miners Protective Association," the loosely official voice of unionism in Virginia City. This, coupled with increasingly hard times in 1864–1865, effectively diluted the miners' strength, and in 1865 a $3.50 day was temporarily instituted with success. But in 1867, when the mines began to revive, a more serious-minded organization was formed, the Miners' Union of Virginia City and Gold Hill.

Their first act was the re-establishment of the four-dollar day. All but one mine in the district complied almost immediately, and the holdout succumbed when a delegation of three hundred miners called on the manager to discuss the situation. From that point until the Virginia City mines were no longer a major force in the mining industry, the Miners' Union maintained the four-dollar standard through good times and bad, and in 1872 added the eight-hour day with no reduction in the daily wage. This was a remarkable achievement for unionism in the mining West; it was, in fact, the *only* such achievement. The rest of the narrative is a depressing chronicle of sporadic conflict, frequently

bitter to the point of warfare, as labor challenged the power of entrenched capital from Grass Valley, California, to Cripple Creek, Colorado—and lost.

Typical was the fate of union activity in Grass Valley and Sutter Creek in California. The formation of the Miners' Union in Virginia City had inspired the creation of similar organizations in the two California camps, and in 1871 the miners of Sutter Creek struck in an attempt to standardize the daily wage at $3.50 for all workers; until then, it had been $3.00 for "first-class" underground workers, $2.50 for second class, and $2.00 for surface workers. The attempt was joined by miners in Grass Valley the following year, but in each case it was in vain. Mine owners, outraged at this interference in executive decision, fired union members and operated their mines with scab labor; unionists responded by beating up on those non-union miners foolish enough to be caught out in the open. The governor called out the militia, and in a matter of weeks the fledgling power of the unions was broken. This, with few elaborations, would be the pattern of such strikes all over the West for the next forty years.

The mines of the American West attracted the largest variety of minority groups outside the warrens of New York City; above, a group of stocky Italian miners from the hills of Tyrol assembles in Utah.

A similar, and even more flamboyant, dénouement took place in Leadville, Colorado, in 1880. Wages there were $3.00 for underground workers, and in May 1880 the Miners' Cooperative Union struck the Chrysolite Mine, owned by H. A. W. Tabor and the Chicago mercantilist Marshall Field, for an increase of one dollar a day. Over the next few weeks, most of the mines in the district were similarly struck. Violence, for the most part, was confined to dramatic flourishes, parades, and such. Tabor and the other mine owners were moved to organize something called the Committee of Safety, a semi-military organization with six hundred members, complete with uniforms donated by Tabor. Colorado's governor, R. W. Pitkin, obligingly supplied rifles and ammunition, and nicely caparisoned, the committee staged a parade and demonstration on June 12, climaxed by a rousing military speech by Tabor himself, who had come a long way from the days when he and his wife ran a grocery store in California Gulch.

The miners remained "exasperatingly quiet," as one mine owner put it, in the face of all this, so the sheriff and prominent citizens requested that Pitkin declare martial law; forever affable, the governor acquiesced. Anti-vagrancy ordinances were used to arrest undesirables—that is to say, union members—165 of whom were offered the choice between a fifty-dollar fine, a fifty-day jail sentence, or departure from town instantly. Most chose exile; "Tramp, tramp, tramp the boys went marching," jeered the Leadville *Democrat*. The strike was broken almost before it had begun.

Ten years later, union efforts in the Coeur d'Alene mines of Idaho seemed more successful than most—at least for a time. In the winter of 1890–1891, the four local unions in Wallace, Burke, Gem, and Mullan merged into one, and in January the new union struck for a $3.50-a-day wage for all underground workers. By July, all mines but the district's biggest, the Bunker Hill and Sullivan, had complied, and by the end of the month even that company agreed. As well, they had agreed to the union's hospital plans. Previously, the individual companies had deducted one dollar a month from wages to pay the services of a company doctor; the

The luckless miner had a choice of crippling and killing disasters, including accidental blasts and runaway cages.

union wanted its own hospital, and one of its demands was that the dollar deduction be paid into a fund to support an institution in Wallace. Again, all but the Bunker Hill and Sullivan agreed, although in August, the mine's manager did agree to put the issue to a vote by its employees; when the ballots were presented, however, only three choices were available: (1) a company hospital in Wardner, (2) no medical service at all, or (3) the current system. Only non-union surface employees bothered to vote, and when a 93-0 vote in favor of a company hospital resulted, the manager announced that "all employees who do not wish $1.00 per month retained for this purpose are not only at liberty but are requested to call at the company's office for their time." One can almost admire the arrogance of the statement; nevertheless, the union struck the mine instantly, and by September the Bunker Hill and Sullivan gave in.

If the union entertained visions of success, it underestimated the determination of mine owners. After the events of the summer and early fall of 1891 calmed down, they organized themselves into a Mine Owners' Protective Association, hired Charles Siringo, a former Pinkerton detective, to infiltrate the union (he became its recording secretary, a tribute to his skill, not

to mention his nerve), and prepared themselves for a major confrontation. At the end of the year, the district's railroads announced a rate increase, and utilizing this as a reason, the Mine Owners' Protective Association announced that all mines would close on January 15, 1892, until and unless the old rates were restored. By March, the railroads rescinded their increase and the mines re-opened—but proclaimed a fifty-cent cut in the daily wage. The union balked, so the owners hired armed guards and began importing non-union help. Fighting broke out in Gem in July, when union members learned that Siringo was a spy (he escaped mutilation by hiding beneath a wooden sidewalk), and Governor Norman B. Willey called out six companies of the Idaho National Guard. More than five hundred union men were arrested over the next few months, and the union's strength was shattered.

By then it was obvious to unionizers in the West that organization on a broader, more significant (and better financed) scale was going to be necessary. In the spring of 1893, forty representatives from fifteen individual miners' unions gathered behind closed doors in the Miners Union Hall of Butte, Montana. When they emerged several hours later, they had created a new organization, the Western Federation of Miners, with the stated purpose of "securing by education and organization, and wise legislation a just compensation for our labor and the right to use our earnings free from dictation by any person whatsoever."*

The new union had hardly been born before disaster struck the mining West with the repeal of the purchase provisions of the Sherman Silver Purchase Act of 1890. This act had required the federal government to purchase no less than 4.5 million ounces of silver per month, nearly the total production of the country at the time—and a subsidy of no little consequence to the silver-mining industry. The silver-oriented states of the West greeted its repeal with howls of outrage, but little effect. The problem was intensified by the crash of

*This last was a dig at the prevalence of company stores; in many places (such as the Bunker Hill and Sullivan's store in Wardner, Idaho), miners were required to shop only at such stores, often at prices superbly inflated over the going rate anywhere else. Similarly, single miners were frequently required to board only at company boarding houses, again at prices over the average.

'93, as 580 banks failed and 16,000 businesses went bankrupt across the nation, and mines, mills, and smelters throughout the Rockies were forced to close; thousands of jobless miners streamed into the few productive gold camps of the West; one of these was Cripple Creek, Colorado, where the Western Federation fought—and won—its first strike; it would be the only such victory.

The owners of the district—some of whom worked their men a ten-hour and some an eight-hour day, but all at a rate of $3.00—apparently could not resist the temptation of a heavy influx of hungry miners. In January of 1894, those mines working an eight-hour day announced a cut in wages to $2.50, which would have made them the lowest-paying mines in the entire West. The federation struck immediately; mine owners retaliated by hiring strikebreakers; and the Federation retaliated to that by taking possession of the Strong Mine on Bull Hill. After several days of sporadic battling with the civilian deputies of Cripple Creek's sheriff, E. M. Bowers, with the resulting death of one miner, Governor Davis H. Waite intervened and negotiated a settlement between the mines and the miners: it stipulated an eight-hour day at $3.00, a policy of non-discrimination against union men, and in effect established the federation as the sole bargaining agent for the Cripple Creek mines. Waite, a populist with obvious sympathies for the working man, had proved to be a valuable ally for the federation.

By the time of its second major strike, Waite was no longer around to lend a hand. In 1896, when federation officials demanded that mine owners in Leadville adhere to the $3.00, eight-hour day established in Cripple Creek, and struck those who refused, the Leadville Mine Owners Association ordered a general lockout and requested state troops from Colorado's new governor, Republican A. W. McIntire. McIntire complied readily, declared martial law, and otherwise so enthusiastically supported the mine owners that the strikers were forced to return to work on employers' terms in February of 1897. Similar defeats followed in Wardner, Idaho, in 1897; in Lake City, Colorado, and in the Coeur d'Alenes of Idaho in 1899 (this last especially marked by the destruction of the Bunker Hill and Sullivan smelter and martial law that remained in effect for nearly two years); and in Telluride, Colorado, in 1901.

By then, the lines were drawn and drawn well. The federation's president, Edward Boyce, had articulated

The stakes in the union wars were high, centering around the fate of men whose lives were ruled by heat, dirt, sweat and danger resulting from their occupation.

one extreme as early as 1898: "Every union should have a rifle club. I strongly urge you to provide every member with the latest improved rifle. . . . I entreat you to take action on this . . . so that in two years we can hear the inspiring music of the martial tread of 25,000

Varieties of death, separated by a generation: above, an avalanche nearly obliterated the King Lease Mill of the Camp Bird Mine of Colorado in February, 1936, killing three men; below, a boiler explosion splintered the hoist room of the Highland Mine in Lead, South Dakota, in May, 1901, killing two men and providing further evidence that a western mine could indeed be "a tragic house," no matter what the generation.

The Western Federation of Miners was headed up in 1901 by Edward Boyce, bottom center, and William D. Haywood, to the right of Boyce; a ruined right eye caused Haywood to keep his left profile to the camera at all times.

armed men in the ranks of labor." His successor, Charles H. Moyer, echoed such militant determinism in 1901: "The Western Federation of Miners will not pause in the determined effort to bring about...change in our social and economic conditions as will result in a complete revolution of the present system of industrial slavery." And Moyer's good right arm, William D. ("Big Bill") Haywood, had already established himself as one of militant socialism's most vigorous proponents ("Sabotage," this one-eyed bull of a man once wrote, "means to push back, pull out, or break off the fangs of Capitalism").

The opposite extreme was expressed in the formation of the Colorado Mine Owners Association in 1902, one of whose openly stated ambitions was the suppression of all labor unions in the state. A subsidiary organization called a Citizens Alliance was established in Denver, and its goals were even more specific: "Labor conditions in Colorado are openly socialistic. The Western Federation of Miners, or as it should be called, 'The Western Federation of Murderers,' is full of socialist agitators.... The Western Federation must go!" Equally obdurate was Colorado's governor in 1902, James H. Peabody, who wrote to none other than Harrison Gray Otis, publisher of the Los Angeles *Times:* "I cannot convince myself to believe in the idea that a laboring man who has several little bodies to

clothe and hungry mouths to feed, may be compelled to labor no more than eight hours.... I disclaim the right of any individual or organization to compel him to cease when the clock strikes the eighth hour, and I will not permit it if it requires the entire power of the state and the Nation to prevent it."

Such muscular opinions were not held lightly nor exercised without conviction—and they inevitably led to what labor historian Melvyn Dubofsky has called "one of the most brutal class conflicts in American history"—the Cripple Creek strike of 1903–1904. In August 1903, the federation declared a strike against the Denver smelter of the United States Refining and Reduction Company, which treated many of the ores from the Cripple Creek district, and coupled this with a demand that the mines of Cripple Creek cease sending ore to the company or face a general strike. The Cripple Creek Mine Owners and Operators Association refused, and on August 8 the federation ordered 3,552 men off their jobs. By the end of the month, most of the mines went back to work with strikebreakers.

Several days of occasional violence, including the burning of a shaft house and the beating of some non-union men, inspired the association to request state troops from Governor Peabody, and on September 5

Bayonet and handgun at the ready to fend off aggressive union miners, a Colorado militiaman stands guard over the Emmett Mine in Leadville, 1896.

The wages of conflict, June 6, 1904: the curious come to gape, as usual, while workmen scour the ruins of the Independence Depot for human shreds.

Adjutant General Sherman Bell, a humorless martinet of a man who had come to glory with Roosevelt's Rough Riders in Cuba, arrived in the district with one thousand troops—equipped with gatling guns, among other things. "I came to do up this damned anarchistic federation," Bell announced, and proceeded to make arrests posthaste, including the entire staff of the Victor *Record,* a newspaper sympathetic to the strike. ("To hell with the Constitution," one of Bell's aides remarked.) Union miners responded predictably; attempts were made to derail carloads of non-union miners on a line of the Florence and Cripple Creek Railroad, and on November 22 the shaft house of the Vindicator Mine was blown up, killing the mine's superintendent and a shift boss. Bell requested martial law, and Peabody complied.

Bell's men enforced the provisions of martial law with enthusiastic rigidity. Wholesale arrests, confinement in a bullpen near Goldfield, and deportation of the more prominent union members effectively thinned the federation's ranks during the next few weeks. Members of the federation in Cripple Creek must have found little comfort in a message from Moyer and Haywood (tucked away in Denver): "Keep your union cards. Refuse to be driven from your homes."

By January, Peabody felt justified in lifting the state

In what was surely the most dramatic gesture in the history of labor conflict in the western mines, the Bunker Hill and Sullivan smelter in the Coeur d'Alenes of Idaho was ripped to shards by dynamite in 1899.

of martial law, and all but fifty troops were withdrawn. Mine owners established a central bureau of employment, effectively blacklisting those few federation members who had not already given up their cards in exchange for the opportunity to provide food for their families. The strike was rapidly becoming meaningless and was further weakened when Bell arrested Moyer in Ouray on a charge of desecrating the flag for printing a pamphlet with Old Glory's stripes displaying sundry lurid slogans.

The long-delayed climax came on the morning of June 6, 1904, when thirteen non-union miners were blown into oblivion by a dynamite bomb at the Independence Depot. Martial law was again declared, and Bell set about the task of cleaning up Cripple Creek for good and all. By the end of July, 238 federation members had been deported to the deserts of New Mexico and the prairies of Kansas; those who had not been deported or forced to renounce their membership in the union were held by the hundreds in the improvised bullpens of the district; civil authority was in the hands

Radical desecration, 1904: Patriot Sherman Bell was outraged by Haywood's exhibition of irreverence for the flag in this luridly descriptive broadside.

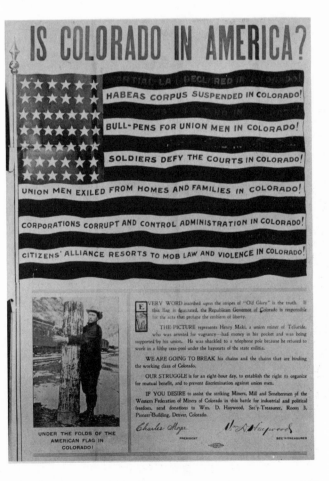

For the most part, the state troops sent into Cripple Creek in 1904 had no one to fight and almost nothing to do with themselves—except practice the arts of war, as in this cavalry saber drill underway at Camp Goldfield.

of the Cripple Creek Mine Owners and Operators Association and its subsidiary organization, the Citizens Alliance; the streets were left in the control of an anti-union mob.

The federation had come to utter defeat in its one major bastion, despite the words of Moyer in December of 1904, after his release on the charge of desecration: "The issues involved . . . remain the same, and the situation is unchanged." He was whistling in the dark and doubtless knew it. In July of 1905 he and Haywood attended an Industrial Congress in Chicago, helping to guide a haggling, dissident-ridden group

When the troops were called in to do something—such as escort prisoners into town for court hearings—they did so with a splendiferous flourish and enough heavy equipment to handle a regiment of unionists.

through to the formation of the Industrial Workers of the World, an organization that would write its own kind of history on the West. The Western Federation of Miners became the "Mining Department" of the IWW.

The final convulsion of union activity in the area of gold and silver mining took place, appropriately enough, in the mining frontier's last boomtown: Goldfield, Nevada. In December, 1906, the IWW-controlled Western Federation of Miners local in Goldfield struck the mines to obtain higher wages and shorter hours, and in three weeks gained their demands. But internal dissensions caused a split between the IWW faction in Goldfield and the WFM, and in April, 1907, the WFM settled a separate agreement with mine owners.

Unfortunately, there was a "hidden" factor in labor-management conditions in Goldfield: the practice of high-grading, which was possibly more prevalent in this camp than in any other on the mining frontier. The tradition of miners' stealing exceptionally valuable chunks of ore and selling them to shady assayers was common wherever high-grade ore was available, but in Goldfield it reached astounding proportions; owners estimated that they had lost as much as twenty million dollars over the years. Among the miners, the practice was regarded almost as a natural right—a kind of fringe benefit, as it were.

Mine owners instituted change rooms, searched lunch pails, constructed jump bars over which naked miners were forced to leap to shake loose any gold hidden between their legs—and even made an appeal to the clergy, as reported by Frank Crampton: "At a Sunday service I attended . . . the preacher extolled to his flock the virtue of honesty and denounced the sin of stealing. . . . I had visions of high-grading becoming something of the past and being ended forever as his flock, deeply attentive, listened in astonished surprise. However, there was obvious relaxation, and a sigh of unrestrained relief, when he closed the sermon by adding: 'But gold belongs to him wot finds it first.' I admit I was somewhat relieved myself."

Such things could not be mentioned in open negotiation, but high-grading was a factor of no little contention between labor and management, and doubtless contributed to the determination of George Wingfield and other mine owners that unionism of whatever brand must end in Goldfield. In November, 1907, they rescinded their agreement with the WFM and began hiring strikebreakers at reduced wages. There was no state militia to speak of, so the Goldfield Mine Owners Association requested federal troops to put down presumed violence, and President Roosevelt sent them in December. By March, 1908, the union was broken, as Wingfield cheerfully reported: "The Western Federation of Miners and the IWW are now eliminated from the camp of Goldfield, and always will be as long as I am identified with it." Union or no union, however, high-grading continued to haunt Goldfield's owners until the town's final decline. Greed is no respecter of institutions.

What can one say of the violence that characterized the rise and fall of labor unionism in the gold and silver mines of the West? Many historians, among them the redoubtable Vernon H. Jensen, whose *Heritage of Conflict* remains the classic study in the field, have attempted to link it in some manner to the traditions of rough-and-ready life on a frontier, a reflection of the free violence that characterized so much of that frontier in all its phases.

This is an easy assumption, based on a traditional view of western history which even historians cannot always escape. It is predicated on the theory that violence, of whatever kind, was somehow endemic to the frontier simply because it took place on that frontier—that a frontier framework somehow enlarged it to the point of uniqueness. Hence, tradition's coloring the Earp-Clanton "feud" with glamor, obscuring the fact that it was nothing more or less than the kind of second-rate gangland struggle that had been common in the urbanized East for more than a generation.

To apply the same reasoning to an assessment of the conflict between capital and labor in the mining West cloaks an important reality: just as western labor unionism was not invented in the West, but adapted from models established long before, the violence that accompanied it was in a long, if not particularly honorable tradition. The miners of the West were the first industrial workers of the West, and a group of them taking over the Strong Mine on Bull Hill in Cripple Creek in 1894 were no different in kind or spirit from the railroad workers who burned the Philadelphia yards in 1877. Both reflected the agonies of a society grown large.

CHAPTER TWELVE

WONDROUS TOWNS
AND INSTANT CITIES

The dynamics of expedience on the mining frontier

"The curses, jeers, and imprecations which were heard on every side; the loud laugh and the obscene joke which was cracked in the crowd below; with the evident glee and humor with which the Committee carried out their bloody purpose, will long remain vivid in the memories of those who witnessed those occurrences of blood...."

Civilization as it was exercised in the towns of the mining frontier has been blessed—or cursed—with a profound amount of discussion through the years. With the exception of the *mythos* of the cowboy, no other real or almost-real phase in the development of the West has come under such fascinated scrutiny, displayed in everything from two-reeler "B" movies to esoteric monographic flagellations. Probed, described, articulated, exploited, questioned, argued, interpreted and misinterpreted, it has been run through every medium of analysis save a computer—and in this age of rampant cybernetics, that probably is not too far behind. The fascination is easily enough explained: such towns were the products of a society re-creating itself in a highly accelerated form—almost as if we were privileged to observe the history of, say, Boston, with all its drama, pathos, conflict, and even nobility, crowded into a few short years. A history condensed is a history more easily comprehended.

Or so it might seem. The trouble is, such condensation brings with it an inevitable exaggeration of what are seen as essential elements—in this case, the drama, the sometimes inspired hijinks, and the insouciant disregard for the prose of life. The history of the mining community was bitten at an early age by Bret Harte, further infected by Charles Howard Shinn, and put into a nearly terminal condition by a small army of local historians, whose loving-hands-at-home chronicles have swaddled it in a tangle of breathless myth. The fact that the western mining town was an institution fully as complicated as its more venerable eastern counterparts is lost in a welter of lambent narratives dealing with gamblers, saloons, whores with platinum hearts, outlaws, gunfights, instant millionaires, miners of Arcadian virtue, and vigilante mobs—a two-dimensional interpretation of three-dimensional history.

This observation is not made out of simple irritation; after all, the process of myth-making is one of our oldest and most revered traditions. But it is necessary to understand that beneath all the patina of legend, lie some truths which may reveal something important about the dynamics of a society transplanted—and even more significantly, perhaps something important about the quality of the American character.

One of the most durable confusions lies in the question of just what constituted a mining camp. The term is utilized with the broad application of a politician discussing the meaning of free enterprise—and with

Reflections in the middle of the definitive desert: the main street of Goldfield, Nevada, mirrored in glass by photographer J. E. Stimson in 1904.

just about the same degree of utility in helping us to understand what it is all about. In fact, the term should be used in its narrowest sense, for the mining camp was a singularly transient and short-lived institution, with a character and quality all its own—a purely extemporaneous exercise in slapping together the basic ingredients necessary for men to function without being done in by the elements or their own natural anarchy. It lasted no longer than it had to last and either disappeared entirely or was transmuted into something else —frequently within a matter of months. Generally speaking, if a camp survived long enough to have a book written about it—or even a magazine article—it was no longer a camp. Last Chance Gulch and Helena were synonymous only in their geography.

The outlines of such communities were as simple as expedience could make them, both architecturally and socially. Most would fit J. Ross Browne's description of the early Virginia City with startling precision: "Frame shanties, pitched together as if by accident; tents of canvas, of blankets, of brush, of potato-sacks and old shirts. . . ." Government, if it could be so dignified, was equally simple, comprising the absolute minimum necessary for the adjudication of immediate needs. In California it was usually placed in the hands of an *alcalde* for such matters as claim arbitration and recording; in later camps "recorders" served the same function. More important things—robbery, murder, et al.—were left up to community action more often swift than precise (more of this later).

Charles Howard Shinn, writing in the 1880s, saw in all this the essence of a kind of noble purpose; put such a community down on a desert island, he said, "and it would organize a government, pick out its best men, punish its criminals, protect its higher interests, develop local institutions, and soon, unless its natural surroundings forbade, there would be a healthy, compact, energetic state. . . ." And even Hubert Howe Bancroft, normally one of the most perceptive—even skeptical—of historians, was moved to write: "Simple, honest, earnest, they affected nothing, and in the direction of self-government attempted nothing which they failed to accomplish. Here was a people who might give Solomon or Justinian a lesson in the method of executing justice. . . . The California miners . . . have

shown to the world more than any other people who ever lived how civilized men may live without law at all."

Such an Edenistic state of affairs did in fact exist in California for a short period of 1848, when the sheer abundance of gold filled every man's heart with good will and when robbery and other crimes were so rare that the most primitive form of self-government was enough to satisfy the situation. But in California, as in all the pinpoints of the mining frontier, such conditions soon reached a state where simple democracy was no longer enough.

Moreover, the "higher interests" and "local institutions" cited by Shinn did not enter the picture; simple expedience was the rationale of any proper mining camp, as outlined by historian David Lavender: "Since no camp conceived of itself as any more permanent than its gold deposits, society was atomistic. Early laws ignored such civic matters as cleaning up the appalling streets and such private affairs as debt, slander, contract violations, and the like. Jurisdiction never extended beyond the immediate boundaries of the camp concerned, and there was no provision for cooperation with other districts."

A mining camp, after all, was not a settlement; it was a collection of men whose principal purpose was to survive long enough to get rich—and it was in such an atmosphere that legends were born. Life was exercised with a ruthless conviction; restraints were few, and the temptations many. Most of those who populated any given camp in the West were young ("I cannot recall ever seeing a man with white hair," one veteran remarked), out on their own for the first time in their lives, and infatuated with dreams, as noted by the *Alta California* in 1850: "Bright visions of big lumps of gold and large quantities of them, to be gathered without any severe labor, haunt them night and day . . . hope to find a land where the inevitable law of God that 'Man shall earn his bread by the sweat of his brow' has been repealed, or at least for a time suspended. They come here with this hope, and it takes but a few short weeks to dispel it. . . . Temptations are about them on every hand. They drink and they gamble. They associate with men who, in their eastern homes, would be shunned by them as the worst of their kind. . . . They sink lower and lower." Such conditions do not make for a stable society, and it is little wonder that mining

(Continued on page 233)

Belmont, Nevada.

TAKEN BY THE WIND

Nothing is more illustrative of the boom-and-bust pathology of the mining frontier than the ghost town, examples of which are scattered in shack-and-shanty profusion from the mountains of Colorado to the rivers of Alaska, together with the deserted machinery, headworks, and mills of the mines whose wealth was considered inarguable and whose permanence was assumed without question. Many of these booming towns evaporated before speculators could consolidate the frontage of their town lots or replace tents with shacks; others lasted long enough to achieve the solidity of brick buildings and elaborate mine workings. Soon or late, most died, their clamoring populations gone, their streets weedgrown, their mine buildings and machinery rusting, their ambitious architecture left to the vagaries of the wind. What follows on the next seven pages is a pictorial tribute to the power of optimism. And the words? They apply to everywhere in general and to nowhere in particular. They are part of the lexicon of the mining frontier, each written in the high gloss of hope—and today serve as obituaries for towns that are no more.

"The rugged cliffs along the road cropped out at
every turn like grim old castles of feudal times,
and there were frowning fortresses of solid rock.
. . . I was particularly struck with the rugged
grandeur of the scenery in the vicinity of Vegas'
quartz mill. . . . Nothing finer in point of
symmetrical proportion, beauty, and finish of the
machinery . . . exists. . . . I had little expected
to find in this out-of-the-way part of the world
such splendid monuments of enterprise."

Abandoned mining machinery in the Talkeetna Mountains, Alaska.

*Mining relic in the high desert
of eastern California.*

"There is so much going in mining circles that it is almost impossible to keep pace with
the developments being made every day. One day it is a rich strike in the Bodie; then a
new hoisting works for the Spaulding; developments which indicate permanency in the
Red Cloud; the Standard still in the front ranks with large bodies of very rich ore;
a whim for the Old Dan; hoisting works for the Goodshaw; the Belvedere Mill going up;
the Standard, Syndicate, and Miners' Mills crushing day and night, and the opening
up of rich veins in the smaller mines, all tend to show that there is an activity
pervading mining matters never before experienced. . . ."

"Times are getting lively in this camp. The honest miner is hard at work tearing up the ground to get enough dust for a Sunday's hurrah in town; the 'girls' and the 'boys' are flocking in by stage coach, train, and on foot; the justice courts are kept hot and our jail is overcrowded. . . ."

Miner's cabin on Ute Creek, Colorado.

Mill and mine, Nevadaville, Colorado.

Jerome, Arizona.

"On the corner are knots of men talking mines and mining, and criticizing the specimens that pass from hand to hand. The stores are thronged with men discussing the locality and merits of the last new thing in strikes. The report of a pistol will bring a hundred men to their feet in an instant, and the saloons will disgorge twice as many more in the same moment, all on the alert to catch a sensation. . . ."

"Gamblers, pimps, prostitutes, and the hangers-on of sporting houses, gambling places, and saloons, none were missing. Welcome were the girls of the line, who gave solace and some brief companionship to men, the hard-rock stiffs, mule skinners, construction stiffs, and others, whose lives were toil, and often danger. There were few women other than those on the line, in the early days of a camp, and to see a woman did something wonderful to lonely men. . . ."

Store building near Ouray, Colorado.

"The streets are lined with freight of every description; heavy teams are constantly coming in with more; buildings are going up everywhere; auction sales are taking place in a dozen localities; men are rushing about in every direction, corner loungers are in crowds, and all is life, bustle and excitement. . . . There is enterprise here, and money enough to build it up rapidly, and when the season becomes more moderate carpenters and masons need not be idle an hour; there will be work enough for all. . . ."

Rhyolite, Nevada.

camps scattered all over the West were ridden by almost uncontrolled crime, gambling, whoring, drinking, and all the other paraphernalia from which our myth-making has come.*

Unfortunately, that myth-making has spilled over into areas that should be viewed in other lights. The mining camp as an institution probably survived in California longer than in any other state, simply because the extent of placer deposits was so large—and placer deposits, by their very nature, lend themselves to quick exploitation, after which the exploiters move on to new territory. In most of the West, however, the mining camp, in the form in which we have been discussing it here, enjoyed a brief spurt of life, then was quickly absorbed if the gold or silver deposits that inspired its existence in the first place showed promise of permanence.

Lode mining, of course, simply speeded the process, since it required time, capital investment, a labor force, supplies, materials, capable management, and all the other elements of industrial development. It also required a stable government and a community that could satisfy the economic needs of corporate mining and the social needs of those who connected themselves with it. Characteristically, the evolution from camp to town—and, in the more ambitious phases, city—was remarkably brief.

Thus, Leadville could be described in early 1878 as consisting of seven log cabins and three hundred miners, only eighteen of which had bothered to incorporate the town itself, and in May, 1879, as a "wondrous town"; and, even more to the point, less than three years later it could be characterized as a dull little industrial city, "like some provincial town," as a visiting Englishman described it. Similarly, swift change came to every camp of consequence in the West, including Denver, Helena, Virginia City (Nevada), Boise, Deadwood, Cripple Creek, and Butte. Some, like Wardner, Idaho, or Ruby City, Nevada, hardly bothered with the camp phase at all, becoming almost instant industrial cities.

Civic improvement was the primary concern of any camp-become-city, possibly the single most telling difference between the two, for it indicates the fact that residents had acquired a stake in the area; they intended to stay, perhaps even to rear up families around them almost in the pioneer tradition, and were willing to sacrifice at least a part of the quick dollar in exchange for a livable environment. Macadamized and cobbled streets, gas — and later, electric — lighting, sewer systems, water lines, and public transportation were among the refinements visible in various mining towns as early as the middle of the 1880s—in regions that little more than a generation before had been as unfamiliar with civilized trappings as the mountains of the moon. Business sections, where practicable, took on the massive solidity of brick or stone architecture, and homes acquired lawns and gardens (although not often trees, at least at first—the first thing any mining district did was strip the area around it of available trees for timbering in the mines and lumber in the town). Fire departments—at first voluntary and later municipally owned and operated—were organized and equipment purchased. They would never be enough for a great many towns, but they were an earnest attempt to control the single worst problem such towns had to deal with.* With such physical improvements came those of a more social or cultural order.

Each town soon acquired one or more major hotels, in many cases of a substantiality and even luxury to challenge the best the East could offer—the St. James in Denver, the Palace in San Francisco, the International in Virginia City, and the Clarendon in Cripple Creek were prime examples. Schools and churches, social clubs and reading societies attended themselves to the higher needs of the mind and soul, while music halls, theatres, and opera houses (few of them having much to do with opera) satisfied the craving for more rambunctious entertainment, although respectable enough.

The opera house, in fact, was a particularly symbolic manifestation of civic arrival; the town that could afford a theatre of such a size and architecture to justify the label of opera house was a town to be reckoned with. It was no accident, after all, that when H. A. W.

*One exception that tests the rule as well as any other was Dawson, in the Yukon Territory. Here, the uncompromising Canadian Mounties made it clear from the beginning that Her Majesty's Government was going to rule the town with a firm hand. As a result, Dawson was the most law-abiding camp in the history of the mining frontier.

*Among the towns that burned down at least once during the course of their careers were Virginia City; Nome; Bisbee; Tombstone; Cripple Creek; Wallace, Idaho; and Helena, Montana.

Sunlight glimmers through the ruined slats of a snowshed outside a mine in the mountains of Alaska.

Creede, Colorado, where there was no night—even in 1890, when this scene was immortalized on glass. Crammed into a narrow mountain canyon in a kind of spontaneous erection, Creede typified the logic-defying mining town.

Tabor, the former grocer of California Gulch, sought some means of conspicuous construction, he chose the opera house as the one structure worthy of his status as one of the richest men in Colorado, if not the richest. The Tabor Opera House in Leadville was built in 1879 and at the time was the most magnificent such structure between St. Louis and San Francisco, where Maguire's Opera House held forth.

Not satisfied with merely conquering the cultural heights of Leadville, Tabor turned his energies on Denver two years later, constructing the Tabor Grand Opera House, a splendiferous affair with Italian tapes-

tries, stained-glass windows, hand carved cherry wood-work, silk plush draperies, and a stirring compliment from the *Rocky Mountain News,* which proudly announced "the grandest Mile Stone in Denver's Career."

Add to such things the fact that nearly every major mining town in the West had some sort of railroad and telegraph connection with the centers of the East by the middle of the 1880s, and it is clear that applying the word "camp" to such muscular exercises in municipal growth is not only inaccurate but misleading. To go further and assume that the peculiarly undisciplined, free-wheeling life of the frontier camp was translated

never change). The "frontier," if it existed anywhere in the mining municipalities of the West after the first flush of boom, existed largely in the minds of its inhabitants—and in the memories of their descendants.

Much has been made of the democracy of the mining camp, particularly in California, and it is true that men did in fact function with relative peace and equity among one another—providing that race and nationality were sufficiently the same. As usual (then or now), democracy tended to be selective in nature. In California it did not include Indians, who were either ignored or hunted down and killed; it did not include Mexicans or *Californios*, who were characterized as "greasers" and consistently cheated, browbeaten, and held in monumental contempt; and most especially, it did not include the Chinese, who were subjected to a campaign of open discrimination as virulent as it was ultimately successful.

Word of the discovery of gold in California reached the China coast perhaps later than most other regions of the world, but by late 1849 and early 1850 it was common knowledge among the residents of Toishan Province, some two hundred miles southwest of Hong Kong. Most of the Chinese who indentured themselves in order to get to California over the next few years were from this province; they were called Gum Shan Hok—guests of the Golden Mountain—and by the end of 1851, there were more than twenty-five thousand of them in California.

During the better part of 1849, the Chinese were accepted as a slightly curious but in no sense threatening element in the California scene. After all, their motives were almost precisely the same as those of the rest of the goldseekers, as Gunther Barth reports in *Bitter Strength:* "The life of Chinese indentured emigrants revolved about three primary objectives: to earn and to save money, to pay off the indenture, and to return home to their families in China for a life of relative ease." Besides, there would be plenty of gold for everyone. The Chinese, quiet, industrious, and infinitely more patient than the Anglo miners, spread throughout the Mother Lode country.

By the end of 1850, it was becoming obvious to all concerned that there was not and would never be enough gold to go around. That being the case, it did

whole into a metropolitan structure is to write history as we like it, not as it was.

While it is true that the social structure of a town like Helena in 1880 was less rigid than that in Boston, with a genuine tolerance—even affection—for idiosyncrasy, it possessed no more vices, and was no more accustomed to random violence than, say, New York City—in fact, it probably was *less* accustomed to it, since New York was ridden with crime and corruption on a fantastic scale in those years, with a hopelessly undermanned police department, teeming ghettoes, and an arrogant and open criminality (some things

In this antic little vignette in the South Paw saloon of Encampment, Wyoming, all the gee-whiz
characteristics of the wildest of the West were parodied by an aficionado of the two-gun system.

Strong-jawed harlots laying in a supply of winter wood in
Dawson, Alaska, 1898—a footnote to mining civilization.

not seem logical to the forty-niners that foreigners
should have the same free opportunity as proper
Americans to get at what was left. So in 1850, a Foreign Miners' License Act was passed by the California
legislature, imposing a monthly tax of twenty dollars
on immigrant miners. This was repealed in 1851, since
its enforcement hurt foothill merchants, but was revived in 1852 at three dollars a month, then raised to
four dollars in 1854. Ostensibly, it was to be applied
impartially to all foreigners, but in fact it was only
enforced with regularity on the immediately visible
foreigners—which is to say, Chinese and Mexicans, and
most steadily on the former.

Sporadic lynchings and semi-pogroms were featured
throughout the state during the generally depressed
period of the 1850s; but the Chinese hung on, and in

The juices of life ran strong, and as long as you could laugh at the situation you could survive anything.
Above, members of the Cottonwood Placer Company satirize the amenities on the San Miguel River.

Gold meant miners, and miners meant there was money to be spread around—a fact not lost on western entrepreneurs of one ilk or another, many of them dealing in respectable goods; above, N. W. Savage opens a subsidiary in Cripple Creek, 1894.

their payment of the Miners' License fees contributed more than one million dollars to the county treasuries of the Mother Lode between 1850 and 1860. Nevertheless, feeling in the 1850s ran sufficiently high for Governor John Bigler to ask the state legislature in 1852 to prohibit further contract immigration; the legislature refused, but his action set the pattern for a systematic program of legislative efforts against the Chinese over the next thirty years, climaxing with the passage of a Chinese exclusion bill by Congress in 1882.

The antipathy against the Chinese exhibited in California was broadcast throughout the mining West, much as California's techniques of placer mining and self-government were transplanted. Samuel Bowles could report in 1865 that such antagonism was common not only in California but in the other Pacific states: "Thus ostracized and burdened . . . they, of course, have been the victims of much meanness and cruelty by individuals. To abuse and cheat a Chinaman; to rob him; to kick and cuff him; even to kill him, have been things not only done with impunity by mean and wicked men, but even with vain glory. . . . " In 1871, riots in Los Angeles killed twenty-two Chinese; in 1877, several Chinese were killed and beaten in San Francisco and

other California towns; in 1878, the entire Chinese population of Truckee was rounded up and driven out of town; in 1880, there were anti-Chinese riots in Denver; in 1885, riots in Rock Springs, Wyoming, killed twenty-eight Chinese; and a pogrom against them was launched in Log Cabin, Oregon in 1886.

This dismal chronicle suggests that the vaunted democracy of the mining frontier had its shortcomings.

Something of the quality of civilization brought to the West by the mining frontier is suggested by the preceding outline of its attitudes towards minorities. Perhaps an even more telling indication of what that civilization meant can be found in the question of law and order, and—most revealing of all—in the tradition of vigilantism which is strung through its history like a dark thread.

In most cases, the dream-seekers plunged into an environment utterly void of government. Since it was necessary to live with one another long enough to reap the benefits of their long searching, they had to come up with some kind of governmental system — and as usual, the pattern for that system had been forged in

Like many another mining town which discovered that helter-skelter construction, unplanned growth, and inadequate municipal services could spell disaster, Bisbee, Arizona, went to glory in 1908.

the California experience. Although it cannot be said that California was totally lacking in government, it was a singularly confused and inefficient one at the time of the Gold Rush—an uneasy mix of Spanish law and military jurisdiction under the aegis of the United States Army, which had neither the means nor the inspiration to adjudicate the private affairs of American citizens, particularly a horde of restless goldseekers.

To fill the vacuum, the miners borrowed from previous frontier experiences and devised what came to be known as "Miners' Law." Its most immediate concern was the establishment of rules concerning the ownership, extent, and transfer of mining claims (see Chapter XIII), but it also applied itself to the question of keeping the peace. Methodology was simple to the point of being primitive: only such serious crimes as murder, theft, and reasonless assault were considered significant enough to be dealt with; once an alleged malefactor was apprehended, he was given the form of a trial by a "miners' jury," which might be twelve good men and true or the entire community, with arguments presented by men extemporaneously appointed to serve as defense and prosecuting attorneys; once a verdict was reached, punishment was swift and

brutally to the point—since there were no jails, the convicted was either executed, branded, flogged, or banished from the district, depending upon the seriousness of his crime.

With very few exceptions, this was the form of law and order carried into the mining camps of the West. It was, to say the least, an imperfect form of justice, however swift and efficient, and for all the fact that it worked well enough to keep men from constantly robbing and murdering one another, it fell considerably short of the accolade given it by Charles H. Shinn in his *Mining Camps: A Study in American Frontier Government* (1884): "Rude mountain courts, rude justice of miner camps, truth reached by short cuts [is truth *ever* reached by short cuts?], decisions unclouded by the verbiage of legal lexicons, a rough-hewn, sturdy system that protected property, suppressed crime, prevented anarchy...."

It may well be that the system did protect property, suppress crime, and prevent anarchy, but one cannot help but wonder at what cost. For these "rude mountain courts" went on too long for too little reason. After 1850, when California began to structure the outlines of a working government, it might have been expected that the camps of the Sierra Nevada foothills would forgo such instant justice in favor of slower, but presumably more reliable forms of government. The men who populated them, after all, were not hard-edged pioneers unaccustomed to the mechanics of civic life; most had come from areas of the East that had been removed from a frontier condition for generations.

But the Miners' Law continued to be a prevalent force in these camps well into the 1850s, and it can only be assumed that they were still too much in a hurry, too concerned over the demands of the present, and too lazy, finally, to work out anything better. "Necessity" was the rationale, and in some places and times this was undoubtedly true; but it was not enough to justify the long life of a system that at best was expedient and at worst a miscarriage of civilization.

The social critic, Josiah Royce, writing just two years after Shinn, assaulted the theory of necessity: "Whose gold, now hoarded by the pound in insecure tents, the prey of every vagabond, might have contributed to build a strong jail at Coloma or at Jackson? Or, perhaps, was it not of a truth felt unnecessary to build a strong jail—unnecessary just because one chose in one's heart, meanwhile, to think ropes a little cheaper than bricks, and, for the purpose, just as strong. . . . Who whines perpetually and tediously, all through these early days, about 'necessity,' and 'the first law of nature,' and the defects of the social order, and all his gloomy social afflictions; even while, in fact, his whole purpose is to store his gold dust, to enjoy his private fun, and then to shake off the viler dust of the country from his feet as soon as possible? Who but the poor outraged miner himself . . .?"

Another factor may have been at work besides expediency and the lack of any real concern over the needs of the social order. The Miners' Law gave every man the opportunity to participate in government of a high order of drama. It would probably be going too far to maintain that it served as a kind of entertainment, a release from the incredible drudgery of mucking about after gold, but it cannot be denied that it provided moments of passion and power, a grim and self-satisfied sense that the goldseeker had taken part in something of great and sober purpose.

"It was regarded," Royce wrote, "as a matter of stern, merciless, business necessity. It was unconscious of any jocular character. Disorderly lynching affairs in some cases do, indeed, appear to have been mere drunken frolics. But nearly all . . . had in them no element of the merely jocular. They expressed an often barbarous fury; but they pretended to be deeds of necessity. . . . No one understands the genuine lynching who does not see in it a stern laying aside of all . . . characteristic American traits of good-humor and oratorical sentimentalism . . . for the sake of satisfying a momentary popular passion, aroused against the forces of disorder." This was heady stuff for men whose normal encounter with the forces of good and evil in their old lives would more than likely have had something to do with taxes or fines for swearing in public. Heady —and perhaps hard to give up.

Be that as it may, the Miners' Law created in the California camps was an essential ingredient in civilization's evolution on the mining frontier. At times, even this singularly extemporaneous form of justice was not considered swift and effective enough, and the spirit that had formulated Miners' Law conceived Vigilante Law—again in California first. As early as July, 1849, the goldseekers had resorted to a form of vigilante justice in San Francisco. When a group of Australian thugs and American ex-soldiers calling themselves the "Regulators" stormed into the camp's little tent community of Chileans and Peruvians, looting, killing, and raping, the decent citizens banded into little vigilante committees, ran down the Regulators, banished their leaders, and collected money to help the victims. It was a noble effort, and probably necessary; San Francisco's embryonic civic government, headed up by a handwringing *alcalde*, was utterly incapable of dealing with such a menace unassisted.

Increasingly arrogant escapades on the part of a large criminal element in the town—including a habit of setting San Francisco on fire from time to time for purposes of loot — inspired the formation of a more formal "Committee of Vigilance" in June of 1850. One of its leaders was Sam Brannan, a backsliding Mormon with all of the instincts of a firebrand, who articulated the committee's point of view: "We are the mayor and the recorder, the hangman and the laws."

In 1851, when it concluded that the situation had gotten out of hand, the committee went to work. It usurped the powers of the regularly constituted—and

Helena, Montana, (née Last Chance Gulch) typified the evolution from camp to city common to all the major districts of the mining West. At the right, downtown Helena is seen just twenty-five years after its founding.

Truth reached by a short-cut: the Miners' Court of Virginia City, Montana, considers the fate of alleged murderer George Ade in December, 1863.

unarguably corrupt — authorities for lack of action, hanged four men, flogged one, deported twenty-eight, later turned fifteen over to the government it had replaced, and released forty-one. Scores of the criminal element hustled themselves out of town voluntarily (one of the principal intents of the committee), scattering into the camps of the Mother Lode and as far south as Los Angeles. Upon their arrival, many of the towns imitated San Francisco's course of action by forming their own committees of vigilance and quickly running the refugees out of camp. For several months, criminals were shuttled from camp to camp in a ludicrous saraband, but many of them returned to San Francisco as soon as things cooled down and were quickly back to their old habits. They would not be significantly disturbed again until 1856, when a second Committee of Vigilance once again "cleaned up" San Francisco.*

*Strictly speaking, this second committee does not come within the scope of this discussion. In the first place, by 1856 San Francisco had long since evolved from the status of camp to that of city, complete with a well-established system of government. As such, the 1856 committee—superbly organized, efficient, utterly powerful, and totally defiant of established authority—was more in the line of a popular revolution than a move for expedient justice.

The San Francisco experience set the precedent for similar actions all over the West, from Idaho to Arizona, as the mining frontier probed into the isolated pockets of the wilderness. None would be quite as dramatic as that in Virginia City, Montana, in 1864. For two years, Bannock and Virginia City had been harrassed by a band of cutthroats whose homicide count reached a total of 102 before action was taken against them. Although President Abraham Lincoln had signed a law creating Montana Territory in May of 1864, there was as yet little in the way of government in the territory and the miners' courts were too slow and unreliable to satisfy what was seen as an immediate need: the elimination of the gang, quickly and once and for all.

Accordingly, after the long trial and ultimate execution of a murderer before a miners' court in December, 1863, a committee of vigilance was formed for "the laudable purpose of arresting thieves and murderers and recovering stolen property." That said, the committee went at it with a will. Between January 4 and February 3, 1864, it captured and either killed outright or executed by due process of hanging twenty-six members of the gang, including Henry Plummer, its leader. They had performed what Charles H. Shinn called "a

Democracy seeking out a scapegoat: in November, 1880, the good citizens of Denver vouch for the adequacy of the American Dream by raging through the Chinese quarter of the town, cutting off pigtails and destroying furniture.

On April 30, 1870, Helena's overworked Hanging Tree was ornamented with two additions when Joseph Wilson and J. L. Compton went to meet their Maker with stiff necks and with hoods removed to record the event.

solemn duty laid upon them as American citizens." There is no questioning the committee's performance; it was the single most expansive vigilante undertaking in the history of the mining West — although it was nearly matched the following year by the performance of Helena, whose committee of vigilance ultimately dangled thirteen men from the branches of its famous Hanging Tree.

For all its color and adaptability to the needs of myth, the tradition of vigilantism in the mining West contributed very little to the evolution of civilization. In fact, it might even be said that it hampered that evolution nearly as much as the criminality it was ostensibly designed to eliminate. It was a disruptive force, not one committed to growth. Those who promoted and participated in it did so not out of any shining dedication to the principles of righteousness but because lawlessness had reached a point where it could directly affect *them* personally—either by killing them or by making off with their property (it is not always easy to determine which was the more important). Up to that point, lawlessness was a purely abstract question, of no great concern to the average citizen, as outlined by historian Roger Olmsted: "When the most substantial citizens thought of nothing but buying and selling, when 'everyone was making money,' what difference did it make that petty bandits and barroom murderers went unapprehended; or if arrested, unindicted; or if indicted, swiftly acquitted; or if convicted, then pardoned, released, or assisted in escape?

"So it went in many places in the West . . . until at some point the arrogance, the insolence of swaggering blackguards provoked a violent revulsion and dramatic overreaction. The populace would acquiesce in cases of flagrant miscarriage of justice, would suffer an active criminal element to operate almost unchecked, would ignore jobbery, bribery, and all kinds of public chicanery—but it would not be *run over*."

There is one more aspect to the question of vigilantism in the West that needs examination—although to look at it at all is slightly unnerving, as if one were lifting the corner of something covering up a dark and unacknowledged blank in the American character. Vigilante action, by its very nature, was a violent business, dealing as a matter of course in such things as crime and punishment and death. For the most part, however, committees went about their business with the kind of grim righteousness described earlier by Josiah Royce. But once in a while, something broke loose in them, freeing almost daemonic bursts of a kind of joyless relish in the mechanics of death.

Consider, for example, this account of the hanging of the Sydney Ducks, Whittaker and McKenzie, by the Committee of Vigilance in August, 1851: "The unfortunate men were conveyed into the upper story of a building, where they were speedily pinioned; ropes were next adjusted out of two beams which protruded over the outside of the building. The noose of these ropes was placed around their necks and they were thrust out of the windows which overlooked the street. The ropes were pulled violently by members inside of the building, which nearly dashed the brains of the doomed men against the beams of which they were suspended. The crowd which had thronged about the building at this time was immense. The curses, jeers,

and imprecations which were heard on every side; the loud laugh and the obscene joke which was cracked in the crowd below; with the evident glee and humor with which the members of the Committee carried out their bloody purpose, will long remain vivid in the memories of those who witnessed these occurrences of blood. . . ."

For another example, consider the fact that a miners' court in Downieville, California, quickly hung a pregnant Mexican girl in 1851 for stabbing an Anglo miner in an argument. Aside from the fact of her obvious guilt, there was no visible justification for the execution; in almost any civilized society of the world, the woman would have been allowed to have her baby before dying—and in some societies would have been spared execution on the grounds of her sex alone. The miners could have banished her; they could have flogged her; they could even have gone out of their way and built a jail in which to house her—but they chose, almost without debate, to hang her, and one can only assume it was because they wanted and needed to see a woman hang.

Finally, consider one incident in the career of the Montana vigilantes. A posse of one hundred men cornered an outlaw in a mountain cabin. Before his capture, the man managed to kill one of his pursuers and wound another. In a nearly unconscious state, he was pulled from the cabin; the man he had wounded was allowed to empty his pistol into the body; a noose was placed around the neck of the already dead man and he was hoisted over the limb of a tree; for the next few minutes, a hundred eager rifles played target practice with the swinging corpse, until it was reduced to bloody ribbons; his cabin was then ignited and the body cut down and thrown on it for cremation. Afterwards, we can speculate that the vigilantes washed their hands, returned home, ate, and presumably slept like warm animals through the night, knowing that they had struck a blow for law and order.

Such incidents did not dominate the story of vigilantism on the mining frontier, but they occurred often enough to color it ghastly in at least some of its parts. That quality was present—sometimes invisible, sometimes evident—in the mechanics of civilization on the mining frontier. If one cares to reflect upon it, as the percipient Josiah Royce did nearly a century ago, it suggests "a world of horror behind the scenes."

CHAPTER THIRTEEN

DIPS, SPURS, AND ANGLES

Mining as a business and some of the finer points of larceny

"A Western mine is a hole in the ground owned by a liar...."

Mark Twain came by the wisdom expressed in the above quotation honestly. As soon as he arrived in the bustling silver camp of Virginia City in 1861, he managed to involve himself in the business of prospecting, laying out the boundaries of claims, registering them, working prospect holes, and selling out—mainly selling out. At the end of a few months, he concluded that mining was not all that it was cracked up to be, that it involved more work than he had counted on, that it paid poorly, if at all, that it was dominated by scoundrels who would cheat a nun on Sunday, and that he had better get into another line of work—like newspapering, which he took up on the muscular *Territorial Enterprise*. Both mining and journalism were better off for the decision; even at the tender age of twenty-six, he was too much of a skeptic and too little of a blackguard to make it in western mining circles.

He left his wisdom with us, however, and it is as good a touchstone as any with which to launch an exegesis on the convolutions of economic and legal questions regarding the mining frontier. It may help to look back on it from time to time as a kind of signpost of sanity in an otherwise confused world of high,

middle, and low finance; of stock jobbing and watering; of bulls and bears; of apex litigation and experting; of dividends and assessments, consolidation and capitalization; and of dips, spurs, and angles—always of dips, spurs, and angles.

First, there is the matter of the claim, the basic ingredient of the western mine. In placer mining, the claim was a fairly simple institution, being comprised of a square or rectangle of ground of locally specified dimensions, into which the miner could dig clear to bedrock and beyond if he chose. The method of regulating such claims fell into the process of Miners' Law described in Chapter 12. Each local area of a strike would form itself into a "district" by the simple expedient of a mass vote. A presiding officer was nominated and elected, together with a recorder, who would list and keep track of all claims.

A code of laws would then be pieced together, amended, and finally voted into existence; most often, these dealt only with matters relating to claim size, requirements of registration, the minimum "development" work a man must maintain on his claim in order to hold title to it (such as laboring on it "one day out of every three"), and usually a final stipulation to the effect that "no man within the bounds of this district shall hold more than one claim," a device calculated

Lest there be any uncertainty as to why the ownership of mining claims could lead to litigation, fistfights, and armed warfare, consider this 1900 map of the surface holdings of mines in Cripple Creek, Colorado.

to give every man an equal chance at the gold. Claim disputes, which usually involved who "got there first" or whether a man had in fact satisfied the working requirements to hold his claim, were adjudicated either by the presiding officer, the recorder, an elected "judge," a committee, or the entire camp. Once again, methodology developed in California became the standard by which the rest of the mining West functioned, and the Miners' Law of California eventually received official recognition by the United States Congress in 1870.

Lode mining was another matter. Since the normal vein possessed perambulatory instincts, the simple placering claim left too much to chance, forcing the miner to guess at where the vein might wander and placing his claim markers accordingly — and in the process perhaps missing the vein altogether. Once again, Californians came up with a solution, maintaining that ownership of the surface part of the vein, or apex, gave the miner the right to follow that vein, together with all its "dips, spurs, angles, and variations," as deep and as far as it led him, even if it took him beneath another man's claim. This became common practice throughout the mining West over the decade that followed the California Gold Rush, and it was given official sanction by passage of the "Apex Law" of 1866.

Unfortunately, the theory presupposed a simple mineral vein between two walls of rock, a vein as consistent and predictable as a slice of ham. Needless to say, this was rarely the case; among other disconcerting habits, veins had a way of "pinching out"—that is, narrowing to nothing—then picking up again somewhere further along—but whether such continuations were part of one original apex claim or another was sometimes almost impossible to tell, and the apex law inspired a growth of litigation over the years, as irate claimants to the same vein or veins tangled in courts from San Francisco to Denver.

"I never knew of such a quarrelsome, law-loving people as the Nevadians," engineer Louis Janin wrote in 1862. "There seem to be half-a-dozen claimants to each piece of property in the Territory, and each must go to law about it. We peaceful citizens think the lawyers keep up the dissensions, especially in mining claims, and often sigh out the wish that they were all hung." Janin was ahead of his time and had the wrong attitude; by the 1880s, many a mining engineer was making an excellent living by testifying for one side

or the other in cases of apex litigation—a procedure not dissimilar to that of psychiatrists testifying at a sanity hearing, and just about as bewildering to juries, whose knowledge of mining law was usually confined to the assumption that it was illegal to jump a claim.

Much of this litigation was purely for purposes of blackmail, as outlined by another engineer in 1890: "There are two characters to the value of mining properties—one mine may have a value, owing to its intrinsic worth; another (having no intrinsic value) may have a value by being so situated as to harass the working of the really valuable mine—in mining camps one is looked upon [sic] as much of legitimate enterprise as the other."

A popular game along these lines was "fractioning." A man would study claim maps of a district and pick himself out a small piece of unclaimed land, sometimes no more than a few square feet in area, between two good working claims. Having recorded his claim, he would either sit back and wait for one or the other of the two mines to start infringing upon "his" vein, or would immediately start to hint loudly at forthcoming litigation; in either case, getting rid of him was worth a small price to one or both of the mines, and many as itinerant entrepreneur made a gambling poke from such dubious activity.

Before it is assumed that Mark Twain's dictum concerning holes in the ground referred only to holes in the ground that were producing no ore, we had better take a look at the traditions of stock jobbery and manipulation as they were commonly practiced on the mining frontier. Operating a mine was not so simple a matter as just taking out profitable ore, breaking it down, refining it, and then selling it to the United States or foreign mints—the whole thing accomplished at a generous profit. Such simple operations occasionally did take place, it is to be supposed, but in a majority of cases, the real money to be made from a western mine was on the stock exchanges of San Francisco, New York, and London-Edinburgh.

The procedure was as simple as it was coolly exploitative, as outlined by John S. Hittell in his *History of San Francisco* (1878): "In a rich mine the quantity and quality of the ore produced and the appearance of the stopes must be regulated by the desire of the direc-

(Continued on page 258)

The Dale Gold Mining Company,

NUMBER
278

SHARES
#1000

CAPITAL, $1,000,000.00. SHARES, $1.00, EACH.

This is to Certify that J. D. Miller is the owner of One Thousand Shares of the Capital Stock of

THE DALE GOLD MINING COMPANY,

full paid and non assessable, transferable only on the Books of the Company in person or by Attorney on surrender of this Certificate.

In Witness Whereof, the President and Secretary have hereunto subscribed their names and caused its corporate seal to be hereto affixed at Marble Colo this 1st day of May A.D. 1900

J. H. Hoffman, Secretary.

L. Hoffman, President.

SHARES
$1.00
EACH

BONDED INSECURITIES...

*Until well into the twentieth century, the business of dealing in gold and silver stocks—
legitimate, semi-legitimate, and downright larcenous—was a large-scale enterprise that
kept many a San Francisco, New York, or London broker in the chips. Unfortunately
for the owners of these intricate wisps of paper, the potential value of a western mine was
unpredictable at best, and at worst had all the adventurous qualities of drawing to
an inside straight. In short, for each mining stock venture that had something solid in its
past or future there were hundreds whose only claim to glory lay in the minds of their
promoters, 99 44/100 percent of whom were a seedy, unreliable bunch. If we cannot
admire mining stocks as a source of steady income, however, we can admire them as art,
as the examples on this page and the following page will attest; the imaginative
flourishes of the average mining stock certificate were some of the earliest examples in
our cultural history of art attempting to surmount reality.*

SILVER LININGS, SLIGHTLY TATTERED...

There was a time, only a little less than a century ago, when the frantic trading of the Leadville Mining Exchange could bring palpitations to hearts in Denver, San Francisco, and New York, not to mention any number of foreign metropolises. Silver was its treasure, and for a time Leadville dominated the markets of the world; stock in its mines—the Highland Chief, the Little Pittsburgh, the Chrysolite, and even H. A. W. Tabor's famous and ultimately futile Matchless—crossed brokerage counters with blinding speed, creating and annihilating fortunes on all sides. Today, "Cloud City" sits quietly beneath its ring of mountains, cut off from the excitements of the past—save those it memorializes for the benefit of passing tourists.

Leadville, a still-functioning city of no mean proportions, is not quite so much of an anachronism as the tramways, headframes, mill buildings, and other mechanistic paraphernalia that dot Colorado's landscape; yet, like all the machinery, its principal impact is that of an echo of a time long past, when men dreamed their silver dreams unhampered by considerations of the future. That future is epitomized by the Homestake Mining Company's Bulldog Mine in Creede, Colorado (seen at the right), one of the few operating silver mines left in the West today. It is owned and operated by a corporation, not a man, and there is little possibility that elements of romance will ever be allowed to intrude. There will be no Tabors here, and there is night, these days, in Creede.

*Further notes on the transience of dreams: "Mines are comparable to humanity," mining
engineer Thomas A. Rickard once wrote. "The new discovery of a prospect is like
an infant, born today, which may die tomorrow, leaving no record, not even a name."
Rickard's career as a lyricist should have been cut short, but he was right.*

"A prospect resembles a young child," Rickard continued, "rich in possibilities but hedged around with all the uncertainties of immaturity. The promising prospect may succumb to the measles of bad management, or the whooping cough of inexperience." Above, the "promising prospect" of the Tomboy Mine, deteriorating near Rhyolite, Nevada.

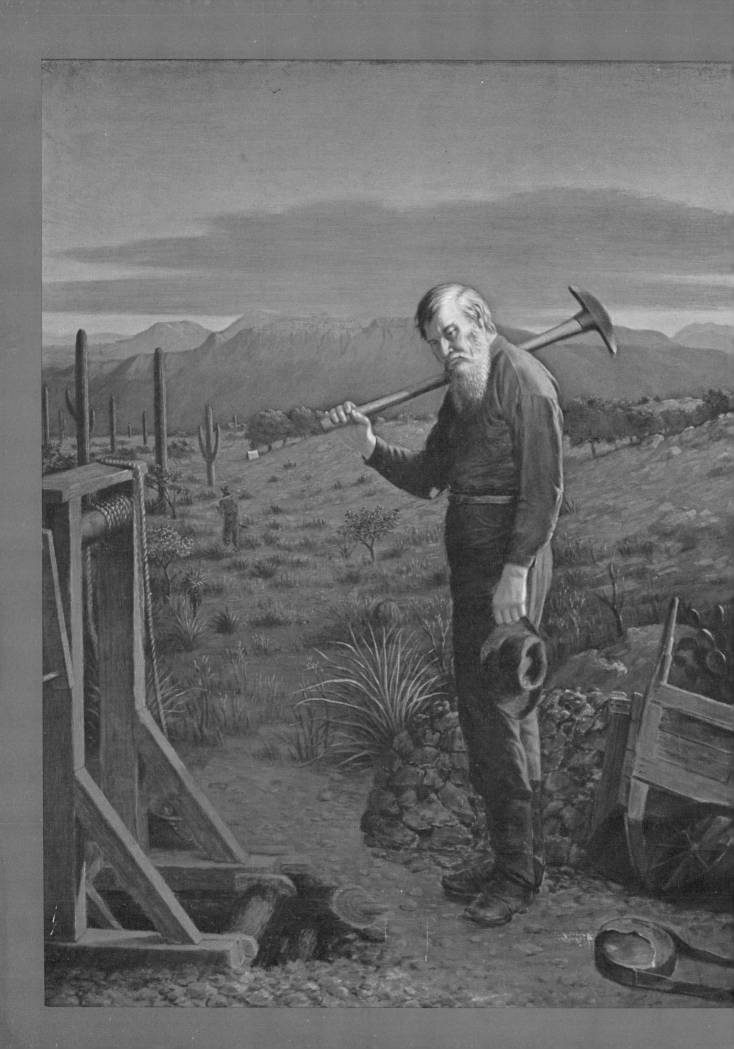

The Prospector

How strangely tonight our memory flings
From the face of the past the shadowy wings,
And we see far back through the mist and tears,
Which make the record of twenty years;
From the beautiful days in the Golden State,
When life seemed taking a lease of Fate;
From the wondrous visions of "long ago"
To the naked shade that we call "now."
Those halcyon days; there were four of us then —
Ernest and Ned, wild Tom and Ben.
Now all are gone; Tom was first to die;
We held his hands, closed his glazed eyes,
And many a tear o'er his grave we shed,
As we tenderly pillowed his curly head,
In the shadows deep of the pines that stand
Forever solemn, forever fanned
By the winds that steal through the Golden Gate
And spread their balm o'er the Golden State.
And the others, too, they all are dead!
By the turbid Gila perished Ned;
Brave, noble Ernest, he was lost
Amid Montana's ice and frost:
And Bennie's life went out in gloom
Deep in the Comstock's vaults of doom,
And we are left, the last of all,
And as tonight the cold snows fall,
And barbarous winds around us roar,
We think the long past o'er and o'er:
What we have hoped and suffered, all,

From the twenty years roll back the pall,
From the dusty, thorny, weary track,
As the torturous path we follow back.
In our childhood's home they think us, there,
A failure, or lost, till our name in the prayer
At eve is forgot. Well, they cannot know
That our toil through heat, through tempest and snow,
While it seemed for naught but a portion of pelf,
Was more for them, far more, than ourself.
Well, well, as our hair turns slowly to snow,
The places of childhood more distantly grow.
And our dreams are changing; 'tis home no more.
But shadowy hands from the other shore
Stretch nightly down, and it seems as when
We lived with Tom, Ned, Ernest, and Ben.
And the mountains of earth seem dwindling down
And the hills of Eden, with golden crown,
Rise up, and we think, in the last great day
Will our claims above bear a fine assay?
From the slag of earth and the baser stains
Will Death's crucible show of precious grains
Enough to give us a standing above
In the mansions of Peace, in the cradle of Love?
And thus do we dream while the tempests beat
While fall on our casement the ice and sleet,
And the fierce winds moan as they sweep the nights
Of these desolate hills, through these desolate nights;
So changed is life since the bright days when
We lived with Tom, Ned, Ernest, and Ben.

— C. C. Goodwin, 1872

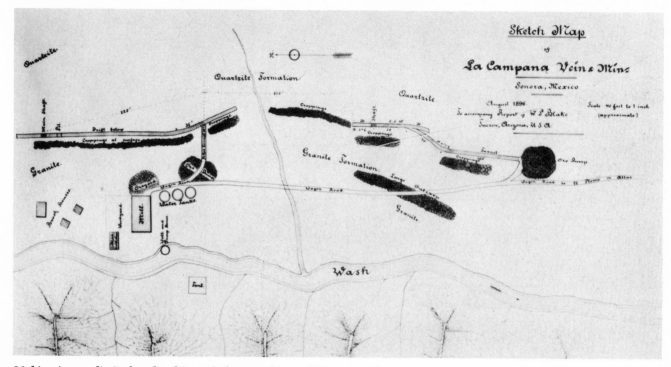

*Making it on a limited scale: this crude but graphic rendition of a mine
and its workings in Sonora, Mexico, in 1896 was typical of thousands of such
skeletal operations scattered across the West.*

tors to buy or sell. The rich deposits were concealed
when the stock was to be bought up, or worked with
every energy when it was to be thrown on the market.
The superintendent of every prominent mine conducted on such principles had his book of ciphers, so
that he could send secret messages to his masters and
let them know whether the ore was growing richer or
poorer, enlarging or diminishing in quantity.... Every
trick that cunning could devise to make the many pay
the expenses, securing to the few the bulk of the profit,
was practiced on an extensive scale, in the most active
of all the stock markets. On such a basis not less than
a dozen of the millionaire fortunes of San Francisco
have been built."*

*One had to be careful of one's superintendents, however, as
William C. Ralston and the Bank of California learned in 1871.
John P. Jones, the "super" at the Bank's Crown Point Mine, it
will be remembered (see Chapter 4), neglected to tell his em-
ployers that the mine was about to come into bonanza; instead,
with Alvinza Hayward, he bought up low-priced shares as fast as
they could be gathered in and ultimately gained control of the
mine. There is no honor among liars who own holes in the ground.

The phenomenon that made such brilliant manipulation possible was an absolute fever of speculation that
characterized the nature of western mining after the
discovery of the Comstock Lode; if California gold was
responsible for reviving the dream in the breast of
Everyman, then the Comstock Lode can be said to be
responsible for inspiring an apparently insatiable desire on the part of investors scattered from Charlotte,
North Carolina, to Edinburgh, Scotland, to speculate
wildly on the supposed fortunes of the American West.
This forty-year fever populated the West with a welter
of hopelessly unproductive mines, made instant millionaires of former shoe clerks, and as instantly wiped
them out, affected the fluctuations of markets from
Great Britain to the Continent, raised and lowered the
price of silver as well as gold, and made the San Francisco Stock Exchange the most active such institution
west of Wall Street.

Everyone speculated, not the least of which were the
miners of the Comstock themselves, as recalled by John
Taylor Waldorf in his reminiscences, *A Kid on the
Comstock:* "The favorite game with our fathers was

*By the time Tonopah entered the lists of western mining excitements, the Miners'
Exchange—seen behind the Goldfield-Tonopah stage—had become an established fact
of life. The Tonopah Exchange, fittingly, was bordered by a saloon and a cafe.*

stocks. We little fellows didn't understand it, but we
thought it would be made clear to us when we grew
up. Since then we've come to the conclusion we never
will be old enough to master it. . . . Women as well as
men put their all in stocks. When the newspaper came
flying over the fence or banged against the front door,
they seized it and turned hastily to the market page.
Though the front page told of the death of the nation's
greatest statesman or the blowing up of a czar, it made
no difference. They paid no attention to the news until
they had looked over the stock quotations."

The place where their hopes turned was a building
on Market Street in San Francisco, at first called the
Hall of San Francisco Board of Brokers, then as it grew
and grew, the Mining Exchange and finally the San
Francisco Stock Exchange—even today the largest west
of Chicago. Mark Twain, perhaps still carrying the
effects of wounds received on the Comstock, visited it
when it was still the Board of Brokers building and
reported his observations to the *Californian*: "The

place where stocks are daily bought and sold is called by
interested parties the Hall of the San Francisco Board
of Brokers, but by the impartial and disinterested the
Den of the Forty Thieves; the latter name is regarded
as the most poetic, but the former is considered the
most polite. The large room is well stocked with small
desks, arranged in semi-circular ranks like the seats of
an amphitheatre, and behind these sit the brokers. . . .
In a few moments the roll call was finished, the pencils
all sharpened, and the brokers prepared for business—
some with a leg thrown negligently over the arms of
their chairs, some tilted back comfortably with their
knees against their desks, some sitting upright and
glaring at the President, hungry for the contention to
begin. . . . Then the President called 'Ophir!' and
after some bidding and counter-bidding, 'Gould and
Curry!' and a babel arose—an infernal din and clatter
of all kinds and tones of voices, inextricably jumbled
together like the original chaos, and above it all the
following observation by the President pealed out
clearly and distinctly, and with a rapidity of enunci-
ation that was amazing: *'Fift'naitassfrwahn fift'nseft-*

five bifferwahn fift'naitfive botherty!' "

"I said I believed I would go home. My broker friend ... asked why I wanted to go so soon, and I was obliged to acknowledge to him that I was very unfamiliar with the Kanaka language, and could not understand it at all unless a man spoke it exceedingly slow...."

Such institutions were hardly unique to San Francisco. Local mining exchanges, most of them constructed with a brick or stone solidity that in no way hinted at the fragile, even ephemeral, nature of the business they served, sprang up in most of the major lode mining areas of the West—in Denver, Butte, Leadville, Colorado Springs, and Cripple Creek, among other places—and the hysteria of the San Francisco Exchange was duplicated with ritualistic enthusiasm in all of them. The West had become a great grab-bag of opportunity, or so everyone supposed, and if the disease of speculation made it possible for capitalists to play with their mines with the greedy instincts of children locked in a game of monopoly, then the hopelessly in-

adequate laws governing the function of corporations in the United States made it possible for people to be swindled outright by flimflam men with gargantuan ambitions.

Swindling, of course, on a greater or lesser scale, was already a practice with a long and suitably sordid history. In its most primitive form, it involved nothing more complicated than "salting" a prospect—that is, injecting it with rich ore from another mine—then selling it to some eager hopeful. Beginning with the California Gold Rush, salting had acquired the weight of tradition in a few years, probably coming to some kind of pinnacle when a group of promoters sought to advance the fortunes of Gregory Gulch in 1859 by salting a prospect for Horace Greeley; the mendacious claim which they showed him so excited the credible journalist that he sent out reams of prose that positively glittered with admiration.

Simple salting was a crude, second-rate sort of thing that lacked the sheer class of the stock swindles perpe-

Clarence King and the Mountain That Sprouted Diamonds

The remarkable success of the California Gold Rush, followed by the Comstock excitement of 1859 and the Big Bonanza of 1875—together with a soupcon of periodic detonations in between—solidly established the American West as the repository of dreams. Here was the treasure trove that had governed the intellectual and emotional thrust of generations; in this misty land of hope anything was possible—even probable. Nothing more thoroughly typified the degree to which dreams had vanquished reality in the West than the great Diamond Hoax of 1872, one of the most transparent frauds in the history of flimflam.

The story began in San Francsico, which is not surprising, considering the fact that she was a city built on dreams. In January, 1872, two slightly grubby miners walked into the Bank of California and deposited a sackful of diamonds, rubies, sapphires, and emeralds. Their names were John B. Slack and Philip Arnold, and their manner was nervous and insecure, in the fashion of men who have stumbled upon the answer to a prayer. Their deposit and their manner were sufficiently uncommon to attract the attention of William C. Ralston, president of the bank, who called them into his presence and listened—and listened. After some prodding, the pair confessed that, yes, they had indeed stumbled upon a major deposit of precious gems, although they stubbornly refused to say precisely where. Ralston convinced them there was a fortune to be made in the

trated throughout the latter third of the nineteenth century and the early years of the twentieth; both had one thing in common, however: a sure reliance on the pulse of larceny that beats in every human heart. The procedure was brutally uncomplicated. A syndicate would take over a worked-out or unproductive mine—or sometimes nothing more than a prospect hole—incorporate itself in a state with low standards of regulation and even lower corporation taxes, announce the issuance of a million or so shares of stock at a dollar a share or less (although the shares were usually printed up only as needed), and award themselves just enough shares to maintain control. They then would turn a team of high-pressure salesmen loose in areas of the country where mining was as unfamiliar an activity as the growing of hashish, bolstering their efforts with cheap advertisements in church bulletins, pulp magazines, newspapers, and any other form of print likely to fall into the hands of salesgirls, widows, spinsters, clerks, mailroom employees, and other "simple-minded people

in a fool's hurry to get rich," as engineer Thomas A. Rickard once described them. They offered a mind-boggling bargain: as many shares as you wanted in a genuine western gold or silver mine at prices as low as ten or fifteen cents the share. When the shares had been sold out, the company regretfully announced that the mine had failed (when they bothered to make any announcement at all), split up the proceeds, and disbanded like Arabs folding up their tents and stealing away in the night. It was a nearly foolproof scheme: the initial investment was minor, the returns were quick, the small number of shares sold to any one person was usually so small that no one was likely to want to pursue the matter, and prosecution was next to impossible.

The nationwide scope of such efforts is illustrated by information gleaned from a rare investigation into an Oregon mine swindle at the turn of the century. Out of 1,250,000 announced shares valued at one dollar apiece (an uncommonly high price for such ephemera),

gem industry, and they reluctantly agreed to let him and a few select individuals in on the venture. Ralston shipped the gems off to Tiffany's of New York for an expert appraisal, and sent two blindfolded engineers with Slack and Arnold to investigate the discovery location itself. Tiffany's reported that the gems were worth $150,000, and the engineers were enthusiastic over finding diamonds sticking out of the earth. The San Francisco and New York Mining and Commercial Company was formed, including Ralston, twenty-five San Franciscans who put up $80,000 apiece, Baron Ferdinand Rothschild of London, and Charles Tiffany and Horace Greeley of New York.

Ralston was a cautious sort, however, and he engaged a young, but respected mining engineer by the name of Louis Janin to investigate the gem field for $2,500, expenses, and an option to buy one thousand shares of the company at an optional price. Janin went, and returned so enthusiastic that he took up Ralston on the stock option. That was all that was needed. The company's stock sold rapidly. San Francisco boiled with talk of western diamond mines. All this high finance proved to be too much for the simple prospectors Slack and Arnold; they sold their interest in the company for $300,000 each and a share in any future profits, and promply faded away. Shortly afterwards, Janin relinquished his shares for $40,000.

In the meantime, Clarence King, a young geologist with the United States Geological Survey (he appears at the far right in the photograph at left), arrived in San Francisco and became intrigued with all the talk about diamond mines.

His interest was natural enough; among other good reasons, he had once written that there were no precious gem deposits in the United States. His reputation was at stake, and to vindicate it, he calculated from newspaper reports that the diamond finds were somewhere in northern Utah and hauled himself and an assistant off to find them. He did and was at first excited; there were diamonds, all right, many of them just under the surface of the ground. His excitement turned to skepticism when the diamonds displayed a tendency to appear in conjunction with rubies, and he became downright cynical when his assistant held up a diamond and exclaimed, "Look, Mr. King! This diamond field not only produces diamonds but cuts them also!"

King returned to San Francisco and issued a report: "Summing up the minerals, this rock has produced four distinct types of diamonds, a few oriental rubies, garnets, spinels, sapphires, emeralds, and amethysts—*an association of minerals of impossible occurrence in nature.*" Slack and Arnold, it developed, had salted the region with $25,000 worth of reject gems purchased from German jewel merchants; Tiffany's was unaccustomed to the evaluation of uncut gems and had overvalued the merchandise. Ralston, a man of conscience, was left with the bag; he paid off each of the twenty-five investors. Clarence King's reputation was not only vindicated but nourished. And Louis Janin? He went on to become a pillar of the mining profession, but one wonders a little about how much he knew of the whole business when he sold off his shares for that healthy $40,000.

The first indication that a mining town had transcended the insecurities of camp status was the erection of a brick building—and the first brick building was often a bank, as shown above in Ouray, Colorado.

it was discovered that 25 shares had been sold in California, 14 in Canada, 11 in Delaware, 106 in Illinois, 25 in Indiana, 422 in Iowa, 61 in Kansas, 16 in Maine, 27 in Maryland, 63 in Massachusetts, 14 in Mississippi, 49 in Missouri, 48 in Nebraska, 18 in Minnesota, 16 in New Jersey, 68 in New York, 95 in Pennsylvania, 70 in Washington, 50 in Wisconsin, and the remainder in other states of the Union—relatively few of them in the mining states of the West, whose residents presumably had learned by then to be cynical of such things.

Not all mining promotions were so blatantly dishonest as the kind of operations outlined above. Some of them actually involved working mines, with real ore, a collection of employees, engineers' reports, and superintendents. Yet even these were inclined to be projects

designed to bring in a quick dollar and run by promotion companies more interested in rape than in development; once the richest ore had been scraped out of them to assure a quick profit, they were abandoned to the vagaries of wind and weather and whatever fly-by-night operation that might follow; employees found themselves without jobs, and investors found themselves holding stock that might or might not have paid one or two quick dividends and was now valueless.

At the other extreme, owners and managers of good mines—mines actually being developed with care to assure a long-term productivity—often found themselves pressured into precisely the same kind of helter-skelter exploitation by investors who cared not a damn for patience and steady, if unspectacular production: they wanted dividends, they wanted them high, and they wanted them *now*. These and other factors con-

262

A solid granitic manifestation of progress, enterprise, and speculation was exhibited by the Mining Exchange Building in Denver, Colorado—the largest between Chicago and San Francisco

The characteristic aspect of the floor of the Cripple Creek Mining Exchange at the turn of the century—as with all such institutions—was a sea of fingers, each of them representing a bid.

tributed to the fact that there were remarkably few mines scattered through the West that were operated on anything close to a businesslike basis—and those few tended to be the giants of the industry, mines so extensive in property and so rich in ore that they leap out of the history of the mining frontier like monoliths thrust up through the surface of the earth—the Empire Mine of California, the Homestake of South Dakota, the El Paso of Cripple Creek, the Bunker Hill and Sullivan of the Coeur d'Alenes, and a handful of others.

For most of the rest, it was a speculator's game, as stable as quicksilver and as predictable as the fall of dice in a Goldfield saloon. As an old-time engineer once put it, "If I were investing in mining companies fifty years ago, I would much rather have the capital that went into the ground, instead of the returns that came out!"

Under the circumstances, it is somewhat astonishing

that the mining West was able to sustain its reputation as an investor's delight for more than forty years—but it did, and one of the regions in which it survived possibly longer than in any other was in England, whose empire may have been crumbling but whose steady, stiff-upper-lip optimism gladdened the hearts of western mining promoters for nearly two generations. England's interest in western mining began early, as noted in Chapter X, with the purchase in 1850 of the Almaden Quicksilver Mine in California by the firm of Barron, Forbes and Company. They were forced to sell out quickly, but British interest had been tantalized. It was further tantalized when Comstock silver began to flood world markets in the early 1870s, depressing prices to such an extent that several European countries, including France, ceased the minting of silver coins in an attempt to hold the price of silver at its old levels. American mining promoters were quick to smell out the sud-

Leadville's Mining Exchange had nothing to feel ashamed of when compared to that of Cripple Creek—although here the fingers seem to be at parade rest.

den urge British investors had acquired, and as early as 1872, they haunted the banking and investment houses of London and Edinburgh.

Benjamin Moran, the more than slightly snobbish secretary to the United States Legation in London, remarked on their presence early in 1872: "I have observed that they are a much lower class now than in any year heretofore in my time. There is seldom a gentleman among them. On the contrary the great majority are badly dressed and badly behaved, with rude manners and poor address. Nearly all are speculators and not a few have silver and gold mines to sell which are generally swindles. But the eagerness with which the British catch at these manifest frauds is remarkable. The result is that our credit is being damaged, and the popular idea that we are rascals—which was dying out —is rapidly being revived."

One of the most spectacular opportunities being

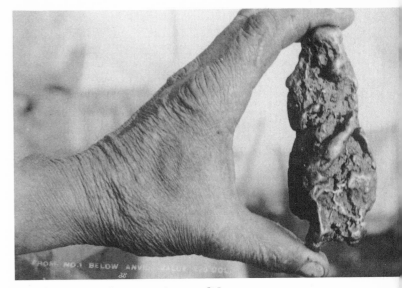

The object of much arm-waving: a solid gold nugget worth $320.

265

offered to British investment by those rude fellows was an enterprise called the Emma Mine, a silver lode that had been discovered in Utah's Cottonwood Canyon in 1868. Its discoverers, lacking the capital to develop it, had gone to investors in San Francisco, Wisconsin, and New Jersey for the wherewithal, and these promoters decided to sell it in England. Armed with a glowing report of the mine's potential from engineer Benjamin Silliman, Jr., of Yale, who had been paid the grand sum of $25,000 for his opinion, the promoters managed to interest British investment to the tune of one million pounds sterling—approximately five million American dollars. The deal was no sooner consummated than rumors that the mine's ores had been gutted began to filter into the country, but these did not discourage at least one investor, who penned the following eulogy to the Emma Mine for the *Mining World* of London:

> Emma's faith and Emma's trust
> Write their characters in "dust":
> Stamp them on the Mormon stream,
> Weight them on the Miner's beam.
> Of her fluctuating scrip
> I will hold a firmer grip;
> She's less changeable I ween
> Than faint-hearted suitors deem.
>
> Her I wooed in her debut,
> Followed when in fame she grew;
> When the bears her downward bore,
> Then I bought her more and more.
> The average of her scrip I ween
> Cost me less than seventeen,
> And my dividends, I'm sure,
> Are enough, and will endure.
>
> Comrades! toast our Emma dear
> Midst our New-Years' festive cheer.
> Henceforth in no monthly driblets,
> But in handsome quarter triplets,
> Shall our Emma's gains be quoted—
> So her guardians sage have voted.
> Emma! best of tochered lasses!
> Emma! drain in peace your glasses.

There will always be an English poet.

Unfortunately, the rumors were all too true: the Emma, poetry notwithstanding, was a swindle of fantastic proportions. Its demise, coupled with the worldwide depression of 1873, stifled British investment for a while—but not for long, given the determination of the English. Clark C. Spence, in *British Investments and the American Mining Frontier* (1958), estimates that at least 274 companies with a capital investment of somewhere between forty and fifty million pounds operated sporadically in the American West between 1860 and 1901.

The returns on this investment were dismal in the extreme. Perhaps one in every nine companies ever paid any kind of dividends, and, as Spence reports, "many of these were but token payments of slight significance; sustained dividend payers are more difficult to locate. Probably no more than ten joint-stock companies registered in London or Edinburgh for operation in the prescribed area ever returned the shareholders' full investment in dividends." It is worthwhile noting, too, that of those companies that could be called successful, or at least not total failures, two of the *most* successful were copper companies.

In all fairness to American mining, it should be pointed out that the British investor got more or less what he deserved. He was one of the worst offenders, in fact, in the formation of ruinously exploitative development techniques—adequately summed up in the spirit of get it and get out. "Obviously," Spence says, "the Englishman consented to pouring his hard earned funds down an unpredictable hole in an unknown wilderness thousands of miles from home but for one reason: he believed profits would result. And all too frequently the English investor was interested only in immediate profits and lost no time in making known his sentiments to his fellow shareholders." The price of such economic colonialism was failure more often than not; but if it was hard on the English investor, it was even harder on the victim of his greedy clamoring: the American West.

I have gone on at such length concerning British investments, not because they were economically important (they probably comprised less than 2 percent of the total capital investment in the mining West), but because they seem to illustrate most dramatically the one major dynamic in the financial history of the min-

Riding away with a small fortune, this teamster and his two young assistants exhibit a degree of forgivable pride in contemplating three profoundly rich nuggets from the Smuggler-Union Mine of Telluride, Colorado, ca. 1890.

ing frontier: its one-sided dependence on the manipulations of men hundreds and thousand of miles removed from the scene of the action.

It was typical of an era that might be called the Golden Age of Rape in the American West—or, as social historian Vernon L. Parrington put it, the "Great Barbecue." It was an age that saw lumbermen launch an assault against the forests of the West, whose legacy we are still trying to live with; it was a time when cattlemen and sheepmen used the public domain so badly that prairies were converted to deserts in a generation; it was a time when industrial farming so overworked the soil of the Great Plains that it ultimately produced the Dust Bowl of the 1930s.

In large part, these industries were financed by capital developed in California, the East, and even Europe, and if industrial mining in the West was somewhat less physically damaging to the environment than clear-cutting, overgrazing, and soil malnutrition, it was nonetheless in the same short-sighted traditions of exploitation. Relatively little of the wealth carved out of the

mountains and deserts of the trans-Mississippi West ever found its way back into the social and economic structure of the region from which it had come. Its gold and silver had helped to finance American wars, had built mansions on San Francisco's Nob Hill and New York's Park Avenue, had fattened the treasury of the Bank of California and the Bank of London, and had enabled former washerwomen to marry their daughters off to noblemen and their sons to princesses.

In the process, it also built cities where cities would have otherwise had no business being, brought railroads and settlements to great sweeps of the West, created government and established territories or states where none had been before, and speeded the process of civilization in mountains and deserts; this is a grace note in the story, but there is no denying the fact that its major theme is one of misuse and exploitation by men who knew little of the American West and cared less.

It was not that the "holes in the ground owned by liars" were so bad, finally; it was that so many of the owners were *absentee* liars.

CHAPTER FOURTEEN

AN EPILOGUE
FOR DREAMERS

Aftershocks, memories, and legacies

"They remind you of the crowd which Vathek found in the hall of Eblis, each darting hither and thither with swift steps and unquiet mien, driven to and fro by a fire in the heart. Time seems too short for what they have to do, and result always to come short 'of their desire...."

In just sixty years, the dream had come to its greatest fruition in the history of man—two generations, a span of time whose events could be experienced and remembered by both fathers and sons. In those sixty years, the hope that had been carried to the New World by *conquistadores,* given new life by the discoveries at Zacatecas, then abandoned by the colonists of New England, had been revived to a level that exceeded all earlier experience.

It was a time filled with the high virulence of fever; men infected by it were imbued with the courage to assault mountains against all logic, driven by the blind desire of greed; incredible financial empires were erected in a matter of months, and as quickly disintegrated; towns, cities, and states were thrust willy-nilly into existence, and even the nation itself was shaken to its roots at times. If the story of this country's pilgrimage is "mad with the impossible," as Bernard DeVoto has written, then no part of that narrative is more robust than the story of gold and silver in the West.

Sixty years of high drama, and then the dream faded to the palest reflection of its former glory. Like any great natural or man-made trauma, however—such as earthquakes and wars—the dream had its aftershocks. In 1933–1934, several thousand hopefuls wandered into the still-hostile Mojave Desert of Southern California following the discovery of gold-bearing veins; each of them was convinced that he would discover a mine as "rich" as the Silver Queen, whose ore assayed at forty-three dollars a ton; only a handful, needless to say, found anything that came close—and this little "boom" died out like all the rest, after stirring a small amount of excitement in the saloons and barbershops of Victorville and Barstow.

The depression years were a time when too many men had little but hope to go on, and this factor doubtless contributed to the creation of any kind of boom at all. It certainly contributed to a phenomenon common throughout the West during the 1930s: the existence of thousands of men, women, and children who spent the summer months supplementing anemic or nonexistent incomes by panning, rocking, and sluicing for gold in gulches and gullies abandoned nearly a century before. Somewhere between ten and fifteen thousand of them scrambled over the foothills of California alone in this decade, and the remarks of one of these part-time goldseekers reveals that if their motives were nothing less than simple survival, some residue of the dream yet remained: "Anyway, it's a clean life. We

269

don't get much gold, average only about 75 cents a day, but it's healthy up here and it's a pretty good vacation. ... It's hard work and at five o'clock you can't very often say, 'Another day, another dollar,' but you can say 'Another day, another four bits, or six bits,' and that's something. And then there's always the chance of really striking it rich."

Always a chance ... The litany of romance was a long time dying, but by the middle of the 1930s the litany was little more than lip service to a dream long past. More prosaic resources had long since replaced the "romantic" minerals of gold and silver in the West. For if the sixty years of frenetic searching in the high and the flat and the wrinkled land of the trans-Missississippi West had done nothing else, it had implanted an image of the West as a vast storehouse of mineral treasure—all kinds of mineral treasure: copper, lead, zinc, aluminum, mercury, manganese, and tungsten, as well as petroleum and a *soupçon* of such esoteric items as molybdenum and vanadium.

If gold and silver were the romantic minerals because of their relatively abstract use as "money," then these were the unromantic minerals, the useful minerals, minerals utilized to build and power the machines of civilization. They were understandable, and they were profoundly more important economically than gold and silver. By the middle of the twentieth century, the relative insignificance of romance to the economics of the West and the nation was painfully apparent. In 1950, gold and silver contributed a little over $122,-000,000 to mineral production in the West—or less than 2.5 percent of the total of more than five billion dollars in minerals produced by the fourteen states that had figured prominently during the halcyon years of gold and silver. Copper in Montana, Nevada and Arizona, petroleum in California, Colorado, Wyoming, and Texas, zinc in Washington, lead in Idaho, coal in Alaska ...

But with the exception of the petroleum industry, which had its own history of booms and busts, wild-eyed speculation, and prospecting, most of these were dull exercises in the mechanics of extraction, possessing

Equipped with all the materials necessary for the implementation of dreams, this "Pikes Peak Prospector" simulates an expedition for treasure.

Posing in 1897 as a living monument to dead hopes, this Montana prospector summarized the common fate of the dream-seeker: barren rock.

little or no romance, nothing to capture the imagination of contemporary America or inspire flights of eloquence from historians. And by 1950 even petroleum, in and of itself never a very appealing mineral, had lost much of its excitement; dreaming seemed to have gone out of western mining, replaced by machines and geologists' reports, the stolid paraphernalia of technology. Then in 1951, the Atomic Energy Commission stepped into the picture, and for the next six years the West experienced one of the most remarkable mining rushes in its history.

Uranium, like gold and silver, is a singularly romantic mineral in the sense that its use is abstract—abstract at least within the comprehension of normal human intelligence. It is used in the manufacture of atomic and hydrogen bombs and in the production of atomic energy for purposes of fueling—both processes having something to do with $E = mc^2$ and other mathematical delights, and both as mysterious to the average mind as the mechanics of transubstantiation.

Known for years, and frequently found in combination with gold and copper in various parts of the West, uranium had been considered almost useless until the early 1940s, when the United States began its secret construction of the atomic bomb; much of the uranium that went into the making of the bombs that were dropped on Hiroshima and Nagasaki in 1945, in fact, was gleaned from the tailings of mills and smelters in Utah, Colorado, and New Mexico—some of it from enterprises that had been throwing away uranium for decades.

With the end of World War II and the emergence of the United States as defender of the world against Communism, the production and stockpiling of bombs

The legacy of waste: man-made earthen turrets and spires in Malakoff State Park, California, testify to the destructive power of hydraulic mining before its own success destroyed the industry in 1884.

steadily increased, until the Atomic Energy Commission considered it necessary to increase uranium mining by offering generous incentives in 1949; these took the form of percentage payments by the federal government based on the uranium content of ore produced. Beginning with a flat fee of $7.00 per ton for ore that contained 1 percent of uranium, a system of premiums and bonuses raised the price to as high as $1,694.50 per ton for ore containing 10 percent of uranium—with corresponding geometric increases for ore that contained an even higher percentage of the mysterious mineral.

These were prices that challenged the best that gold and silver had offered in the most affluent years of their domination, and the result was predictable: hundreds of former shoe clerks, dude ranch operators, cowboys, stockbrokers, and garage mechanics leaped into the wilderness of Nevada, Utah, Colorado, Wyoming, and New Mexico, equipped with jeeps, house trailers, beans, beer, and geiger counters for the detection of radiation-loaded treasure.

The boom remained a generally local excitement until the spring and summer of 1952, when Charles Steen, a professional—but by no means affluent—geologist, and Vernon Pick, a former car dealer, each made spectacular discoveries near Moab, Utah. Steen named his the Mi Vida, and it was estimated to be worth no less than one hundred million dollars; Pick called his the Delta, and promptly sold it for ten million dollars to the Atlas Corporation, which proceeded to rename

The excrescence of mining in Cripple Creek—as in all other mining regions of the West—was exhibited in 1904 by dump-piles that looked like the work of gigantic gophers; muted by weeds, most are still visible today.

its new acquisition the Hidden Splendor.

Here was the stuff of glory once again, and the local adventure soon became one that approached national dimensions. Newspapers from San Francisco to New York, as well as such national magazines as *Look, Life,* the *Saturday Evening Post, Reader's Digest,* and *McCall's* gave this curious new Golconda pages and pages of nearly hysterical coverage. Eastern and far western investment firms found a new opportunity. Sleepy little desert hamlets like Moab and Grants, New Mexico, found themselves booming. "Atomic Motels" popped into existence and bars renamed themselves the "Uranium Club."

By the middle of the decade, there were eight hundred mines hauling out uranium ore of varying quality in regions scattered from the Big Indian district of Utah to the Gas Hills district of Wyoming, from the deserts of Nevada to those of New Mexico. Atomic Energy Commission geologists cruised over the mountains in airplanes equipped with scintillators for the detection of "hot spots," and ten thousand or more amateurs stumbled around in dismal wilderness country equipped with little more than blind optimism and sundry electronic gadgets that whirred, buzzed, clicked, and beeped when in the presence of uranium—or so their manufacturers promised.

Every year, the government purchased nearly $150,000,000 worth of uranium ore. Hundreds of millions of dollars in uranium stocks crossed the counters of brokerage houses and the bars of taverns. Claim disputes and outright swindles proliferated, and at least one murder was perpetrated in the name of greed. As described by Edward Abbey in his *Desert Solitaire,* these were "years of feverish struggle, buying and selling, cheating and swindling, isolation, loneliness, hardship, danger, sudden fortune and sudden disaster."

And then, after starting the whole business with its openhanded generosity, the AEC proclaimed in 1957 that the government had almost all the uranium it needed, thank you, and that no ore would be purchased from any mines discovered after that year. Prospecting died; geiger counters were placed on closet shelves, and deeds to undeveloped claims were tucked away in bureau drawers. A hundred paper millionaires were left

The detritus of a momentary civilization: an abandoned mine shaft in Cerillos, New Mexico, 1970.

with a wealth of paper. In the middle of the 1960s, the boom was revived with the emergence of nuclear-fueled power plants for the generation of electricity, but by then big business thoroughly dominated the industry, as corporations like Homestake, Union Carbide, Anaconda, Newmont, and Phelps-Dodge shouldered aside the part-time prospector and the small-time operator in a pattern common to western mining for more than a century.

In just fifteen years the great uranium rush had repeated the old boom-and-bust cycle in an intense, almost miniatured form. The dream had enjoyed one last flourish.

Copper, king of the West: an overview of the Sacramento Pit today in Bisbee, Arizona.

In 1965, the last of California's great gold quartz mines, the Sixteen to One of Alleghany, closed down operations. The mine's attorney articulated the problem for gold mining all over the West when he said, "You cannot produce gold at a cost of $50 an ounce and sell it for $35 an ounce and stay in business forever." During and after the years of World War II, hundreds of mines closed down one by one, sinking beneath the pressure of rising production costs—costs that were not matched by a corresponding increase in the purchase price of gold.

Silver mining faced a similar dilemma, one compounded when the United States ceased the minting of silver dollars and cut back on its use of silver in other coins. The federal government, which for decades had supported both industries with its purchases, felt that the nation's currency was sufficiently backed by gross national product, and no longer saw any need to support it with either gold or silver reserves.

Some of the pressure was taken off gold mining when the government allowed the private purchase of gold in 1968; the resulting "free" market* introduced some flexibility in the purchase price of gold, which fluctu-

*The market is not quite so free as, say, shoes or bottle openers. Under strict licensing, gold may be purchased privately only in specific quantities and for specific purposes.

"He believes in hope, but thinks he has lived on that long enough, and would now like something a little more substantial." The words are from 1861, and the picture from more modern times, but the core of truth remains.

ates between $37.00 and $43.00 the ounce in the private sector; what little government purchasing is left is still based on the old standard of $35.00. Silver rarely rises above $2.00 the ounce, and today is at about $1.75. In neither case do such prices reflect a proper balance between production costs and potential profit; one estimate has it that for the average gold mine to produce at a profit, the purchase price of gold would have to rise to $175.00 the ounce. As a result, gold and silver mining have declined to an embarrassingly low point.

Today, most silver is mined strictly as a by-product of various "base" minerals, such as lead and copper, although the Homestake Mining Company has opened a producing silver mine in Creede, Colorado, presumably hoping for the best, and a few similarly big companies have silver operations going in the San Juan Moun-

tains. And while gold dredging and hydraulicking still take place—principally in Alaska—there are only two major gold mines left in the United States.

The Homestake Mine of Lead, South Dakota, the largest, still produces more than two million ounces of gold every year (if it survives the vicissitudes of the economy, the mine will soon celebrate its centennial). In northern Nevada, the Carlin Mine of the Tuscarora Mountains (owned by the New York–based Newmont Mining Corporation, not surprisingly) has developed refining techniques that enable it to recover gold in particles that can only be seen through an electron microscope. Spreading for miles over the Nevada landscape, this wonderfully destructive operation is one of the largest open-pit mines in the world; an indication of the earth-moving involved in its processing is given

276

by the fact that it requires the removal of seven tons of rock to obtain one ounce of refined gold.

There are those who insist that gold and silver will someday have a revival, *must* have a revival. With this country's gold reserves down to about ten billion dollars and with the annual gold drainage to foreign countries through foreign aid, military spending, and imbalance of payments approaching eight hundred million dollars every year, there obviously must come a time when the government will have to resume large purchasing to make up for the difference—unless the country decides to abandon the concept of treasure reserves entirely, a not impossible happenstance in this unpredictable world. Some maintain that this cannot happen, and perhaps it can't. Yet it is significant that both the Homestake Mining Company and the Newmont Mining Company, the two largest gold and silver mining corporations in the country, are covering their bets with expansive operations in uranium, lead, zinc, and iron—and even in such pragmatic items as potash and aggregate. Faith is not enough.

If the future of gold and silver in the West is dim, perhaps even moribund, then what of its past—its legacy? Economically, there is little to celebrate. All the gold and silver mining in all parts of the West in the 120 years since 1849 probably has not produced more than twenty billion dollars in treasure (although precise figures are impossible to calculate)—an amount equal to less than two years of the West's annual *agricultural* product alone, much less the output of its other industries. If gold and silver mining created cities and states where none had been before, it remained for less romantic enterprises to settle and develop them for the future; the mining itself left little more than the memory of rape, for it took as much as it could as fast as it could, and it gave back as little as possible.

The physical remnants of the dream may have some air of romance about them, but they can hardly be called attractive: open cuts scar the landscape of the Black Hills; mountainous molehills of dumps and tailings clutter the mountains of Colorado; crumbling ghost towns dot the deserts of Nevada; abandoned piles of rusting machinery litter the wilderness of Alaska; man-made canyons and badlands in California attest to the destructive power of hydraulic mining, and ancient windrows of tailings from gold dredges lace river bottoms in Montana. If such things make up a legacy, then it is a legacy of waste.

What is left of the dream that we can cherish, finally, is a memory—the memory of a great adventure that had no precedent and will have no repetition. The mechanics of the dream have fallen to storytellers and historians, and to commercial entrepreneurs who are making a very good thing indeed of the elements of the past. Towns in which men once "toiled and wrestled, and lived a fierce, riotous, wearing, fearfully excited life," as they were once described, have taken to recreating their past for the sake of tourists; today, for an appropriate fee, you can tour abandoned mines in Virginia City (Nevada), Tombstone, Cripple Creek, and Deadwood. Weekenders don skin-diving outfits and swim around in mountain rivers in search of gold for the fun of it, and children squat by the sides of Sierra Nevada streams and pan for gold, playing at a dream for which men once died.

And that is what is left of a compulsion that called men across mountains. If they had known what would become of their fond visions, it would not have made the slightest difference, we can be sure. Such cosmic reflections were beyond them; there were fortunes to be made, empires to be built. James Bryce, British ambassador to the United States and one of the most perceptive observers of the American scene ever to visit these shores, described them in 1889 in his brilliant *American Commonwealth;* his words will serve as well as any for an elegy to dreams: "This constant reaching forward to and grasping at the future does not so much express itself in words . . . as in the air of ceaseless haste and stress which pervades the West. They remind you of the crowd which Vathek found in the halls of Eblis, each darting hither and thither with swift steps and unquiet mien, driven to and fro by a fire in the heart. Time seems too short for what they have to do, and result always to come short of their desire. . . . Sometimes in a moment of pause . . . one is inclined to ask them: 'Gentlemen, why in heaven's name this haste? You have time enough. No enemy threatens you. No volcano will rise from beneath you. Ages and ages lie before you. . . . You dream of your posterity; but your posterity will look back to yours as the Golden Age, and envy those who first burst into this silent, splendid Nature.' "

A GLOSSARY OF
MINING TERMINOLOGY

Adit: The entrance to a mine; if driven into the earth vertically, or on a steep incline, the adit is called a "shaft"; if driven horizontally, it is called a "tunnel."

Amalgam: The combination of mercury (quicksilver) with one or another metals after milling, generally gold.

Apex: The "edge" or "crest" of an ore vein that is nearest the surface.

Arrastra: A Spanish device used for the free milling of gold or silver; a circular pit whose bottom was lined tightly with rock facing, over which heavy stones were dragged, usually by horse- or mule-power, to grind ore.

Assay: A chemical procedure by means of which the commercial value of ore is determined.

Auriferous: Earth that contains particles of gold, or gold in combination with some other mineral.

Blossom rock: Float ore that has decomposed from outcroppings.

Bonanza: The discovery of rich ore; in Spanish, "blue skies."

Borrasca: The opposite of bonanza; in Spanish, "barren rock."

Breasting: The process of removing ore from the face of a drift or stope.

Bullion: Gold or silver that has been milled and smelted to a form approaching purity, then molded into bars.

Cage: An elevator compartment raised and lowered in a shaft for the moving of men and ore.

Cazo process: An ancient Spanish method of treating silver ores, in which the ore was placed in a copper-bottomed vat or kettle, and boiled with salt and quicksilver to speed the process of amalgamation.

Chili Mill: A refinement of the *arrastra* that utilized large stone wheels in place of the heavy boulders.

Chlorination: The method of removing gold from its gangue by the injection of chlorine gas to milled and roasted ore.

Chute: An inclined opening from a stope to a drift through which to slide ore.

Claim: The boundaries that encompass the ownership of a piece of ground presumed to contain a mineral vein or placer deposit.

Claim-jumping: The illegal appropriation of another man's claim.

Gold mining: The removal of ore using only hand tools and muscle.

Cornish Pump: A simple, if cumbersome and powerful device, the Cornish Pump was based on the design of the simple farm well pump and was used in most of the deep mines of the West at one time or another.

Country rock: The permanent, "natural" rock that encloses a vein, usually itself barren.

Coyoting: A method of placer mining utilized to remove gold from its resting place on bedrock; a vertical shaft was sunk, then radial tunnels bored out along the surface of the bedrock.

Cradle: A simple extension of the pan method of washing gold, the cradle was rocked steadily while a stream of gold-laden dirt and water was funneled through it; cleats on its bottom were designed to catch the gold as it passed through.

Crevicing: Probably the simplest method of all of mining, although rarely successful; the process required only a strong knife for prying bits of gold loose from the cracks and crannies of rocks.

Crosscut: A short, lateral tunnel in a deep mine used for exploratory, ventilation, or communication purposes.

Cyanide process: A method of precipitating gold from slimes or tailings by dissolving it in potassium of cyanide and then depositing it on plates of zinc.

Dip: The angle at which a vein inclines down from the horizontal.

Double-jacking: Hand-drilling of blasting holes by two (and sometimes three) men; one holds the drill rod, turning it after each blow from an eight-pound sledge, while the other hammers at it with a steady rhythm.

Dredge: A shallow-draft barge used in one highly efficient method of placer mining; crawling over a water-soaked and presumably rich landscape, it washed a steady stream of gravel, depositing the waste behind it in windrows.

Drift: A deep-mining tunnel that "drifts" with the course of the vein.

Dump: A place for the deposition of waste rock from a mine; or the waste rock piles themselves (which may still be seen over much of the West).

Face: The solid, unbroken surface of a vein at the head of a drift or stope.

Fitcher: The event in which a drill is seized in the grip of rock while being pounded in for a blasting hole.

Fire-setting: A process of cold mining developed by Spanish miners; a fire was built against the face of a vein and at the appropriate moment, cold water was dashed against the rock, and the ore broken up by the action of thermal stress.

Float: Decomposed ore from an outcropping that has been deposited at some distance from its source (*see* Blossom rock).

Flume: A wooden trough designed to carry water, sometimes at great distances.

Foot wall: The country rock on the underside of a vein.

Gangue: The base material of a vein that holds more valuable minerals in place.

Hanging wall: The country rock on the upper side of a vein.

Hard rock: Ore that must be blasted as opposed to ore soft enough to be worked with hand tools.

Headframe: A steel or wooden frame at the top of the shaft that supports the cage for lowering or raising.

Headworks: The collection of buildings—shaft house, hoist house, pump house, offices, blacksmith shop, and so on—clustered near the adit to a mine.

High grade: Ore of uncommon richness.

High-grading: The act of stealing exceptionally rich pieces of ore from a mine and selling it to assayers with more greed than honor. It was a common practice among hard-rock miners whenever such ore was available—something in the way of a fringe benefit.

Hoist: The engine that raised or lowered the cage of a deep mine by the driving of a large drum around which cable was wound; a fishing reel for people and ore.

Horse: Waste rock found deposited within a vein.

Hydraulic mining: A form of placer mining that involved the use of powerful jets of water to wash away hillsides where alluvial deposits of gold occurred.

Leaching: The removal of minerals from gangue by dissolving them in chemicals or percolating water (see Cyanide process; Lixiviation).

Lead: The visible course of a vein; pronounced to rhyme with greed.

Ledge: A visible portion of rock that contains rich ore; also called a "lode."

Level: One of the "stories" of a deep mine, providing access from the shaft to drifts and stopes.

Lixiviation: A process of removing silver from refractory ores that involved the roasting and chlorination of the ore, followed by leaching with water, and finally leaching with sodium hydrosulphite and cuprous sodium hyposulphite to precipitate the final product.

Lode: A vein of larger than normal proportions, although it is frequently used synonymously with vein to describe a body of ore.

Long Tom: A wooden sluice used in placer mining, usually about twenty feet long and eighteen inches deep, fitted with cleats in its bottom, and often designed with a tapered end, so that several could be fitted together.

Mercury (quicksilver): A metal derived from cinnabar that exists in liquid form at normal temperatures; its affinity for amalgamating with gold and silver made it an essential element in the story of western mining.

Mill: A plant where ore is reduced by crushing and, where applicable, valuable minerals are extracted from waste rock by one or more methods of refining.

Mucking: Loading ore that has been blasted from the face of a vein.

Outcropping: A vein exposed at the surface of the earth.

Pan: A shallow metal device used for washing gold in placer mining.

Patio process: Method invented by a Spanish miner in 1557 in order to treat silver ores in greater volume than could be handled in the cazo process. After being crushed in an arrastra, the ore was spread in large circles, and teams of horses were driven through it to crush it further and mix it with quicksilver for amalgamation.

Placer mining: The extraction of free gold from alluvial deposits by one or more of several methods: crevicing, panning, rocking, sluicing, hydraulicking, or dredging.

Quartz: An ore composed of gold or silver trapped in a gangue of crystallized silicon dioxide; the term was commonly applied to any hard gold or silver ore.

Riffle. A series of cleats in the bottom of a rocker or sluice designed to catch free gold passing through, frequently with the aid of quicksilver.

River mining: The act of damming and diverting a stream in order to get at the gold deposits in its bed.

Replacement deposits: Ore that has been deposited in veins that actually replaced the host rock, rather than just filtering into it in cracks and fissures.

Reserves: Major ore bodies known to exist that have not yet been worked.

Rocker: See Cradle.

Shaft: An adit sunk either vertically or on an incline.

Shoot: The portion of a vein rich enough to be considered "payable"; any portion of the vein that is significantly richer than that around it.

Single-jacking: Hand-drilling of blasting holes by one man, holding and turning the drill with one hand and hitting it with a four-pound sledge with the other.

Slickens: The debris or tailings deposited by hydraulic mines or stamp mills.

Slimes: The highly pulverized ore, mixed with water to a fine, mud-like condition during milling.

Sluice: Either a ditch or a wooden device, as a Long Tom, used to wash gold in large quantities in placer mining.

Smelting: The process of melting ore in order to release the desired minerals from their gangue.

Spitter: A short length of fuse used to ignite the timed fuses in dynamite blasting.

Square-set timbering: A method of supporting unusually large stopes, invented in 1861 by Philip Diedesheimer; timbers were mortised and tenoned so that they could be fitted together in cubes, which were then stacked one upon the other in whatever combinations were necessary.

Stamp mill: A device that crushes ore by means of a series of pestles, or stamps, raised and lowered by a camshaft; also used to denote the building in which the machinery is housed.

Station: The end of a level that connects with the shaft for the movement of men or material.

Stope: An excavation in a deep mine whose dimensions are dictated by the width of the vein being mined.

Stoping: The process of creating a stope by mining out a body of ore.

Sump: The bottom of a shaft at which underground water gathers for pumping to the surface.

Tailings: The waste material deposited by mills and smelters.

Toplander: A man who handles ore cars at the surface of a mine.

Tramway: An aerial device that transports ore cars to the top of a dump, where waste rock is then disposed of.

Tunnel: A horizontal adit; any drift or crosscut in a mine that is open at one end.

Vein: A clearly-defined body of ore lying between walls of country rock; frequently used synonymously with lode.

Washoe Pan Process: A method of reducing silver ores on the Comstock, invented by Almarin B. Paul and utilizing both the California stamp mill and a refinement of the cazo process.

Widowmaker: A compressed air drill; the term was one of affection used by miners who had to operate it.

Winze: An underground shaft, either vertical or horizontal, which has no direct connection with the surface; frequently a connection between two levels.

A CHRONOLOGY OF GOLD AND SILVER

1519-1841: For more than three centuries, both the North and South American continents have been harassed by treasurer-seekers whose imaginations are inflamed by rumors and hope; *conquistadores* and peons, New England colonists and American farmers, all scrabble about after gold and silver. Only twice during this period does reality come close to matching dream—once when the kingdoms of the Aztecs and Incas are looted in 1521 and 1533, and a second time when rich silver deposits are discovered in the Zacatecan mountains north of the City of Mexico in 1546. For the rest of the time, only such minor discoveries as those in North Carolina in 1799, New Mexico in 1828, Georgia in 1829, and Southern California in 1841 keep the dream alive.

1848: *California*—James Marshall, an itinerant carpenter, discovers what he later describes as "something shining in the bottom of the ditch" of a mill race he is building on the American River for Johann Augustus Sutter; it is gold, and a new era of frantic dreaming is born.

1849: *California*—America's definitive Gold Rush begins, as thousands crowd the ports of the East Coast for sea passage and thousands more gather at "jumping-off" points on the Missouri River for the land journey; by the end of the year, at least ninety thousand have arrived in California. *Kansas Territory*—Gold is discovered beneath the eastern shadow of the Rocky Mountains by a group of California-bound forty-niners; they decide to move on to the richer diggings on the Pacific Coast. *Arizona*—Again, near the Gila River, gold is discovered by forty-niners who elect to move on to California.

1850: *Washington*—Expeditions of disappointed miners from California discover promising placers on the Spokane and Yakima rivers. *Nevada*—Mormon miners work diggings in the Carson Valley, then move on to California; later in the year, their place is taken by a group of Sonoran Mexicans *from* California.

1851: *Oregon*—Comparatively rich placers are discovered in the Rogue River Valley, and similar discoveries are later made south of Coos Bay.

1856: *Arizona*—American entrepreneurs begin developing old Spanish silver mines in the mountains around Tubac.

1858: *British Columbia*—Twenty-three thousand miners rush to newly discovered gold placers on the Fraser River. *Kansas Territory*—Gold is found on a tributary of the South Platte River, and by the end of the year, several hundred miners have dug in for the winter. *Arizona*—A small rush to placers on the Gila River develops.

1859: *Colorado*—The "Pikes Peak" rush begins, with at least fifty thousand miners streaming across the Great Plains to the Rocky Mountain goldfields. *Nevada*—Silver is discovered near Mount Davidson by a group of gold miners who had been throwing away the "damned blue stuff" for years.

1860: *Nevada*—Ten thousand or more cross the Sierra Nevada to the new silver mines of the Comstock Lode, founding the town of Virginia City. *California*—Gold in rich quartz deposits is discovered on the eastern slopes of the mountains, and Bodie rises as a boomtown. *New Mexico*—Placers are discovered near Pinos Altos.

1861: *Oregon*—Gold placers are found on the John Day and Powder rivers, inspiring the state's second significant rush.

1862: *British Columbia*—Placer deposits are discovered and worked on the Kootenai River in south central British Columbia. *Montana*—Similar placers are discovered by disappointed California miners on Grasshopper Creek in the southwestern corner of region. *Idaho*—Very rich gold fields are developed on tributaries of the Snake River.

1863: *Montana*—Gold is discovered in Alder Gulch, and the boomtown of Virginia City is born. *Nevada*—A similar rush creates the town of Austin in the valley of the Reese River.

1864: *Montana*—North of Virginia City, Last Chance Gulch—later Helena—relinquishes gold in paying quantities, and a thousand miners stream in immediately.

1865: *Utah*—Gold placers are discovered in Bingham Canyon south of Salt Lake City.

1867: *New Mexico*—Rich lode deposits of gold are developed in the Morenos District in the north central part of the territory.

1868: *Nevada*—Incredibly wealthy deposits of hornsilver are uncovered in the White Pine District, and the town of Treasure Hill erupts. *Utah*—Silver in replacement deposits is discovered in Little Cottonwood Canyon, and the Emma Mine becomes world famous.

1875: *Nevada*—After years of floundering in borrasca, the Comstock is electrified by the discovery of the "Big Bonanza," vast quantities of new ore bodies.

1876: *South Dakota*—The rush to the Black Hills begins, as thousands clamber into the tangled gulches of the Holy Wilderness. *Arizona*—Silver deposits are discovered at Globe, in the south central portion of the territory. *New Mexico*—Similar silver mines are developed at Silver City, in the territory's southwestern corner.

1877: *Arizona*—Ed Schieffelin discovers silver in the southeastern pocket of the territory and names his discovery Tombstone, perhaps the most rambunctious camp in western history.

1878: *Colorado*—Silver in replacement deposits is uncovered in the mountains north of South Park, creating the territory's first bonanza discovery.

1881: *Alaska*—"Seward's Icebox" enters the annals of western gold and silver mining with the discovery of gold on the Alaskan Panhandle, leading to the founding of Juneau.

1885: *Idaho*—Silver-lead deposits of great wealth are found above Coeur d'Alene Lake in the northern panhandle, the region's first—and last—true bonanza.

1892: *Colorado*—Rich lode mines of gold are developed in a mountain basin just southwest of Pikes Peak, and the Cripple Creek District soon emerges as the greatest gold mining region in the history of the Rocky Mountains.

1897: *Alaska*—Heavy deposits of placer gold are discovered in the Klondike region of Canada's Yukon Territory, and the last great gold rush in the history of the West erupts the following year as more than one hundred thousand enter the wilds of Alaska from all parts of the United States.

1899: *Alaska*—Free gold is found in the sands of the beach at Nome; it is the last significant free placer opportunity in the history of gold and silver in the West.

1900: *Nevada*—The state re-enters the chronicle of western mining with discoveries in the southwestern part of the region; the consequent rush for lode claims creates the town of Tonopah.

1904: *Nevada*—Gold is discovered in the Columbia Mountains, south of Tonopah; fifteen thousand people eventually rush to the area, and the town of Goldfield is thrown together as the last boom city of consequence in the history of gold and silver.

1933: *California*—In the state where the dream had been revived more than eighty years before, a final, minor rush for quartz gold in the Mojave Desert develops—and soon dissipates. There is little left of the dream now but memory.

A NOTE ON SOURCES

Of all the subjects and periods of American history, I can think of few that have been more thoroughly and enthusiastically recorded in both contemporary and secondary materials than the story of mining in the West. The California Gold Rush alone has inspired several *thousand* books over the past 120 years—guides, diaries, journals, reminiscences, thinly-disguised romances, journalistic reports, histories (traditional and revisionist), social studies, economic studies, and even medical studies. And this does not take into account the fantastic miasma of periodical literature. To burden the reader with a complete listing of the material consulted during the preparation of this book, then, would be to threaten him with premature glaucoma. Instead, I will confine myself to a brief discussion of several works of a general nature, those dealing with the mining frontier in a broad fashion and those dealing with some particular aspect of that frontier. Those who wish to learn in more detail about any given mining region or period, I can only direct to the card catalogue section of a major university library—and wish good luck.

Given the attraction of the subject, there are remarkably few general surveys of mining in the West, and these are of widely variant quality. *Pay Dirt: A Panorama of American Gold Rushes* (1936) by Glenn Chesney Quiett is a rich, anecdote-laden account that remains a joy of readability, even though it is correctable now and again. Equally readable, but with a much less cohesive narrative, is the handsome *Gold Rushes and Mining Camps of the Early American West* (1968) by Vardis Fisher and Opal Laurel Holmes; as its title suggests, it is limited in scope and has much more to do with mining camps than with mining. *A Pictorial History of American Mining from Pre-Columbian Times to the Present Day* (1970) by Howard N. and Lucille Sloane is short on text and long on pictures; some of the pictures are excellent, some adequate, and some very poor, but they all possess a documentary appeal—even though the book's design, in comparison to the Holmes and Fisher volume, is a disaster area. In *The Mining Frontier: Contemporary Accounts from the American West in the Nineteenth Century* (1967), Marvin Lewis has gathered a collection of primary sources (reports, newspaper articles, letters, et al.) covering various aspects of the mining frontier; some may argue with the logic of his selections but for myself, I found them meaty and well presented. A "scholarly" approach to the subject has been attempted by William S. Greever in *The Bonanza West: The Story of the Western Mining Rushes, 1848-1900* (1963). In spite of the fact that it is one of the most unreadable books in our literature, it is the single most comprehensive survey yet attempted —with the exception that the Southwest is not covered, for reasons best known to the author and his Maker (the book offers no explanation for the lapse).

The best single book on the subject of the mining West, of course, is still Rodman Paul's *Mining Frontiers of the Far West, 1848-1880* (1963), a masterwork of synthesis that correlates and compares the social and economic factors of every major development in mining in the West for the years of his coverage. The perception, thought, and literary skill he brings to bear on the mining frontier has not yet been matched and probably never will be. Anyone familiar with Paul's work will recognize my indebtedness to him in the present volume.

In the history of the mining frontier, as in so many other areas, no study can properly begin without recourse to the several volumes in Hubert Howe Bancroft's *History of the Pacific States of North America*. As Bernard DeVoto has written, "I cannot imagine anyone's writing about the history of the West without constantly referring to Bancroft. His prejudices are open, well known, and easily adjustable . . . I have found that you had better not decide that Bancroft was wrong until you have rigorously tested what you think you know."

The technical aspects of western mining have been handled somewhat pedantically by Thomas A. Rickard in his *History of American Mining* (1932), and with considerably more flair (and no less expertise) by Otis E Young, Jr., in *How They Dug the Gold: An Informal History of Frontier Prospecting, Placering, Lode-Mining, and Milling . . .* (1967). Young has expanded his work recently (1970) in *Western Mining: An Informal Account of Precious Metals Prospecting, Placering, Lode-Mining, and Milling on the American Frontier;* written with the technical assistance of Robert Lenon, *Western Mining* is an indispensable and often charming handbook on the subject. Mining as a working industry is catalogued in great detail in Jack R. Wagner's *Gold Mines of California* (1970), a series of biographies of twelve of the most productive quartz mines in California history, as well as some hydraulic and gold-dredging operations of more than passing significance. Mildred Fielder's biography of the Homestake Mining Company, *The Treasure of Homestake Gold* (1968), has all the earmarks of an "authorized" version, but it is nonetheless indispensable to an understanding of the inner workings of the largest gold mine in the United States, past or present.

The professional hard-rock miner has not yet been given his own book, but at least three come fairly close to full treatment. *The Cornish Miner in America* (1968) by Arthur Cecil Todd, is a relatively dull treatise, but rich in detail and source material. A. L. Rowse's *The Cousin Jacks: The Cornish in America* (1969) is more of a literary success, although the author does have the rather dismal habit of listing Cornish names from city directories frequently; may his drill fitcher. Frank A. Crampton's *Deep Enough: A Working Stiff in the Western Mine Camps* (1956) is one of the great unsung autobiographies in western history; muscular in prose, sharp in its prejudices, and enormously evocative of what it was *like* to work a hard-rock mine, the book comes with as high a recommendation as I can give it. Management's side of the story is told in encyclopedic detail and with a wealth of primary sources in Clark C. Spence's seminal study, *Mining Engineers and the American West* (1970); one of his many significant contributions in the book is the discussion—presented here for the first time in any significant detail—of the joys and agonies of managing a mine in the West.

The history of labor conflicts in the West has been told in a number of books, most of them prejudiced in favor of one side or the other (as the histories of labor conflicts usually are). The best is still Vernon H. Jensen's *Heritage of Conflict: Labor Relations in the Non-ferrous Metals Industry Up to 1930* (1950), a book whose internal prose is infinitely more graceful than its title. A recent and excellent addition to the literature of the subject is *We Shall Be All: A History of the I.W.W.* (1969) by Melvyn Dubofsky, whose beginning chapters on the formation and struggles of the Western Federation of Miners are superb.

The society, morals, and quality of civilization displayed in western mining camps and towns is covered in a number of sources, particularly Quiett's *Pay Dirt* and Fisher's *Gold Rushes and Mining Camps*, mentioned above. More serious study is given the urban nature of western mining communities by Duane A. Smith in *Rocky Mountain Mining Camps: The Urban Frontier* (1967). The tradition of vigilantism has been overdone to the point that singling out any one narrative source would be gilding a gilded lily—save to note that the mechanics and implications of vigilantism have never been given more thoughtful and incisive treatment than in "San Francisco and the Vigilante Style," a two-part article by Roger Olmsted that appeared in the January and March, 1970, issues of *The American West*.

The particularly smarmy field of economics in western mining has never been thoroughly unraveled. An early attempt was Thomas A. Rickard's *The Economics of Mining* (1905), a collection of essays that first appeared in the *Engineering and Mining Journal*, of which he was editor. They are as remarkable for their attempts at lyricism as for any real insight into the nature of mining finances, but they are nevertheless valuable. Better, if less lyrical, attempts have been made in more recent years, including *Bostonians and Bullion: The Journal of Robert Livermore, 1892-1915* (1968), edited by Gene M. Gressley; a chapter on the Hornsilver Bonanza by Leonard J. Arrington and Wayne K. Hinton in *The American West: A Reorientation* (1968), also edited by Gene M. Gressley; and *British Investments in the American Mining Frontier, 1860-1901* (1958) by Clark C. Spence, whose *Mining Engineers and the American West*, noted earlier, also contains many nuggets of hard and sometimes delightful information on the subject.

A final word must be said regarding the statistics on production and populations used in this book. As Rodman Paul has pointed out, sources for such figures have all the certain reliability of drawing to an inside straight: "Superlatives come easily—too easily—to anyone who is writing about the mining West. Contemporary accounts are so strewn with inflationary phrases that the adjectives lose their force....Obviously, no precise figures are possible when dealing with so volatile a subject as the mining West." In all cases, I have relied upon what seems to be a consensus among the more reliable historians, and have tried whenever possible to check these figures against Paul himself, whose cautionary instincts in this regard provide a beacon in an otherwise murky world.

PICTURE CREDITS

Cover: David Muench

Endpaper maps: C. E. Erickson

Introductory section: pp. 2 & 3: Honeyman Collection, Bancroft Library; pp. 4 & 5: Homestake Mining Company; pp. 6 & 7: Honeyman Collection, Bancroft Library; p. 8: Ronald Ruhoff.

p. 12: Wittick Collection, Museum of New Mexico.

Chapter One: pp. 14, 18: Bancroft Library; p. 20: map by C. E. Erickson; p. 22: Georgia Historical Commission; p. 23: map by C. E. Erickson.

Chapter Two: p. 24: Mackay Collection, Bancroft Library; pp. 27-31: Bancroft Library; p. 33: map by C. E. Erickson; p. 34: Honeyman Collection, Bancroft Library; pp. 36 & 37: Mackay Collection, Bancroft Library; pp. 38-40: Bancroft Library.

Color section: pp. 41-43: Honeyman Collection, Bancroft Library; p. 44: Mrs. Harry Lehman, Kentfield, California.

Chapter Three: p. 46: Bancroft Library; p. 47: Western Collection, Denver Public Library; p. 48: map by C. E. Erickson; pp. 49-59: Western Collection, Denver Public Library.

Color section: p. 61: Western Collection, Denver Public Library; pp. 62 & 63: State Historical Society of Colorado; p. 64: Honeyman Collection, Bancroft Library.

Chapter Four: pp. 66-68: Bancroft Library; p. 71: Cann Collection, Nevada Historical Society; pp. 72 & 73: Bancroft Library; p. 75: California Historical Society; pp. 76 & 77: Bancroft Library; p. 78: California Historical Society.

Color section: p. 81: Tom Tracy; p. 82, top: David Muench; pp. 82, bottom, & 83: Tom Tracy; p. 84: Idaho Historical Society.

Chapter Five: p. 86: Bancroft Library; p. 88: Montana Historical Society; p. 89: Idaho Historical Society; p. 90: Montana Historical Society; p. 91: Idaho Historical Society; pp. 92 & 93: Montana Historical Society; p. 95: Bancroft Library; p. 96, top: General Library, University of California at Berkeley; bottom, & p. 97: Western Collection, Denver Public Library; p. 98: Stimson Photo Collection, Wyoming State Archives and Historical Department; pp. 99 & 105: Western Collection, Denver Public Library.

Color section: pp. 101-104: all photographs by Ronald Ruhoff.

Chapter Six: p. 106: Stimson Photo Collection, Wyoming State Archives and Historical Department; p. 108: Bancroft Library; p. 109, top: Matthew Brady Photo, National Archives; bottom: Illingsworth Collection, South Dakota State Historical Association; pp. 110 & 111: William H. Jackson Collection, State Historical Society of Colorado; p. 112: Stimson Photo Collection, Wyoming State Archives and Historical Department; p. 113: Bancroft Library; p. 114: Homestake Veterans Association (print courtesy of Mildred Fielder); p. 115: Stimson Photo Collection, Wyoming State Archives and Historical Department; p. 116: Larry Cooper (print courtesy of Mildred Fielder); p. 117: Adams Memorial Museum (print courtesy of Mildred Fielder); p. 118: Stimson Photo Collection, Wyoming State Archives and Historical Department.

Chapter Seven: p. 120: Wittick Collection, Museum of New Mexico; pp. 122 & 123: Bancroft Library; pp. 124-127: Wittick Collection, Museum of New Mexico; p. 128: Bancroft Library; p. 129: Arizona Pioneers Historical Society Library; pp. 130-134: Museum of New Mexico; p. 135: Arizona Pioneers Historical Society Library.

Color section: pp. 137 & 138, top: David Muench; p. 138, bottom: Joan Parker; p. 139. David Muench; p. 140: Ed Cooper.

Chapter Eight: pp. 142-144: Bancroft Library; p. 145: Western History Research Center, University of Wyoming; p. 146: Bancroft Library; pp. 148-150: University of Washington Library; pp. 151-155: Bancroft Library.

Color section: pp. 157-159: Ed Cooper; p. 160: David Muench.

Chapter Nine: p. 160: Stimson Photo Collection, Wyoming State Archives and Historical Department; p. 162: map by C. E. Erickson; pp. 163 & 165: Bancroft Library; pp. 166-169: Stimson Photo Collection, Wyoming State Archives and Historical Department; p. 170: Western Collection, Denver Public Library; p. 173; Montana Historical Society.

Chapter Ten: p. 174: Western History Research Center, University of Wyoming; p. 186: Bancroft Library; p. 187: Rio Grande Collection, State Historical Society of Colorado; pp. 188 & 189: Bancroft Library; p. 190, top: Stimson Photo Collection, Wyoming State

Archives and Historical Department; middle: Schmidt Collection, Museum of New Mexico; bottom: State Historical Society of Colorado; p. 191: Bancroft Library; p. 192, top: Special Collections, University of Arizona Library; bottom: California Historical Society; p. 193: Stimson Photo Collection, Wyoming State Archives and Historical Department; pp. 194-196: Western Collection, Denver Public Library.

Color section: pp. 177-179: Honeyman Collection, Bancroft Library; pp. 180-184: Homestake Mining Company.

Chapter Eleven: p. 198: Bancroft Library; pp. 210-213: Western Collection, Denver Public Library; p. 214: Bancroft Library; p. 215: Arizona Pioneers Historical Foundation; p. 216, top: Western History Research Center, University of Wyoming; bottom: J. Arthur Lobe (print courtesy of Mildred Fielder); pp. 217-218: Western Collection, Denver Public Library; p. 219, top: Idaho Historical Society; bottom: Western Collection, Denver Public Library; p. 220, top: State Historical Society of Colorado; bottom: Western Collection, Denver Public Library.

Color section: pp. 201 & 202: Honeyman Collection, Bancroft Library; p. 203: Art Division, the Oakland Museum; pp. 204 & 205: Honeyman Collection, Bancroft Library; pp. 206-208: David Muench.

Chapter Twelve: p. 222: Stimson Photo Collection; p. 234: Western Collection, Denver Public Library; p. 236, top: Western History Research Center, University of Wyoming; bottom: Bancroft Library; pp. 237 & 238: Western Collection, Denver Public Library; p. 239: Arizona Pioneers Historical Society Library; p. 241: Montana Historical Society; p. 242: Western Collection, Denver Public Library; pp. 243 & 244: Montana Historical Society.

Color section: p. 225: Frank Mitrani; pp. 226 & 227: Ed Cooper; p. 228: David Muench; p. 229: Ronald Ruhoff; p. 230, top: David Muench; bottom: Ronald Ruhoff; p. 231: David Muench; p. 232: Ed Cooper.

Chapter Thirteen: p. 246: Bancroft Library; p. 258: Arizona Pioneers Historical Society Library; p. 259: Stimson Photo Collection, Wyoming State Archives and Historical Department; p. 260: Bancroft Library; pp. 262-265, top: Western Collection, Denver Public Library; p. 265, bottom: Bancroft Library; p. 267: Western History Research Center, University of Wyoming.

Color section: p. 249: University of Wyoming Library; p. 250: Western Collection, Denver Public Library; p. 251: David Muench; p. 252, top: Ronald Ruhoff; bottom: David Muench; p. 253: Homestake Mining Company; pp. 254 & 255: Frank Mitrani; p. 256: Arizona Pioneers Historical Society Library.

Chapter Fourteen: p. 268: Newmont Mining Corporation; p. 270: Western Collection, Denver Public Library; p. 271: Montana Historical Society; p. 272: Bancroft Library; p. 273: Stimson Photo Collection, Wyoming State Archives and Historical Department; p. 274: Todd Webb (print courtesy of Museum of New Mexico); p. 275: Special Collections, University of Arizona Library; p. 276: Montana Historical Society.

ACKNOWLEDGMENTS

The author wishes to thank the following individuals and organizations, whose help was indispensable in manipulating this book into existence: John Barr Tompkins and the entire staff of the Bancroft Library, University of California at Berkeley; Alys Freeze and James Davis, of the Denver Public Library's Western Collection, Denver; Shirley Alley, of the State Historical Society of Colorado, Denver; Gene M. Gressley and Lila Krump, of the Western History Research Center, University of Wyoming, Laramie; Laura M. Hayes, of the Wyoming State Archives and Historical Department, Cheyenne; Mildred Fielder, of Lead, South Dakota; Donald Howe and James Dunn, of the Homestake Mining Company, Lead; Betty Tarvin and Harriett Meloy, of the State Historical Society of Montana, Helena; Judy Austin and Robert L. Romig, of the Idaho Historical Society, Boise; Ross McLachlan, of the Special Collections Department, University of Arizona Library, Tucson; Heather Hatch, Margaret Sparks, and Sidney Brinkerhoff (Director), of the Arizona Pioneers Historical Society, Tucson; Carlos Nagel (Director) and Arthur Olivas, of the Museum of New Mexico, Santa Fe; and Donald Parks, of the Newmont Mining Corporation, New York.

Special thanks must go to Gerry Beyer, who typed most of the manuscript under conditions that too often approached hysteria, and to Ferol Egan and Richard H. Dillon for reading the book in manuscript and discovering a number of gratuitous errors in fact and interpretation; they are in no wise responsible for any errors that may remain, which are the sole and exclusive property of the author.

Portions of this book appeared in the following publications and are here used with permission: *Deep Enough: A Working Stiff in the Western Mining Camps,* by Frank A. Crampton (Sage Books, Denver, 1956); *The Diary of a Ninety-Eighter,* by Basil Austin (John Cumming, Mount Pleasant, Michigan, 1968); *The Poems of Robert Frost* (Random House, New York, 1946).

INDEX

The type selected for this book is Baskerville, designed by English master craftsman John Baskerville in the mid-eighteenth century. Lithography and color separations are by Graphic Arts Center of Portland, Oregon; typography by Paul O. Giesey/Adcrafters; binding by Lincoln & Allen book manufacturers of Portland.